"As it did years ago, the Church is undergoing another Great Awakening. In this landmark volume, Brunner, Butler, and Swoboda have provided the theological resources, inspiration, and vision for a Green Awakening. Weaving together personal stories, biblical readings, theological insights, confessional backgrounds, and practical advice, this co-authored work will prove immensely useful for Christians of all theological persuasions."

—**William P. Brown**, Columbia Theological Seminary; author of *The Seven Pillars of Creation: The Bible, Science, and the Ecology of Wonder*

"I believe *Introducing Evangelical Ecotheology* is the most carefully constructed and comprehensive work of its kind to date. If you have been waiting for a text centering ecotheology in solidly biblical and historic Christianity, the wait is over."

—**Randy Woodley**, George Fox Seminary; author of *Shalom and the Community of Creation: An Indigenous Vision*

"*Introducing Evangelical Ecotheology* is a highly readable and insightful exploration of new evangelical thinking about the task of 'ecotheology,' that is, Christian theology that re-thinks the Bible and church tradition with constant reference to God's good gift of creation. Written by three leading figures in this emerging field of study, this book features illuminating sidebars that address the authors' disagreements about difficult topics in contemporary ecotheology including the role of inclusive language for God, the question of evolution, and the problem of 'stewardship' language for a Christian environmental ethic. An excellent volume for college students, church groups, and general readers alike."

—**Mark Wallace**, Swarthmore College; author of *Green Christianity*

"The interlocking ecological crises stalking us confront Christians with a stark choice: denial or discipleship. This engaging and thoughtful collaboration offers a wide-spectrum overview of the biblical, theological, historical, scientific, and practical issues at stake. Butler, Brunner, and Swoboda have established a new baseline for committed evangelical ecotheology and praxis."

—**Ched Myers**, Bartimaeus Cooperative Ministries

INTRODUCING

Evangelical Ecotheology

Foundations
in Scripture, Theology,
History, and Praxis

•

Daniel L. Brunner,
Jennifer L. Butler,
and A. J. Swoboda

B
Baker Academic
a division of Baker Publishing Group
Grand Rapids, Michigan

© 2014 by Daniel L. Brunner, Jennifer L. Butler, and A. J. Swoboda

Published by Baker Academic
a division of Baker Publishing Group
P.O. Box 6287, Grand Rapids, MI 49516-6287
www.bakeracademic.com

Printed in the United States of America

Library of Congress Cataloging-in-Publication Data is on file
at the Library of Congress, Washington, DC.
Brunner, Daniel L.
    Introducing evangelical ecotheology : foundations in scripture, theology, history, and praxis
  / Daniel L. Brunner, Jennifer L. Butler, and A. J. Swoboda.
        pages cm
    Includes bibliographical references and index.
    ISBN 978-0-8010-4965-1 (pbk.)
    1. Ecotheology. 2. Evangelicalism. I. Brunner, Daniel L. II. Butler, Jennifer L., 1981–
III. Swoboda, A. J., 1981– IV. Title.
BT695.5.B775 2014
261.8'8—dc23   2014020075

14   15   16   17   18   19   20   7   6   5   4   3   2   1

To Kenley, Dylan, Elliot, and Moses

Contents

Foreword

I've been following the progress of our struggles to come to terms with our environmental struggles most of my life—when I was still in my 20s I wrote the first account for a general audience of what we then called the greenhouse effect and now call climate change. Along the way I've gotten to know a great many scientists who are using the gifts God gave them to understand our predicament; they are curious, careful, and persistent, and it's been a joy to make their acquaintance.

I've also had the pleasure of accompanying many people on various parts of their individual faith journeys, from hiking with orthodox rabbis as they made what for many was their first ascent of a mountain, to visiting with the Orthodox patriarch Bartholomew in his Turkish redoubt. A Methodist myself, I've gotten to know many Christians as they work to carry out the command that we steward the earth, and that we love our neighbors.

So far, it must be said, we're not doing as much as we need to in order to fulfill these commandments. To give just one of a thousand examples, ocean water, absorbing carbon from the atmosphere, is now 30 percent more acidic than it was just four decades ago. That is to say, our habits and lifestyles are dramatically altering the "face of the waters" described in the second verse of Genesis—and with it the ability of those ocean waters to support the small creatures at the base of the marine food chain. One could make much the same argument about Arctic ice, about spreading deserts, about deepening storms.

Changing these trends is not easy, but also not impossible. Human ingenuity has provided us with answers: solar panels and windmills, say, to replace coal and gas and oil. But the transition won't be seamless or simple, and it will require changes in our expectations and demands on the earth. That's one reason that religious people and theological thinkers will play such an important role: they are specialists in human transformation, and in building communities that can cope with—and delight in—change for the better.

I can remember, in my days as a Sunday school teacher, the pleasure of taking the kids on hikes and watching them exult in the miraculous abundance that God has provided around us. For us adults, that exultation is shadowed by the knowledge that it will take care and commitment to safeguard Creation. But that responsibility is our glory: the commands to "keep" the beautiful place and to exercise dominion over this gift we've been given were our original charges after all!

Bill McKibben
May 2014

Part I

Why
Ecotheology?

1

Introduction

The Stories behind the Story

Nathan[1] and I (Dan) pulled into the Mbanhela community in the Gaza province of Mozambique and were greeted by the high-spirited singing of six women who form the livestock association of that small community. A Christian relief and development organization, of which Nathan is the country director, provided funds for a large chicken coop, feed, supplies, and 300 chickens for the Mbanhela community. In addition, it furnished training in basic animal husbandry and marketing. Every two months the community starts a new cycle with 320 chicks. Raising chickens for income empowers that community and helps it toward health and sustainability. But the goal of raising livestock is not just for community development. The Mbanhela community decided that God had called them to provide a home for twenty-nine orphans and other vulnerable children. (One woman, Pastor Ramira, said to us matter-of-factly, "God tells us to care for the orphans and widows, and so we do.") Profits from the sale of the chickens help those children attend school and buy books and school supplies.

And yet Mbanhela faces many hurdles on its journey. In its first two years of operation, it lost two whole cycles of chickens, one to an abnormal heat wave and the other to the second "hundred-year" flood in thirteen years. Drought,

---

1. For more on Nathan's story, see chap. 7.

floods, and irregular rains—all primarily the result of climate change—are disrupting the planting and harvesting patterns of rural farmers.[2] Roberto Zolho, coordinator of World Wildlife Fund in Mozambique, says that other ecological ills negatively impacting Mozambique include deforestation and species depletion through poaching.[3] The nation's impoverished are burning forests at an alarmingly high rate in order to produce and sell charcoal. About 80 percent of Mozambicans use charcoal for heating and cooking. Driven by hunger, they are exchanging trees for maize. In addition Mozambique has the highest rate of illegal wildlife trade in the world, a practice connected globally to human and drug trafficking. In spite of efforts by nongovernmental organizations (NGOs) to protect "flagship species"—elephants, wild dogs, sea turtles, and dugong (a large marine mammal similar to a manatee)—poachers in 2012 killed over 3,500 elephants for their ivory and 680 rhinos for their horns. Poachers get $500–$1,000 for a rhino horn, which sells for $65,000–$85,000 on the black market in Asia. Corruption and issues surrounding law enforcement undermine efforts to protect the land and its biodiversity. Zolho emphasizes that ecological degradation, such as climate change, deforestation, and animal trade, is inextricably entwined with poverty. Mozambique ranks 185th out of 187 countries on the Human Development Index (HDI) of the United Nations Development Programme.[4]

Stories like this lie behind this book, stories of a Creation that is groaning, of Christ-followers whose discipleship increasingly involves "keeping" the Earth, and of communities like Mbanhela that live out of hope and a hunger to serve the poorest of the poor. More and more it is becoming apparent that the story of Western Christians is inescapably interconnected with Mbanhela's story, with the Creation's story, and indeed with God's story.

Our Stories

Tell me the landscape in which you live and I will tell you who you are.

—José Ortega y Gasset[5]

2. Alexander Huw Arnall, *Understanding Adaptive Capacity at the Local Level in Mozambique* (n.p.: Africa Climate Change Resilience Alliance, 2012), 4.

3. Interview with Roberto Zolho, coordinator of the World Wildlife Fund Coastal East Africa Initiative, Maputo, Mozambique, June 28, 2013.

4. Khalid Malik et al., *Human Development Report 2013: Summary* (New York: United Nations Development Programme, 2013), 18. Out of the 26 countries on the bottom of the HDI, 24 are in Africa.

5. Cited in Belden C. Lane, *Landscapes of the Sacred*, expanded ed. (Baltimore, MD: Johns Hopkins University Press, 2001 [1988]), 20.

The lifeblood of this book is our common story as a writing team. In the writing process we have tried to model the redemptive tension that community brings and the kind of hospitality, honesty, and bridge building that we hope the text itself will engender. We are two men and one woman, dedicated to mutuality, yet each with his or her own unique story and writing style. Out of a commitment to a writing process that both preserves our own unique voices and at the same time yields a readable and coherent narrative, each of us contributed something to every chapter, then each chapter was edited and woven together in community.

As authors we broach the topic of ecological theology (hereafter, ecotheology) from within evangelicalism. Each of us has evangelical roots; we secure our theology in the *euangelion* ("good news") of Jesus Christ.[6] David Bebbington offers a framework that best captures our understanding of "evangelical," lifting up four marks of evangelicalism: "*conversionism*, the belief that lives need to be changed; *activism*, the expression of the gospel in effort; *biblicism*, a particular regard for the Bible; and what may be called *crucicentrism*, a stress on the sacrifice of Christ on the cross."[7] These qualities are explicitly woven into this book. Repeatedly in this text we voice a call to conversion, to life change, to obeying the invitation of Jesus Christ to a more encompassing discipleship. The third part of the book, on *doing* ecotheology, is pointed toward activism and expressing the gospel with our lived experiences and action. In grounding our ecotheology, we hold to the authoritative nature of Scripture and the creeds. Lastly our desire is to center our writing in Jesus Christ, recognizing that through his life, death on the cross, and resurrection God has acted definitively for the salvation and reconciliation of the world.

All of us are ordained: two (Dan and Jen) in mainline denominations, one (A. J.) in the Pentecostal/charismatic tradition. Our common call to earthkeeping is a part of our call to discipleship, and our call to discipleship is nothing more than a call to Jesus Christ. "The greatest issue facing the world today, with all its heart-breaking needs, is whether those who, by profession or culture, are identified as 'Christians' will become *disciples*—students, apprentices, practitioners—*of Jesus Christ*, steadily learning from him how to live the life of the Kingdom of the Heavens into every corner of human existence," writes the late Dallas Willard.[8] The call to write this book arises out of our desire to respond together to Christ's claim on our lives, to ask what Jesus might

6. Robert Webber, *The Younger Evangelicals* (Grand Rapids: Baker, 2002), 14–15.
7. David Bebbington, *Evangelicalism in Modern Britain* (New York: Routledge, 1989), 3.
8. Dallas Willard, *The Great Omission* (New York: HarperCollins, 2009), xv.

want to say, and ask from us, today. Even as we share a common call to this endeavor, each of us has his or her own story to tell.

Dan Brunner

My single favorite thing as a child growing up was my tree house. When I was nine or ten years old, my dad built a platform in a large maple tree, about twelve feet in the air. Over the years I added a roof and walls. I hardly let anyone come up into that tree house, especially not my sisters. Most often I would climb the tree to get away, to breathe, to seethe, to "simmer down," as my mom would say. One of the walls was nicely sloped, and I could bring my knees up to my chest, lean back against the sloped wall, and just sit there by myself. I loved that tree house, and I loved that maple tree. Our only pets growing up were tropical fish; that maple tree was one of my most loyal friends.

My parents were raised in the Depression. Like many of their generation, they took "conservation" to an extreme we kids considered excessive. Most of the things they did to conserve—raise a garden, drive a fuel-efficient car, not throw away anything that might one day be useful—were done predominately to save money. Yet those practices formed me.

In retrospect the single most ecologically intensive time of my life was when in my mid-thirties my family and I lived in a wilderness community called Holden Village in the North Cascades of Washington state. In this remote setting without telephone or television, we spent unrushed time in spectacular natural beauty, ate low on the food chain, worshiped daily, studied spirituality and discipleship, kept Sabbath, and lived a simplified rhythm of life. Most importantly, gifted teachers led our small community in intentional dialogue about ecology and the state of the planet. Never before had I spent such focused time on such a vital issue with such well-informed and passionate people.

Like my coauthors, I have favorite places in the glory of God's Creation: the coastline and Cascades in my home state of Oregon, Tuolumne Meadows and Half Dome in Yosemite, the Dungeness Spit and Lake Chelan in Washington state, the Black Forest and Bavarian Alps in Germany, Iona and Loch Ness in Scotland, and Betws-y-Coed and Snowdonia in Wales. On the other hand, I have encountered large-scale environmental degradation. Before the fall of the Berlin Wall, I saw the widespread ecological fallout—air and water pollution, acid rain, etc.—of a burgeoning chemical industry in Halle (Saale), East Germany. In Burundi I witnessed the crushing effects of deforestation, land degradation, and soil erosion on rural peoples in the upcountry.

In 2010 a long-term dream came to fruition when my colleagues and I launched the Christian Earthkeeping (CEK) program at our seminary (George

Fox Evangelical Seminary).[9] For nearly a year beforehand a small group of dedicated students and I hammered out the vision and framework of the program. Its mission is to form evangelical leaders who cultivate the care of Creation in their communities. Our rationale for the program can be summarized simply:

- The Earth is endangered.
- The church, and in particular the evangelical church, has by and large been silent.
- The Bible speaks to our relationship with the created order.
- The church must respond to God's command to "keep" the earth (Gen. 2:15).
- Christian leaders need a theological and biblical basis for earthkeeping.

Students are exposed to a broad spectrum of authors, experts, and practitioners as we engage theological reflection, spiritual disciplines, and intentional praxis.[10] As much as anything, this book arises out of the community of learning at our seminary, out of the students—including my two coauthors—who have poured themselves into what it means to be a follower of Christ and a loving caretaker of Creation.

I am a lifelong Lutheran; my father and mother were lifelong Lutherans. Our home was rooted in an evangelical, pietistic spirituality, something for which I remain grateful. Today I am an ordained pastor in the Evangelical Lutheran Church in America, teaching full time at an evangelical seminary with Wesleyan Holiness and Quaker roots. My prayer is that this book will be a small part of building ecotheological bridges in a spirit of hospitality and grace.

Jennifer Butler

My grandmother is a birder. For as long as I can remember, she's kept a pocket-sized red Audubon guide and a pair of binoculars by her rocker. When I was a child she exclaimed: "Jennifer! Come look at this!" I obliged her, peering through the binoculars to get a closer look at common Ruby-crowned Kinglets

9. For more on the program, see the description at George Fox Evangelical Seminary, Christian Earthkeeping Concentration, http://www.georgefox.edu/seminary/programs/christian-earthkeeping/index.html (accessed July 27, 2013). A two-year, 12-credit CEK concentration includes two yearlong seminars ("Theology and Stewardship of Creation" and "Eschatology, New Creation, and Communal Ethics") and two summer immersion intensives ("Theology and Ethics of the Land" and "Poverty and Restorative Earthkeeping").

10. The *Oxford English Dictionary* (hereafter, *OED*), "praxis, n.," defines praxis as "the practice or exercise of a technical subject or art, as distinct from the theory of it." Praxis arises from theology, or, as we will see, can transform our theology. Ecopraxis embodies ecotheology.

and Black-capped Chickadees. Inwardly I groaned, making oaths never to turn into a crazy old bird-watcher. Today if I had an icon, it would be some kind of bird, maybe the Vesper Sparrow, whose song has so often carried me to sleep and greeted me in the morning.

I don't remember the moment it happened, but one day I looked up and noticed birds everywhere. I spent a summer watching baby birds hatch outside my bedroom window. I spent one spring pilgrimaging to where swifts formed a great funnel and descended from the sky in a furious dive toward the brick chimney of a deserted movie theater.

These days I escape down a country road that dead-ends in front of a farmhouse. There are alfalfa fields on either side, and in the winter, when the grass has been harvested, a flock of sheep roam and cats prowl for rodents. I go there for the birds. A Great Blue Heron stalks the field—reminding me of a tall old man, torso and shoulders hunched from age and covered by a bluish tweed suit jacket, holding his hands together behind his back as he takes slow, deliberate steps.

Once, I found an injured juvenile Red-tailed Hawk on the side of the road. It moved almost gratefully, willingly, into a cardboard box and sat silently in the backseat of my car, head rotating ever so slowly from side to side, its great, glassy eyes blinking as we drove in silence to the wildlife rehabilitation center.

I have observed strange sights: fat robins pecking at the ground when spring is nowhere near; enormous formations of geese flying south as late as midwinter; and seagulls that just appeared one day—in a wet, frosty grass seed field (far from the ocean) standing in icy little streams as though they'd found the sea. I don't know what they were doing there, but every time I drove by, I couldn't help thinking they were canaries in the coal mine—our early warning system, showing up in places they ought not to be at times that were ominously curious.

Each sighting—even strange and foreboding ones—enchants me. To be honest, I like the sparrows best, and the wrens. Common birds remind me of the places I come from—the lakes of Northern Idaho, the fields of Eastern Washington, and the Blue Range of Northeastern Oregon.

I've been running away from myself and my history for a long time, but the truth about who I am and where I come from shows up in what I can no longer help noticing: birds in flight, the way my hands look identical to my mother's when I'm digging in the garden, and the way I feel most like myself when I'm walking in silence down that quiet, country road.

I used to be embarrassed of the landscape I grew up in—miles away from a library or a grocery store, chores that involved pulling weeds and picking berries, reading *Little Women* instead of *Seventeen* magazine. I spent a long time trying to forget growing up as an evangelical in rural America. I finally began to know something about who I was around the same time I noticed the birds.

I am a minister in the United Church of Christ. I care about women and the loss of wild spaces. I am a political idealist. I accept the science that tells us we're facing a human-made apocalypse. I take Scripture seriously but not always literally. And I am an evangelical. I believe in the message of the gospel, in personal relationship with Christ. The people I cherish most believe in a literal, seven-day creation and are suspicious of science and politicians. I've lived with communities losing their local identities once Walmart came to town, and I've experienced deliverance when Walmart provided desperately needed jobs to unemployed loggers. I know what it's like when a rancher loses half his herd to wolves protected by the law. I had friends who never went to college because they spent their afternoons and weekends baling hay and driving a combine.

Sometimes I feel overwhelmed by the awkwardness, but more often I am convinced that this balancing act is home—exactly where I am meant to be. This book is part of that awkward rooting—a commitment to bringing my two worlds closer.

I am the granddaughter of Virginia Grace, watcher of birds; the daughter of Robert Lee, blue-collar worker, card-carrying Republican; and Karen Lee, stay-at-home mother, gardener, and born-again Baptist. I grew up in pickup trucks, tagged along on hunting trips, and worked at Walmart as a teenager. And somehow, perhaps through divine intervention, I have become a witness to wonder—an amateur bird-watcher.

A. J. Swoboda

We're all born into great debt, I suppose. Our clothes, our food, and our fingerprints are all handed to us. Words are no different. We're borrowers. My parents afforded me my experience of God's Creation long before memory kicked into gear: walks through Oregon forests, the gathering of leaf piles, a love for roses. I guess, in a way, I've borrowed my love for the Earth from someone else too: the One who made it.

During childhood, summers always meant Montana. The pilgrimage—which brought me from Oregon, and my father from New Mexico, to Billings, Montana, where my grandfather lived—ended somewhere up a windy canyon road along the Boulder River. There a dainty, dusty cabin awaited us fit with a small kitchen and a perpetually half-ripped fly net. It was perfect. The Boulder was our shared religion. With liturgical predictability, we three Swoboda men would awake at five o'clock in the morning to watch the sun, the trout, and our expectations rise. And with each scaly resurrection above the tombs of the rushing water, we knew a long day of work was before us.

Grandpa Rudy was a master fly-fisherman and a World War II vet. Just like God, he could make flies. Raised by the ancients, Rudy knew not just where the fish *were* but how they *thought*. He had a trout-like mind. I recall the texture of his wrinkled hands as he helped me place a fresh handmade fly on my line when I'd lost one on a snag below. Then there was my old man, a courageous and bold child of the sixties. He'd wade into deep waters only, at times, to be overwhelmed by the torrent. Grandpa rolled his eyes. A lot. But we were all together. To be careful, I'd remain in the safe liminality between the two, casting my net into the cold Montana waters. Those trips were magical, transfixed in time. The smell of the river, the sound of the rocks, and the color of the sky made it feel as though God were peeking over the mountains' edge just to see what was happening.

My grandpa died just hours after he put my twenty-fifth birthday card in the mail. After the funeral, I read it. He'd signed it, "Grandson, I love you. Keep your health. Love, Rudy." With my grandfather's end came an end to our yearly pilgrimages. My father and I still talk about the Boulder and how Grandpa taught us the way of fish and how he's probably still rolling his eyes. In a way, the Boulder made us one: three generations of men, one a World War II soldier, another a doctor, and another a confused young man. We were that river. And we always will be.

I became a Christian as a sophomore in high school and then joined a Pentecostal church. My earliest encounter with Pentecostalism was reading cursorily about Pentecostals in the Appalachian Mountains who audaciously drank poison and handled snakes.[11] Needless to say, this was a peculiar (yet stimulating) introduction to Pentecostalism. Later, in college, I attended a Pentecostal ministry on campus and soon became its pastor. Along the way, I came to believe that Pentecostalism and Creation care were not incompatible. In fact Pentecostals love the same Spirit that hovers over Creation. It hovers over us. And seeks to reconcile us.

I write because change is imperative. Without question change is needed within my Pentecostal/charismatic family, which has often been caricatured as having nothing to contribute to the ecological conversation. There's some truth to that. In some ways my heritage has canonized a harmful theological mind-set that not only perpetuates but encourages destruction of the Earth in order to usher in Christ's return. Yet, along the way, I've come to believe that Pentecostal communities can both contribute to and offer hope within this crisis. Notably the founder of Earth Day was a Pentecostal.[12]

11. Dennis Covington, *Salvation on Sand Mountain* (New York: Penguin, 1995).
12. John McConnell Jr., the originator of Earth Day and son of founding members of the Assemblies of God, believed that Earth Day was an opportunity to "show the power of prayer, the validity of their charity and their practical concern for Earth's life and people." Darrin J. Rodgers, "Pentecostal Origins of Earth Day," Flower Pentecostal Heritage Center website, http://ifphc.wordpress.com/2010/04/22/pentecostal-origins-of-earth-day/.

We're borrowers of this land, not owners. I've always known the God of the stream. Now I know the God of the home, the classroom, the church, and the Bible. But it's the same God. My father and I still visit the Boulder. Not as much, though. Now I have a son too. And there will be a moment, somewhere down the river's flow, when we will take him to the cabin; he'll smell the river, see my father's wrinkly hands, and watch his own dad learn how to swim a river. *His* grandpa will roll his eyes too. There the rocks will shout, leaves will meander down the river, and God, by grace, will peek over the mountains.

The Structure of This Book

> The reconstruction of worldviews and the redirection of praxis and spiritual life are all required in meeting the long cycle of decline that contributed to the present state of ecological systems.
>
> —Anne Marie Dalton and Henry C. Simmons[13]

Jürgen Moltmann describes a major component to the process of how his theology developed after his conversion to Christ as a German soldier in a World War II allied prison camp. He terms his work a "theology of the way," or *theologia viatorum*. This kind of theology "emerged only as I walked it."[14] Like a walk in the woods or a hike up a mountain, this book has unfolded as we have walked with it. Its structure corresponds to a core assumption we bring to our writing: that theology and practice must go hand in hand.

Outline: Theology and Practice

This book is structured as three main sections (with a final, short section): part I—"Why Ecotheology?"; part II—"Exploring Ecotheology"; and part III— "Doing Ecotheology." It is important to note the rationale behind the book's structure. Parts I and II *explore* methodology, biblical foundations, ecological realities, historical roots, and central theological concepts for building a Christian ecotheology. Part III, then, is dedicated to moving from academic reflection to concrete action. In the West, with our privileged, intellectualized, and compartmentalized lives, theorizing and theologizing can become ends in themselves. Therefore we advocate *doing* ecotheology. Social psychologist David Myers writes, "We are as likely to act ourselves into a way of thinking as to think ourselves into action. Not only do we often stand up for what we believe, we also come to

13. Anne Marie Dalton and Henry C. Simmons, *Ecotheology and the Practice of Hope* (Albany: State University of New York Press, 2010), 70.
14. Jürgen Moltmann, *Experiences in Theology* (Minneapolis: Fortress, 2000), xv.

believe more strongly in what we have stood up for."[15] Regular ecological practices (like drying laundry on a line, gardening, composting, living in community,
commuting by bicycle, etc.) are capable of transforming our theology and ethic
as we do them. Our actions not only give evidence of a caring relationship with
the planet but also shape our loves, affections, and desires. Doing ecotheology
may be the truest way to a conversion of both mind and lifestyle. Orthodoxy
can lead to orthopraxy, but orthopraxy can also lead to orthodoxy.

Part I (chaps. 1–3) establishes the rationale for our endeavor. In this first
chapter we share some of the stories that underlie the work and provide a
general overview of this book's structure and how it can be used. In chapter 2
we discuss the complex problems we faced in this project; our basic methodology, especially as it relates to Scripture and our biblical hermeneutic; and core
biblical reasons for caring for the Earth. In chapter 3 we examine the grandeur
of God's Creation and provide an overview of its groaning, of some of the
symptoms of ecological degradation.

Part II delves into an array of historical and theological considerations for
a Christian ecotheology. Chapter 4 provides an overview of Christianity's
"ecological" heritage. History helps us understand how we might think and
live in our historical moment. Theology forms the content of chapters 5 and
6. In chapter 5 we consider how our understanding of the Trinity, Christology,
and pneumatology lays the groundwork for a Christian ecotheology. Following
that, in chapter 6, we dive into the doctrines of creation, sin, salvation and
redemption, and eschatology.

In part III we strive to bring our history and theology down to earth by considering how individual Christians and the church might live them out in the
twenty-first century. Chapter 7 establishes the foundation of ecological practice
by exploring key characteristics of an ecological mind-set and the broad vision
of ecojustice. The next two chapters revolve around ecological practice (hereafter, ecopraxis), first by looking at our lifestyles as individual Christ-followers
(chap. 8) and then by offering concrete ways of "greening" the church (chap. 9).
Finally, in part IV (chap. 10) we reflect on how we live as people of resurrection
hope in a broken and hurting world. At the conclusion of the text we provide
a bibliography to make the reader aware of further resources available.

A Word about Words

In writing this book, we had to make a few decisions about language.[16] We
have chosen to use inclusive language for God and people; however, we have

---

15. David G. Myers, *The American Paradox* (New Haven: Yale University Press, 2000), 285.
16. Other than those listed here, most words and concepts are defined in the text itself.

not altered historic documents, direct quotations, or the biblical text (we have used the New Revised Standard Version). We believe that gendered language for God is complex and carries with it a history of neglect. At the same time, we know that human language fails when speaking of the Holy. What we are left with are words and metaphors, whether that imagery speaks of God in human ways (mother, father, friend, comforter) or other-than-human ways (light, dove, rock, water). Whatever language we choose proves problematic, so we ask for grace from the reader as we enter into the fraught, yet holy, task of describing God.

We will use both "earth" and "Earth" (or "Creation"). The word "earth" refers to the land, water, soil, and atmosphere of our planet—the ground beneath our feet and the air we breathe. When we capitalize "Earth" (or "Creation") we are aiming to include all living creatures (including humans) and emphasizing the interconnected nature of the created community. The household (Gr. *oikos*, from which the word "ecology" derives) of Earth encompasses all scales—planetary, bioregional, ecosystemic, human, and microbial—as necessary and related components of the broad community of life. While we understand that humanity is part of the natural world, our use of "nature" or "natural world" is primarily in reference to the other-than-human part of Creation.

Using This Book in the Classroom

We are educators who believe in the power of education. The word "education" derives from the Latin roots *e* ("out") and *ducare* ("to lead"). Both Exodus and education are primarily about the same thing: God's people being "led out" from the Egypt of slavery and the Egypt of ignorance. Education, like wandering in the desert, can be painful, burdensome, and confusing. Education creates new problems. It deconstructs in order to reconstruct. Years ago Paulo Freire asserted that the goal of education was not transferring information or sermonizing but "conscientization," through which people carefully reexamine injustice in order to take just action.[17] Good education is proven by a changed world. This book assumes that teaching and learning are about the conscientization to what is going on with God's Creation and taking steps to deal with it.

Our hope is that this book will open up ways for every reader—whether in undergraduate, graduate, seminary, or church settings—to bring his or her own experiences and beliefs to the conversation. Over the course of formal

---

17. Paulo Freire, *Pedagogy of the Oppressed*, 30th anniv. ed., trans. Myra Bergman Ramos (London: Bloomsbury Academic, 2010), 119.

education, students will scour, dissect, and mine hundreds of texts and lectures, but the "texts" that will leave the greatest impression on the trajectory of their future are those of real people who do real life, who teach what they have learned in their doing. People learn best from people who are actually doing the material. We are aware that the nature of this content often creates problems and questions. We recommend making adequate space for disagreements as they arise.

We have written this book in community; we have disagreed, argued, cried, laughed, and reconciled over and over again in coffee shops, on planes, in hotel lobbies, and in Google hangouts. Some of those debates did not make the book. Others, however, have. Throughout this book there are intermittent boxes we have named "Tension Points." These boxes illustrate some of the challenges we had in finding commonality and agreement around certain issues. While the tension points represent our differences, our broader commitment to hold hospitable space for dialogue exemplifies our overarching responsibility to each other and this work.

We encourage creativity in going through the content of this book. Contemplate, dream, and discover unique ways of exploring *and* doing ecotheology. For instance:

- Hold a class outside—Connect learning about God's Creation by being in God's Creation.
- Schedule a praxis day—As part of a class exercise, do something that was discussed in the classroom. Go pick up garbage. Carpool to class one day.
- Engage in a class project—Discover a useful way for the whole class to do a project. One idea would be to start a recycling program over the course of the semester.

We hope that in reading and engaging this text, whether alone or in learning communities, people will discover how vitally interconnected their stories are to the Earth's story, to the stories of places like Mbanhela and Mozambique, to the church's story, and to Christ's story.

2

In the Beginning

Listening to the Voice of Scripture

When my wife and I (A. J.) purchased our home, we had no idea what we had gotten ourselves into. After countless hours of walk-throughs, prayer, counsel from family and friends, and talks with the realtor, we were certain we were buying the best house we could in the neighborhood; everything *looked* perfect. After scrounging together a down payment, we bought the house and moved in with the excitement of any new homeowner. But before too long, it became evident there were many hidden problems with the house. Lights stopped working, the dishwasher continuously broke down, and the gate fell off its hinges countless times—I cannot list all the problems. Doing some homework, I learned that the previous owners had flipped the house for great profit. "Flipping" is the process of buying a house, fixing it up (sometimes with lower quality items), and putting it back on the market to make, at times, a big profit.

You do not flip something you plan on living in. And yet, for generations humanity has been *flipping* Creation. Real work has been postponed. Decade after decade, for this or that excuse, we have abdicated real responsibility and real care for the integrity of the Earth, leaving our children and grandchildren to mop up. In trading stewardship and husbandry of the land for quick profit, we have now come to a crossroads. The consequences of our irresponsibility are upon us. Things are starting to fall apart. How could we have done this? Could it be that we assumed we would never have to live in *that* place again, that we could just move on to another space? If the people who flipped our house had been forced to live on the property for three decades, they would have made different choices in caring for it. We might think of it like this: Because of sin, humanity has increasingly exhibited a short-term, utilitarian relationship to Creation, the same way many of us treat a hotel room. We stay for a short time, make a mess, pack up, and go somewhere else, all the while believing someone else will clean up after us. When it comes to God's beautiful Creation, the problem is that too many of us think someone else is paid to be the housekeeper.

The Problem

> One thing is clear: if current trends continue, we will not. And that is quali-
> tatively and epochally new. If religion does not speak to [these things], it is an
> obsolete distraction.
>
>   —Daniel C. Maguire[1]

The "problem" underlying this book is actually an array of interconnected problems. First and foremost, we begin with the widespread conviction, especially among scientists and other experts, that our planet is facing an acute ecocrisis and that its causes are overwhelmingly anthropogenic, or human-caused. While there are certainly disagreements as to the scope and specific causes of the trouble, we are convinced that this crisis is indeed the next "great work" facing both humanity and the Christian faith.[2]

A second problem, especially for a book about Christian ecotheology, is the church's own internal strife and theological inflexibility. All along the continuum of Christian traditions—from "liberal" mainline churches to "progressive" and "conservative" evangelical churches—we too often find a rigidity of conviction and a lack of generosity when dealing with others. In both the right-wing and the left-wing sides of Christianity there is the tendency to stereotype, to overlook the nuance in differing opinions, or to distrust the good intentions of others. Diana Butler Bass distinguishes between tolerance and hospitality when dealing with differences.[3] Tolerance *allows* divergent opinions to exist; hospitality *welcomes* and *invites* others into dialogue in a

1. Daniel C. Maguire, *The Moral Core of Christianity and Judaism* (Minneapolis: Fortress, 1993), 13.

2. Thomas Berry, *The Great Work* (New York: Bell Tower, 1999), 7, writes, "For the success or failure of any historical age is the extent to which those living at that time have fulfilled the special role that history has imposed upon them."

3. Diana Butler Bass, *A People's History of Christianity* (New York: HarperOne, 2009), 286–88.

spirit of love and trust. Our hope is to build bridges of hospitality, generosity, and civility when dealing with potentially divisive subjects. In the ethos of Protestantism's *ecclesia reformata et semper reformanda* ("the church reformed and always reforming"), we desire to remain authentic to Scripture and creedal orthodoxy while looking for common ground with fellow Christ-followers without side-stepping genuine differences.

Even within a movement broadly described as evangelical there are stark differences of opinion regarding climate change. Katharine Hayhoe, an evangelical Christian and climate scientist, is concerned about the impacts of global warming: "Climate change really is happening, and most of it really is because of human activities."[4] On the other hand, the evangelical Cornwall Alliance calls the environmental movement "radical" and claims "this so-called green dragon is seducing your children in our classrooms," while "millions [are] falling prey to its spiritual deception."[5] It is no wonder evangelicals have been "laggardly" (so John Stott) in responding to the imperatives of Creation care.[6]

A third problem is how politicized ecological conversations have become; it would seem that our faith convictions have little impact on our ecological opinions. One national observer writes, "Surveys have consistently shown that while faith-based groups may draw attention to what they characterize as the biblical imperative to be good stewards of the Earth, their efforts don't move public opinion on what is now one of the most deeply divisive, politicized issues in America."[7] For example, an evangelical friend of ours received generally favorable responses to the following post on Facebook: "The more deeply I search for the roots of the global environmental crisis, the more I am convinced that it is an outer manifestation of an inner crisis that is, for lack of a better word, spiritual."[8] Later, after our friend clarified that the quote was from Democrat Al Gore, the comments turned less complimentary. We believe this issue must move beyond political polemics. In this text, we certainly could consider the differences between the ways "progressive" and "conservative" evangelicals approach the ecocrisis and our responsibility (or lack thereof) to act. We could discuss how mainline and nondenominational

4. Katharine Hayhoe, "The Secret Life of Scientists and Engineers: Katharine Hayhoe," Nova PBS, April 22, 2011, https://www.youtube.com/watch?v=g-ngBJGHtnM.

5. Cornwall Alliance, "Resisting the Green Dragon," YouTube video, October 15, 2010, https://www.youtube.com/watch?v=vAA2sLtzXJM.

6. John Stott, Foreword to *The Care of Creation*, ed. R. J. Berry (Leicester, UK: Inter-Varsity, 2000), 7.

7. Liz Halloran, "On Climate Change, Americans May Trust Politics Above Preachers," Political News from NPR, January 28, 2013, http://www.npr.org/blogs/itsallpolitics/2013/01/28/170484601/on-climate-change-americans-may-trust-politics-above-preachers.

8. Albert Gore, *Earth in the Balance* (Boston: Houghton Mifflin, 1992), 12.

congregations are engaging (or not engaging) this work. We could examine
how partisan politics co-opts religion and influences what we believe about
this subject. But these culture wars cannot bring healing to Creation. We are
weary of knowing more about describing the kind of Christians we are *not*
than the kind of Christ-followers we are. Division exhausts us. We are more
interested in engaging and embracing the wide stream of the body of Christ,
seeking common ground to discover what our own tradition might teach us.

We face, fourthly, numerous theological problems. Within much of the evangelical Christian community the doctrine of redemption has taken priority
over the doctrine of creation, and spirituality has been raised above earthiness.
Cosmology, the study of the universe's origins, is a particularly delicate question
for evangelicals who hold either to young earth or intelligent design creation
theories. Are evangelical Christianity and evolution incompatible? Can Christians who hold to a young earth and Christians who hold to a 4.5-billion-year-
old earth work together for the care of the created order? Max Oelschlaeger,
referring to the substantial differences of belief within Christianity, nonetheless
expresses the hope that "caring for creation . . . *might* serve to unite all traditions of faith in setting an environmental agenda."[9] We concur.

Fifthly, another problem in writing a text like ours is the *wealth of the
first* (minority) *world*. Our affluence allows us to deprioritize the ecological
crisis while the two-thirds (majority) world is disproportionately affected by
it and unable to overlook its ramifications. Simply put: first world peoples
do not (yet) *have* to face the consequences of our decisions on the planet as
a whole. Our wasteful, rampant consumerism is powerfully addictive and at
times seems almost irresistible. Ultimately what is it—biblically, morally, ethically, spiritually—that will motivate us to care for the earth and for all those
whose well-being is so interconnected with it?

Lastly, the enormity of the ecocrisis itself poses a difficult motivational
dilemma for every Christ-follower. In the face of transnational economies and
global ecological realities, any personal action can seem inconsequential and
meaningless. But the notion of ecology carries with it the idea that everyone
and everything are downstream from everyone and everything else. Small actions and incremental changes *do* have huge ramifications. Only inaction is
meaningless. The overpowering temptation is to withdraw passively into sentimental escapism, a space in which our only hope seems to be a miraculous,
eschatological intervention by God. Where do we find the courage, hope, and
strength to become partners with the God of the universe in the redemption
and reconciliation of all things in Christ?

9. Max Oelschlaeger, *Caring for Creation* (New Haven: Yale University Press, 1994), 120.

God's Two Books

> If I profess with the loudest voice and clearest exposition every portion of the truth of God except precisely that little point which the world and the devil are at that moment attacking, I am not confessing Christ, however boldly I may be professing Christ.
>
> —Martin Luther[10]

We write this book in an attempt to confess the gospel of Jesus Christ boldly in the midst of the contemporary ecological challenge, that place where the world and the devil are at this moment attacking. This is what Christ's church has always done. New dilemmas and dangers have faced Christians throughout history and summoned the church to renewal. By confronting such challenges, concerned Christians seek to contextualize the gospel of Jesus Christ in ways that are conversant with the historical moment. Our method in this text is to listen to both of God's books—Scripture and Creation—and then to put into practice what we have learned. Therefore we approach the ecological challenge in three ways. The first is an appeal to Scripture, historical tradition, and our evangelical theological heritage. Secondly, an aspect of our process is to "listen" to the Earth. Our desire is to bring Scripture, tradition, and theology into dialogue with those who speak on behalf of the ecocrisis our planet faces—scientists, theologians, historians, poets, storytellers, and artists—and with our own experiences of nature. Finally, in responding to the ecocrisis and building on Scripture, history, and tradition, we place a strong emphasis on praxis, the proverbial seam where reflection and action are bound together.

Reading Scripture

Reflecting on the disciples' journey to Emmaus (Luke 24:13–35), Benedictine nun Maria Boulding has provided a metaphor for how we choose to engage Scripture, Christian theology, and the church's own history.[11] The two travelers on the Emmaus road represent the church, the first Easter community. For these travelers it was a long journey, filled with sorrow and incomprehension, knowing and yet not knowing. Then the risen Christ set their hearts aflame as he revealed the Scriptures, breaking open the bread of the Word even as he would break the bread of the Eucharist. Boulding observes that the Word is not always clear; it is mysterious because it is the very presence of God; it

---

10. Martin Luther, cited in Douglas John Hall, *Confessing the Faith* (Minneapolis: Fortress, 1996), vi.
11. Maria Boulding, *The Coming of God* (Collegeville, MN: Liturgical Press, 1982), 75–76.

is creative and disruptive. We are only able to hear it, and be converted, over the long journey.

Those two original travelers were so certain in their knowledge of the Scriptures. "Don't you see?" Jesus replied. And he opened their minds to understand what the Word was saying in *their* historical moment. They had just missed it—yet they had been so sure of what they thought they knew. Their fellow divine traveler says, "Don't you see that it had to be like that? Was it not written? Isn't it what all the Scriptures are about, from end to end?" But they had not been able to see the truth that Jesus would enable them to see. It is as if Jesus were saying, "You have to jettison your small plans, because the Father's plans for you are unthinkably greater and more wonderful."[12]

A heart turned to Christ's Spirit must be open to seeing what is fresh for today's real world. French author Marcel Proust notably wrote, "The only true voyage . . . would be not to visit strange lands but to possess other eyes."[13] The Spirit continuously opens the Word anew, preparing our hearts to hear it and forming our minds into the mind of Christ. Such is the ongoing gift of the risen Christ. Gerhard Ebeling (alluding to Paul's words in 2 Cor. 3:6, "the letter kills, but the Spirit gives life") has written: "As existential life continues, so the understanding of the scripture is a continuous task which can never be brought to a conclusion. For there is a constant threat that an understanding once achieved will cease to be the Spirit, and return to being the mere letter, unless it is constantly attained anew and made one's own. Thus unceasing progress is necessary in understanding the scripture."[14]

Our goal is to return consistently to the biblical witness. In arguing for the involvement of Christ-followers in the stewardship of Creation, New Testament scholar I. Howard Marshall writes, "Just as the responsibility of Christians for political and social involvement rests not on direct command but on an application of the examples found in Scripture (especially the Old Testament), so the responsibility for care for the world rests not on direct command but on application of the principles which are to be found in Scripture."[15] The God of the Old Testament *is* the God of the New Testament, and there is continuity in the development of doctrine from the Old Testament to Jesus Christ to the early church. Yet the biblical writers could not have predicted later global issues, including the ecocrisis; therefore we search for biblical principles in

---

12. Ibid.
13. Marcel Proust, *In Search of Lost Time*, vol. 5, *The Captive and the Fugitive*, trans. C. K. Scott Moncrief and Terence Kilmartin, revised by D. J. Enright (New York: Random House, 1993 [1923]), 343.
14. Gerhard Ebeling, *Luther*, trans. R. A. Wilson (London: Collins, 1970), 99.
15. I. Howard Marshall, "Commitment to Creation," in *Care of Creation*, 97.

Tension Point: Gender Language

Gender inclusive language about God can stir up passion and biting debate within both mainline and evangelical communities. We acknowledge that the predominate language for God within Scripture and historical sources is male, although there are examples where this is not the case. We also recognize that the image of God as male is troubling and problematic for much of the Christian community. Likewise, we are sensitive to those who similarly find language about God as female problematic. However Madeleine L'Engle once criticized this sweeping attempt for sexual neutrality as fruitless—what she called a false search for "vague androidism."[a]

Because this book is not a project about language inclusivity, we had to decide what our common "voice" would be. We agreed that God has no gender—God is Spirit (John 4:23–24). Therefore we must be careful not to anthropomorphize God or limit God to human characteristics. This posed quite a conundrum regarding historical sources, which commonly refer to God in male terms. To avoid anachronism and out of respect for historical and literary integrity, we have chosen not to edit historical sources and have left their male or female terminology for God unchanged. However in what we wrote, we intentionally chose not to use either male or female pronouns in reference to God (or in reference to nature).

- What is your reaction to our process and decision? Would people have noticed if we had not drawn attention to it?
- What are the implications for a Christian ecotheology that, often in our history, we have used male language for God and female language for nature?
- What is your response to L'Engle's description of gender neutral language as "vague androidism"?

a. Madeleine L'Engle, *Walking on Water: Reflections on Faith and Art* (Wheaton, IL: Harold Shaw, 1980), 43.

---

our constructive process. With Marshall, we affirm the enduring authority of revealed Scripture, while recognizing "that Scripture needs interpretation and fresh application, both in our doctrine and in our practice."[16]

At the same time, we want to keep a healthy dialogue with our own traditions. After all we stand on the shoulders of those who have gone before us. It is far too easy to say, "If I had been there at *that* point in history, I would have thought or interpreted or acted differently." We recognize the arrogance, or historical hubris, of such statements. We want to be wary of anachronism. Phyllis Trible characterizes the biblical text and its gospel message as a pilgrim

16. I. Howard Marshall, *Beyond the Bible* (Grand Rapids: Baker Academic, 2004), 78–79.

wandering through history to merge past and present: "As Scripture moves through history, it is appropriated for new settings."[17] We cannot reject the pilgrim for being rooted in his or her own place and time. Neither can we allow past cultural norms to hold the text captive and dictate our present understanding, since theology divorced from our social context is hollow.[18]

Our context *is* different from the biblical writers and from Christian thinkers, pastors, leaders, and writers in times past. Our context requires us—in a spirit of openness to the risen Christ who travels with us—to petition continually "the breaking of the bread of the Word," by which he opens our minds to understand the Scriptures.[19] While we embrace the Bible for its compelling revelation of salvation and justice, we must resist applying it through a model that views interpretation as timeless and transcultural.[20] Scripture is inspired; our interpretations are not. Thus in dialogue with other Christ-followers, we want to "glean" from the Bible and from our traditions' insights and practices what may have been missed or left behind by dominant structures and voices. Experience teaches us that all too frequently the majority voice—those in power, the "winners" of debates and wars—overlooks, neglects, or suppresses the minority voice—the "losers," the weak. We approach our theological task in repentance, aware that our tradition has been (in part) responsible for perpetuating the ecocrisis and for silencing marginal voices.[21]

And so, while embracing Christian orthodoxy with prayerful humility and in community with other seekers, we return to Scripture and tradition to glean what might have been left behind. To do this work necessitates highlighting the voices of the silenced Other. It does not mean that the Other is categorically correct or that the marginalized are innocent but that their perspective is critical because, in the words of Eleazar Fernandez, "in principle they are least likely to allow denial of the critical and interpretive core of all knowledge."[22] It is essential to bring the voices and experiences of the minority into conversation with the voices and experiences of the majority. The Other includes, but is not limited to, women, those marginalized by sexual orientation and/ or gender identity, indigenous peoples, people of color, the politically and religiously disenfranchised, the economically underprivileged, and those who are not able-bodied—everyone who has historically been excluded, ignored, or

17. Phyllis Trible, "Depatriarchalizing in Biblical Interpretation," *Journal of the American Academy of Religion* 41, no. 1 (March 1973): 48.

18. Kevin Giles, *The Trinity and Subordinationism* (Downers Grove, IL: InterVarsity, 2002), 260.

19. Boulding, *Coming of God*, 75.

20. Giles, *Trinity and Subordinationism*, 261.

21. Catherine Keller, "The Lost Fragrance: Protestantism and the Nature of What Matters," *Journal of the American Academy of Religion* 65, no. 2 (Summer 1997): 366.

22. Eleazar S. Fernandez, *Reimagining the Human* (St. Louis: Chalice, 2004), 24.

silenced. In our own context, in this *kairos* moment, the Other includes God's other-than-human Creation. Admittedly, to "listen" to the Earth is subjective; still, there are those who speak on its behalf. By "gleaning" from the minority we hope to create theological dialogue about our own future, our children's future, and the future of the planet itself.

Reading Creation

When the Pharisees told Jesus to silence his disciples, Jesus replied, "I tell you, if these were silent, the stones would shout out" (Luke 19:40). Does Creation speak? Can it be heard? Can it be read?

The Christian community has long held that the Scriptures of the Old and New Testaments are "inspired" (*theopneustos*, 2 Tim. 3:16) by God and the basis for faithful reflection in the church. At the same time, Christian writers have maintained that Creation can be read as a text about God and that God has presented us with "two books"—Scripture and the natural world. From the desert wisdom tradition of the fourth century we read: "A philosopher asked Saint Anthony: Father, how can you be enthusiastic when the comfort of books has been taken from you? He replied: My book, O Philosopher, is the nature of created things, and whenever I want to read the Word of God, it is usually right in front of me."[23] Augustine wrote, "Others, in order to find God, will read a book. Well, as a matter of fact there is a certain great big book, the book of created nature. Look carefully at it top and bottom, observe it, read it. God did not make letters of ink for you to recognize him in; he set before your eyes all these things he has made. Why look for a louder voice? Heaven and earth cries out to you, 'God made me.' . . . Observe heaven and earth in a religious spirit."[24] Thomas à Kempis likewise suggested, "If your heart is right, then every creature is a mirror of life to you, and a book of holy learning, for there is no creature—no matter how tiny or how lowly—that does not reveal God's goodness."[25] And Meister Eckhart wrote:

> Every single creature is full of God
> and is a book about God.
> Every creature is a word of God.[26]

23. *Desert Wisdom*, trans. Yushi Nomura (Maryknoll, NY: Orbis, 2001), 68.

24. Augustine, "Sermon 68," in *Sermons III (51– 94)*, trans. Edmund Hill, OP, ed. John E. Rotelle, OSA (Brooklyn, NY: New City, 1991), 68.6, p. 225.

25. Thomas à Kempis, *The Imitation of Christ*, trans. Joseph N. Tylenda, SJ, rev. ed. (New York: Vintage, 1998), II.IV.1, p. 52.

26. Meister Eckhart, "God in All Things," quoted in *Earth Prayers from Around the World*, ed. Elizabeth Roberts and Elias Amidon (New York: HarperCollins, 1991), 251.

It is easy for a "literate" society to forget that the vast majority of people centuries ago could not read, and yet God could still speak to them through Creation. Indeed we have the remarkable gift of encountering God through the written Word, but could it be that the Reformation emphasis on *sola Scriptura* (Scripture alone) has desensitized us to God's other book, one that has spoken truthfully for millennia?

Of course Creation can be misread just as Scripture can be misread. Howard Snyder points to four false readings of the natural world: (1) Romanticizing nature—believing that nature in its beauty is the primary and profoundest font of truth; (2) Commodifying nature—presupposing that nature exists purely as product or property; (3) Worshiping nature—deifying Creation; and (4) Spiritualizing nature—envisioning Creation as having no intrinsic value other than pointing to some external spiritual truth outside it.[27] How, then, do we read Scripture and Creation? It is best to read Scripture and nature in dialogue with one another.[28] Without such a tension, our reading of the other will be misinformed. We do not argue for harmonization necessarily but rather that both be allowed to bear witness. In the same way that the Bible offers four distinctive accounts of the gospel story, so Scripture and nature offer two accounts of God's story.

As we grow in our ability to read Creation, we will discover that it has much to teach us. The created world has the power to reveal to us something of God, to awaken us to the presence of the divine, shouting out to those with eyes to see and ears to hear. Walt Whitman, reflecting on how he might describe grass to a child, wrote:

> Or I guess it is the handkerchief of the Lord,
> A scented gift and remembrancer designedly dropped,
> Bearing the owner's name someway in the corners, that we may see and
>   remark, and say *Whose?*[29]

Nature is truly a "remembrancer" of the One who is its Creator and Owner.

The book of Creation teaches us to praise God (see Ps. 148:7–13). Breathing and inanimate, tempestuous and serene, mighty and unheeded—by nature of being faithful to its very nature, all Creation praises the Creator. Paul of the Cross (1694–1775), founder of the Passionists, penned these thoughts: "When

---

27. Howard A. Snyder, *Salvation Means Creation Healed* (Eugene, OR: Cascade, 2011), 42–45.
28. It is helpful to remind ourselves that John Wesley held that Scripture, tradition, reason, and experience should be "read" in dialogue with one another.
29. Walt Whitman, "The Song of Myself," in *An American Anthology, 1787–1900*, ed. Edmund Clarence Stedman (Boston: Houghton Mifflin, 1900), http://www.bartleby.com/248/366.html.

you are walking alone, listen to the sermon preached to you by the flowers, the trees, the shrubs, the sky, and the whole world. Notice how they preach to you a sermon full of love, of praise of God, and how they invite you to glorify the sublimity of that sovereign Artist who has given them being."[30] Steven Chase summarizes it well: "In stripping creation of all we 'imagine' it to be, we will see it as it is, as pure doxology."[31]

■ ■ ■

Our method is rooted in listening to God's Creation and to those who speak on its behalf, exploring Scripture and our historical tradition—with both majority and minority voices represented—and placing high priority on living out our values through praxis. By these means we aim to confess Jesus Christ and to help the Christian community engage the most pressing crisis of our time—"precisely that little point" at which the whole of God's Creation is being attacked.

Biblical Reasons for Creation Care

> Our predicament now, I believe, requires us to learn to read and understand the Bible in the light of the present fact of Creation.
>
> —Wendell Berry[32]

Our conviction remains that our contemporary context demands—ethically and theologically—that we reorient our way of reading the Scriptures through an ecological lens.[33] Although historically Christians have at times read the Bible in anthropocentric and even Earth-damaging ways, the Scriptures also provide support for a comprehensive ecotheology and ecopraxis. Throughout this book we will reference the Old and New Testaments frequently; here we want to provide a summary of key biblical reasons to care for Creation.

Earthkeeping

My (Jen's) oldest nephew is in love with LEGOs®. His current favorite projects are castles and pirate ships. As he builds, he narrates aloud the story forming in his mind. I am sometimes asked to hold the female-looking LEGO

---

30. Paul of the Cross, *In the Heart of God*, I, 418, in *The Heart of Catholicism*, ed. Theodore E. James (Huntington, IN: Our Sunday Visitor, 1997), 495.

31. Steven Chase, *Nature as Spiritual Practice* (Grand Rapids: Eerdmans, 2011), 27.

32. Wendell Berry, "Christianity and the Survival of Creation," in *The Art of the Commonplace*, ed. Norman Wirzba (Berkeley: Counterpoint, 2002), 306.

33. David G. Horrell, *The Bible and the Environment* (Sheffield: Equinox, 2010), 9.

character and voice her distress when the castle comes under pirate attack. My nephew plays the parts of all the other characters, but I suspect his favorite is the castle guard—that stubby, square-shaped swashbuckler who protects the royal family from ferocious marauders. His cheeks flush and his eyes sparkle as he describes the way the guards safeguard the castle during attack. I ask him if he knows what this is called. "Yeah, fighting!" he responds. "It's keeping," I tell him. "The keep is the heart of the castle and the people who protect the royal family are 'keepers.' You can also keep a lighthouse or . . ." He's lost interest, so I stop my educational ramble. But I think about just how widespread the use of the word is: innkeeper, zookeeper, bookkeeper, peacekeeper, gamekeeper, scorekeeper, housekeeper, groundskeeper, "am I my brother's keeper?" (Gen. 4:9), etc. To be a keeper carries the notion of care and watchfulness, of being charged with a responsibility. Earthkeeping too is just such a responsibility.

After Adam was created, "the LORD God took the man and put him in the garden of Eden to till it and keep [*shamar*] it" (Gen. 2:15). The Hebrew word *shamar* means to guard, protect, keep watch, preserve. The same word is found in Aaron's blessing, so often used as a benediction in our worship services: "The LORD bless you and keep [*shamar*] you" (Num. 6:24). Calvin DeWitt writes, "The keeping we expect of God when we invoke the Aaronic blessing is one that nurtures all of our life-sustaining and life-fulfilling relationships with our family members, with our neighbors and our friends, with the land, air, and water, and with our God. We ask God to love us, to care for us, and to sustain us in relationship to our natural and human environment."[34] Earthkeeping springs from grace: we keep because God first kept (and keeps) us.

The psalmist writes, "The earth is the LORD's and all that is in it, / the world, and those who live in it" (Ps. 24:1). The planet ultimately belongs to the One who created and sustains it. Humanity was not given the Earth to possess; rather Adam and Eve were given the divine responsibility of caring for (tending and keeping) the land. To keep God's garden, to work, to cultivate and nourish the earth, to get dirt under our fingernails is *not* a burden resulting from sin but a vocation of dignity and partnership. As humans, our primary vocation is taking care of—keeping—what belongs to God for the mutual flourishing of all life.

Mutuality

In the late 1980s a major controversy arose over the Northern Spotted Owl that lived in the "old growth" forests of the Pacific Northwest. Because of

---

34. Calvin DeWitt, "Creation's Care and Keeping," in *Simpler Living, Compassionate Life*, ed. Michael Schut (Harrisburg, PA: Morehouse, 1999), 177.

extensive logging, only 10 percent of those forests remain, mostly on federal lands. As the ancient forests have diminished so have the owls. After years of heated exchanges between conservancy groups and the logging industry, the owl was listed as an endangered species—its population had dwindled to about 2,000 pairs—resulting in considerable logging restrictions. Oregon's timber industry fought these limitations, claiming they would damage an already beleaguered industry—rural logging and millwork communities have suffered for decades from high unemployment and reduced lumber harvests. The ethical issues surrounding the spotted owl are complex, but the political and legal arguments are generally presented in stark, either-or terms: environmentalists versus the timber industry, Northern Spotted Owls versus loggers, old growth forests versus rural communities.[35] What is too often missing in these debates is an acknowledgment of the interdependence of owls, forests, humans, and communities—of social systems and ecosystems.

A principal reason to care for Creation is *mutuality*: the well-being of humankind is dependent on the well-being of the planet. And vice versa. After the Genesis flood, God addressed Noah and his children: "This is the sign of the covenant [*berith*] that I make between me and you and every living creature that is with you, for all future generations: I have set my bow in the clouds, and it shall be a sign of the covenant between me and the earth" (Gen. 9:12–13). Like other biblical covenants, the Noahic covenant is instigated by God; in response to God's covenantal commitment, humans bear covenantal responsibility.[36] However unlike other covenants and promises, this one is universalized to include *all* creatures; it is essentially an ecological covenant.[37] To keep covenant or to fail to keep covenant has consequences for the whole Earth community.

The biblical theology of covenant means that when it comes to the planet's welfare, we are all in this together. It is possible to view this mutuality in entirely anthropocentric terms: in order for the survival of our own kind, we need to recognize our interdependence with the rest of Creation. Because we have a moral obligation to ourselves, our cultures, and the future, we have a corresponding duty not to destroy the ecological groundwork of our lives.[38] But mutuality is also an opportunity to begin to see the world from a "subject-subject" perspective.[39] Mutuality, rooted biblically in God's covenant with Noah, offers us

35. Claire Andre and Manuel Velasquez, "Ethics and the Spotted Owl Controversy," *Issues in Ethics* 4, no. 1 (Spring 1991), http://www.scu.edu/ethics/publications/iie/v4n1/, accessed Jan. 4, 2014.

36. R. Larry Shelton, *Cross and Covenant* (Tyrone, GA: Paternoster, 2006), 19.

37. Bernhard Anderson, *From Creation to New Creation* (Minneapolis: Fortress, 1999), 157.

38. Kathleen Dean Moore and Michael P. Nelson, *Moral Ground* (San Antonio: Trinity University Press, 2010), 2.

39. See the section "From Object to Subject" in chap. 3.

hope of visualizing our relationship with Creation in brand new ways. Dan Erlander calls this mutuality "cosmic koinonia," in which "every part of creation participates in the life and shalom that God intends for every other part."[40]

Artistry

Imagine an artist putting on an art display for friends. Striking, compelling paintings line the walls of the studio. People are sipping wine, conversing amiably, milling around, and admiring each creation. A sweet sense of joy, friendship, and beauty fills the room. All of a sudden an angry stranger bursts into the studio, takes out a pocketknife, and slashes three or four of the splendid canvases. People react in horror. The artist simply weeps over the destruction of her handiwork, the work of her hands.

In the process of creating the world, God regularly took a break to observe the created things and "saw that it was good." The Hebrew word for "good" (*tov*) can also be translated "beautiful." So God paused each day to see how good or beautiful the Creation is. In this way, we can think of the Creator as both the first Artist and the first Appreciator of beauty. In Proverbs 8, God, personified as Wisdom, is called *amown* (v. 30), a rare Hebrew word translated as "master worker" (NRSV), "master craftsman" (NJB), or "architect" (NLT). God is the Artist of all that is, in heaven and on earth: "The heavens are telling the glory of God; / and the firmament proclaims his handiwork" (Ps. 19:1). As human greed and domination slash that handiwork, the Artist weeps.

In Ephesians we read, "For we are what he has made us, created in Christ Jesus for good works, which God prepared beforehand to be our way of life" (Eph. 2:10). The Greek word for "what he has made us"—other translations read "handiwork" (NIV) or "workmanship" (NASB)—is *poiema*, from which we derive "poem." As human creatures bear witness to a master Poet or Potter (Rom. 9:21), so the whole Earth gives evidence of an imaginative Artist (Job 38–41; Ps. 104; Rom. 1:20). Augustine saw God as the Composer and Conductor of a glorious hymn, as one who knows "what at a particular time he ought to give, add, remove, subtract, increase, or decrease until the beauty of the whole world, whose parts are those things that are suited for their own times, is played out alike a great song of a certain ineffable artist."[41]

God is indeed the inexpressible Artist—Poet, Potter, Composer, Conductor—whose untamed imagination is imprinted everywhere. To ignore Creation's

---

40. Daniel Erlander, *Manna and Mercy* (Mercer Island, WA: The Order of Saints Martin & Teresa, 1992), 92, comments that he got the phrase "cosmic koinonia" from Michael Poellet.

41. Augustine to Marcellinus, [c. 411–412], *Letters 100–155 (II/2)*, trans. Roland Teske, SJ, ed. Boniface Ramsey (Hyde Park, NY: New City Press, 2003), Letter 138.5, p. 228.

fierce beauty, to disrupt its intricate interrelatedness, to oversee its accelerating demise, must grieve the Artist. To see and wonder and admire, to defend and conserve and keep, to love and steward and care, is to respect and honor the Artist. Elizabeth Barrett Browning (1806–1861) captures the humility of engaging the artistry of the Creator in these famous lines:

> Earth's crammed with heaven,
> And every common bush afire with God:
> But only he who sees, takes off his shoes,
> The rest sit round it, and pluck blackberries,
> And daub their natural faces unaware. . . .[42]

It is a gift of grace to see every common bush afire with God, to search for the imprint of the Artist. Having seen, may we know the grace to remove our shoes.

Character

In the 1980s and 1990s, "What would Jesus do?" bumper stickers and neon-colored bracelets were found in abundance on the SUVs of Christian suburbanites and their adolescent offspring. Its intention and effects were largely concerned with individual Christian morality. But the roots of the theological question run much deeper and are connected with the social justice movement in evangelical Christianity. Over a century before bumper stickers and statement-making accessories, novelist Charles Sheldon published *In His Steps*, a novel with the subtitle *What Would Jesus Do?* addressing issues of social inequities in an industrialized society; thus the famous phrase entered Christian ethical conversations. Today a restored emphasis on the humanity of Jesus Christ raises a complementary question: What kind of person was Jesus? The first question points to conduct, the second to character. These ways of understanding Jesus are not incongruous; in fact, both are necessary. Each one draws attention to Jesus as someone to be imitated, a key aspect of Paul's theology and practice: "And you became imitators of us and of the Lord" (1 Thess. 1:6), and "be imitators of God, as beloved children, and live in love" (Eph. 5:1–2).

Steven Bouma-Prediger describes two basic ethical viewpoints: a concentration on rules and duties (deontology) or a focus on consequences (teleology).[43] Bouma-Prediger lifts up virtue theory (areteology) as an overlooked resource

---

42. Elizabeth Barrett Browning, *Aurora Leigh: A Poem* (London: J. Miller, 1864), in "A Celebration of Women Writers," ed. Mary Mark Ockerbloom, http://digital.library.upenn.edu /women/barrett/aurora/aurora.html, accessed May 21, 2013.

43. On what follows, see Steven Bouma-Prediger, *For the Beauty of the Earth*, 2nd ed. (Grand Rapids: Baker Academic, 2010), 131–54.

for Christian ecological ethics. For Aristotle, to speak of virtue (*arête*) was to speak of excellence. We are reminded of Paul's clear statement on excellence and virtue: "Finally, beloved, whatever is true, whatever is honorable, whatever is just, whatever is pure, whatever is pleasing, whatever is commendable, if there is any excellence [*aretē*] and if there is anything worthy of praise, think about [*logizomai*] these things" (Phil. 4:8). Here Paul challenges the Philippian people to think *logically* about excellence and the virtuous life. In verse 9 he balances thinking with imitation: "Keep on doing the things that you have learned and received and heard and seen in me." What we do is rooted in who we are; conduct arises out of character. And yet, at the same time, habits form character. Virtue, then, "is a state of praiseworthy character, formed by habits over time, that disposes us to act in certain excellent ways."[44]

Bouma-Prediger's conviction is that certain character traits are essential for Earthcare. To that end he forwards seven pairs of ecological virtues: respect and receptivity, self-restraint and frugality, humility and honesty, wisdom and hope, patience and serenity, benevolence and love, and justice and courage. To build an ecological character requires two things. First, we need stories or narratives with which we can identify. Our culture offers us numerous framing stories, including consumerism, materialism, and prosperity. As Christ-followers, our dominant narrative must be that of Jesus and his vision of the kingdom of God. Secondly, ecological character is developed chiefly in community. Our social and ecosystemic communities play central roles in forming our character. What we do to care for God's Creation must be rooted in who we are in solidarity with God's Creation.

The Underprivileged

In 2008 I (Dan) traveled to Burundi to teach at Hope Africa University in Bujumbura. During the end of our stay, my friend Scott and I were driven to the upcountry to visit the source of the Nile River. As we climbed to about 6,000 feet, we witnessed gorgeous landscapes and terraced gardens along steep, hilly terrain. Women dressed in brightly colored dresses walked along the road, with mystifyingly heavy loads balanced on their heads. In village after village we saw scores of large, stuffed white sacks beside the road. We learned they were filled with charcoal. Like neighboring Rwanda and Democratic Republic of Congo, charcoal is the main source of fuel for cooking in Burundi. But their methods for producing charcoal are inefficient, resulting in pervasive deforestation and soil erosion. My heart ached as I witnessed an

44. Ibid., 134.

impoverished people faced with the dilemma of choosing between feeding their families and destroying their land.

The truth is that the underprivileged in the world experience the desolating effects of ecological degradation *disproportionately* in comparison to the economically privileged. Many Western peoples can choose whether or not they will recycle, conserve water, eat less meat, or purchase carbon credits for air travel, while those in upcountry Burundi must choose whether to feed their loved ones or pillage their beloved land. Yet throughout the Old and New Testaments we are reminded that God is on the side of the poor. The psalmist writes, "I know that the LORD maintains the cause of the needy, / and executes justice for the poor" (Ps. 140:12). James chastised readers who had "dishonored the poor" (James 2:5–6).

And Jesus himself said, "When you give a banquet, invite the poor, the crippled, the lame, and the blind" (Luke 14:13). On another occasion he spoke to his followers (and ultimately to the whole Christian community) about the eternal ramifications of what they did "to one of the least of these"— the hungry, the thirsty, the stranger, the naked, the sick, and the imprisoned (Matt. 25:31–46). With words like these, Jesus aligned himself with the Hebrew prophets, who reprimanded those "that trample on the needy, / and bring to ruin the poor of the land" (Amos 8:4) and called them to "show kindness and mercy to one another," and not to "oppress the widow, the orphan, the alien, or the poor" (Zech. 7:9–10). The practice of showing singular compassion to the widow, the orphan, the alien, and the poor was a tradition kept by the early church. In the fourth century, Basil of Caesarea (330–379), one of the Cappadocian fathers, wrote a unique exposition on "the least of these," in words pertinent to Western Christians today:

> Is not the person who strips another of clothing called a thief? And those who do not clothe the naked when they have the power to do so, should they not be called the same? The bread you are holding back is for the hungry, the clothes you keep put away are for the naked, the shoes that are rotting away with disuse are for those who have none, the silver you keep buried in the earth is for the needy. You are thus guilty of injustice toward as many as you might have aided, and did not.[45]

The poor, neglected, and outcast of today are suffering disproportionately from the planet's ecological predicament. Following in the tradition and practice of Jesus, it is the responsibility of those with power and privilege to care for the Earth and, by doing so, the economically underprivileged.

45. St. Basil the Great, *On Social Justice*, trans. C. Paul Schroeder (Yonkers, NY: St. Vladimir's Seminary Press, 2009), 70.

Harmony

On a visit to modern Israel, theologian Joseph Sittler's car broke down. He took it to a mechanic who was a Sabra, a native-born Israeli. When he returned several hours later, the mechanic was smiling. He lifted the hood, showed Sittler a flawlessly running engine, and said, "Sedaka." Sittler asked him to repeat the word, and the mechanic said, "Sedaka"—which Sittler recognized as the biblical word for "righteous" or "righteousness." Dan Erlander, who relates the story, comments that God's promise is righteousness, "a universe which functions like that engine. Every part works in harmony with every other part; all parts work for the good of the whole."[46]

Erlander bases this vision of a righteous harmony throughout the universe on the declaration in Ephesians that God "has made known to us the mystery of his will, according to his good pleasure that he set forth in Christ, as a plan [oikonomia] for the fullness of time, to gather up [anakephalaiosasthai] all things in him, things in heaven and things on earth" (Eph. 1:9–10). The fascinating and rare word, anakephalaiosasthai, derives from ancient mathematics.[47] The total sum of a string of numbers was known as the anakephalaiosasthai, a number that gathered up all the other numbers. "This is the work of Jesus Christ—to gather together every part of the universe, to bring everything together in one harmonious household."[48] Erlander's idea of "one harmonious household" draws on the Greek word oikonomia (v. 10). Translated as "plan" (NRSV), its basic meaning is "stewardship."[49]

The Pauline depiction of the reconciliation of "all things [ta panta]" through Christ's death on the cross reinforces this vision of harmony (Col. 1:15–20). James Dunn writes, "What is being claimed is quite simply and profoundly that the divine purpose in the act of reconciliation and peacemaking was to restore the harmony of the original creation."[50] Such a restoration of harmony and shalom is reminiscent of an indigenous understanding of harmony that includes humanity, social structures, ecosystems, and the created order.[51] Over fifty years ago, Sittler, a pioneering ecotheologian, gave a prophetic address, based on Colossians 1:15–20, that lifted up the theological and biblical

46. Erlander, *Manna and Mercy*, 93.
47. The only other use of the word is in Rom. 13:9: "The commandments . . . are summed up in this word, 'Love your neighbor as yourself.'"
48. Erlander, *Manna and Mercy*, 93.
49. See the section "Stewardship" in chap. 7.
50. James D. G. Dunn, *The Epistles to the Colossians and to Philemon* (Grand Rapids: Eerdmans, 1996), 104.
51. Randy S. Woodley, *Shalom and the Community of Creation* (Grand Rapids: Eerdmans, 2012), 14.

foundation of this harmony: "For it is here declared that the sweep of God's restorative action in Christ is no smaller than the six-times repeated *ta panta*. Redemption is the name for this will, this action, and this concrete Man who is God with us and God for us—and all things are permeable to his cosmic redemption because all things subsist in him. . . . He is not only the matrix and *prius* [a necessary prior condition] of all things; he is the intention, the fullness, and the integrity of all things."[52]

The Future

In 1992 twelve-year-old Severn Suzuki offered the closing address at one of the plenary sessions of the United Nations Earth Summit in Rio de Janeiro. She and a small group of friends had raised their own funds to attend the Summit. Thomas Friedman calls her speech "one of the most eloquent statements I have ever heard about both the strategic and the moral purpose of a really green revolution."[53] Here are just a few excerpts:

> Coming here today, I have no hidden agenda. I am fighting for my future. Losing my future is not like losing an election or a few points on the stock market. I am here to speak for all generations to come. . . .
>
> I'm only a child and I don't have all the solutions, but I want you to realize, neither do you! You don't know how to fix the holes in our ozone layer. You don't know how to bring the salmon back up a dead stream. You don't know how to bring back an animal now extinct. And you can't bring back the forests that once grew where there is now a desert. If you don't know how to fix it, please stop breaking it! . . .
>
> Do not forget why you're attending these conferences, who you're doing this for—we are your own children. You are deciding what kind of world we are growing up in.[54]

Someone has wisely said that not only do we inherit the Earth from our ancestors, but we are also borrowing it from our children. Professor John Ikerd has turned to Jesus's Sermon on the Mount—"In everything do to others as you would have them do to you" (Matt. 7:12)—to offer biblical support for the importance of considering future generations when making ecological choices: "The concept of sustainability applies the Golden Rule across generations: we

---

52. Joseph Sittler, "Called to Unity," in *Evocations of Grace*, ed. Steven Bouma-Prediger and Peter Bakken (Grand Rapids: Eerdmans, 2000), 45.
53. Thomas L. Friedman, "Who We Really Are," in *Moral Ground*, 189.
54. For a video of her speech, see "Severn Suzuki speaking at UN Earth Summit 1992," YouTube, May 29, 2007, https://www.youtube.com/watch?v=uZsDliXzyAY.

should do for those of future generations as we would have them do for us, if we were of their generation and they were of ours."[55] Are we, in our short-sighted decadence, inhibiting the ability of future generations to provide for themselves and their own children? Some eco-ethicists call this the principle of the seventh generation—meaning that our actions must take into account not just our children and grandchildren, but all future children of the Earth.

An ethic of love, grounded in God's ageless love for the world (John 3:16), moves us beyond self-interest to the welfare of others, beyond anthropocentrism to interconnectedness, beyond this generation only to those for whom we are forebears. Chief Oren Lyons, of the Seneca Nations of the Iroquois Confederacy, has written, "We are looking ahead, as is one of the first mandates given us as chiefs, to make sure and to make every decision that we make relate to the welfare and well-being of the seventh generation to come, and that is the basis by which we make decisions in council."[56] In a stock market age of quarterly reports, to make decisions for the well-being of the seventh generation is counterintuitive, revolutionary, and subversive. Its long-term logic and orientation to the Other disrupt a society built on short-term, egocentric fulfillment. The only thing that can empower such an ethic is love. A commitment to love, like to marriage, is founded on a promise. Indeed "the gate is narrow and the road is hard that leads to life" (Matt. 7:14), and it is only love, as Wendell Berry reminds us, that promises hope for the future: "Making a promise binds one *to someone else's future*. If the promise is serious enough, one is brought to it by love, and in awe and fear."[57]

■ ▓ ▒

For all the good that science has accomplished in our world, it has repeatedly failed to motivate the kind of expansive change needed to make a significant impact on the ecocrisis. It is our conviction that Christianity provides the coherent framework we need to integrate our experiences of the natural world with the values of our faith to foster such a transformation. Our own biblical reasons to care for the Earth are certainly not meant to be comprehensive or exhaustive. Yet these are the rationales that undergird our loyalties, affections, and convictions. And they are the reasons that turn our faith in the direction of action on behalf of all Creation.

55. John Ikerd, *Crisis and Opportunity* (Lincoln: University of Nebraska Press, 2008), 40–41.

56. Oren Lyons, "An Iroquois Perspective," in *American Indian Environments*, ed. Christopher Vecsey and Robert W. Venables (Syracuse: Syracuse University Press, 1994), 173.

57. Wendell Berry, "A Promise Made in Love, Awe, and Fear," in *Moral Ground*, 389.

3

The Voice of Creation

The Grandeur and the Groaning of the Earth

In the summer of 2012, I (Jen) found myself doing something unusual for someone not very interested in sports. At the insistence of eight-year-olds from my church I spent a late night watching the opening ceremony of the Olympics. The children had convinced me that the rumored showdown between Lord Voldemort and Mary Poppins would be worth watching.

The ceremony opened with Caliban's speech from Shakespeare's *The Tempest*. Embodying the archetypal "natural" man—wild and unintelligent, grotesque and deformed—Caliban represents those indigenous to the island. In the Olympic production, Caliban stood in front of a giant tree atop a tall hill in the center of the arena, which was covered in verdant, rolling fields. The opening prose was Caliban's "Be not afeard" speech, a monologue during which we become acutely aware of his love for his island home and the deep connection he feels with the natural environment.

> Be not afeard. The isle is full of noises,
> Sounds and sweet airs that give delight and hurt not.
> Sometimes a thousand twangling instruments
> Will hum about mine ears, and sometime voices
> That, if I then had waked after long sleep,
> Will make me sleep again; and then, in dreaming,

> The clouds methought would open, and show riches
> Ready to drop upon me, that when I waked,
> I cried to dream again.[1]

As Caliban's final line hung in the air, the English pastoral scene was deconstructed. The giant tree disconnected from its root system and floated into the sky, while hundreds of people (actors) arose from the ground, walking a winding path down the tall hill. They took the landscape apart piece by piece,

---

Tension Point: Stewardship

As common as it is to talk about the "stewardship" of Creation in Christian circles, it may be surprising to many that the term is actually quite controversial. By no means is our team in unity as to the ongoing viability of the concept of stewardship for our ecological future.

On the side of those who think stewardship has outlived its usefulness is the fact that the word "stewardship" in our churches means little more than an annual fund drive, in spite of all efforts to make the idea more inclusive and universal. Even more so, however, is the conviction by some that the notion of stewardship reinforces a hierarchical worldview, one in which humans steward the Earth from positions of power and domination.

On the other side are those who believe that stewardship, when practiced with humility and solidarity, is a perspective that recognizes our God-given responsibilities as humans. It acknowledges that even as we are the principal cause of the ecocrisis, we have a primary obligation for its restoration.

- Do you think it is possible for the concept of stewardship to be redeemed from its dominant meaning in most Christian communities? If not, what are the implications? If so, how?
- If we choose no longer to use the term "stewardship," what other options are available to us that would motivate Christ-followers toward earthkeeping?
- If we continue to employ the idea of stewardship, how can we reimagine it in ways that don't buttress hierarchy and unhealthy attitudes of dominion?

---

ripping out and rolling up sod and leaving what looked like broken and scorched cobblestones. Large, smog-pumping smokestacks replaced the tree. The actors who earlier descended the hill wearing overalls and suspenders, long skirts and

---

1. William Shakespeare, *The Tempest*, 3.2.148–56. References are to act, scene, and line. Folger Shakespeare Library, "The Isle Is Full of Noises," http://www.folger.edu/template.cfm?cid=2081, accessed January 21, 2013.

aprons, now wore gas masks as they erected smokestacks, worked on factory lines, and continued to make manifest the majesty of industry.

One of the news commentators made an aside, "We can't forget that the progress of the Industrial Revolution came at a great price." That single sentence represented the only reference to the darker history of the Industrial Revolution, the only acknowledgment of the devastation that period of history wreaked on the natural environment. No moment of grief was observed for the tree that disintegrated while smokestacks rose and earth was ripped from the ground. Caliban's isle full of noises was warped by the din of progress, of a world being forever changed by technology and modernity's mark. Another well-known piece of literature also depicts the earth full of noises: "The whole creation has been groaning in labor pains until now" (Rom. 8:22). In the Olympic pageantry the noise of industry and progress sounded more like "groaning" than "sweet airs that give delight."

Should we not experience some degree of cognitive dissonance as we watch the destruction of the planet while celebrating the progress of industry, science, and technology? If we stop and listen, to both the voice of God and Earth's sweet sounds and groaning, we just might acknowledge the ambiguity of events like the Industrial Revolution, gain a sense of the ways in which the planet has suffered mistreatment, and repent of how we have failed to be responsible stewards of Creation. In this chapter, by considering the grandeur and the groaning of the Earth, we hope to inspire a responsible stewardship, grounded in love.

The Grandeur of Creation

> Beauty is the experimental proof that the Incarnation is possible.
>
> —Simone Weil[2]

To learn to love the created order, and steward what we love, we begin by experiencing and reflecting on its grandeur—its beauty and wonder, its wildness and fierceness. To cultivate a sense of wonder for God's creation, states David Orr, "takes us to the edge of mystery where language loses its power to describe and where analysis, the taking apart of things, is impotent before the wholeness of Creation, where the only appropriate response is a prayerful silence."[3] The entire Creation, in all its grandeur, becomes our teacher, if only

2. Simone Weil, *The Notebooks of Simone Weil*, trans. Arthur Wills (New York: Routledge, 2004), 440.
3. David W. Orr, "Recollection," in *Ecological Literacy*, ed. Michael K. Stone and Zenobia Barlow (San Francisco: Sierra Club, 2005), 99. Mary-Jane Rubenstein, *Strange Wonder* (New

we will surrender to its wisdom. Malcolm Margolin observes, "The world contains things that we need to know that are too important to be left solely to human beings, and these essential lessons are embedded in the animals, plants, mountains, and rivers around us."[4] Margolin echoes Job: "But ask the animals, and they will teach you; / the birds of the air, and they will tell you; / ask the plants of the earth, and they will teach you; / and the fish of the sea will declare to you. / Who among all these does not know / that the hand of the LORD has done this?" (Job 12:7–9). Learning and understanding are not about control or manipulation as they often are in the Western scientific worldview. Learning *about* Creation *from* Creation is how we learn to love and to care *for* Creation. When we fall in love with the beauty, we will know what to do. In the words of C. S. Lewis, "We do not want merely to *see* beauty, though, God knows, even that is bounty enough. We want something else which can hardly be put into words—to be united with the beauty we see, to pass into it, to receive it into ourselves, to bathe in it, to become part of it."[5]

Childlike Wonder

On a blustery Oregon morning I (Dan) was walking to pick up my four-year-old granddaughter Kenley. Friday is my Sabbath, and most Friday mornings I hang out with Kenley, making pancakes and doing whatever we feel like doing. Her house is a half-mile from mine, and on my way that morning I noticed a tree with a particularly animated flock of birds in it. I made a mental note to point the birds out to Kenley on our way back. Setting out from her place I told her that I wanted to show her something. "That's great, Grandpa," was her eager response. We hadn't gone far before she piped up, "Grandpa, look at all these different rocks. One's brown, one's gray. What colors do you see, Grandpa? Rocks are really hard."

"Yes, rocks are hard," I said. "It is one of their finer qualities. Let's keep going. I've got something to show you."

A little farther down the sidewalk she stopped and commented, "Grandpa, look at these chestnuts. Squirrels really like them. You can crack them open when you stomp on them. Look at all the squirrels on that tree across the street."

"That's right, Kenley. Squirrels eat chestnuts, but we don't, unless they're roasting on the open fire. Let's keep walking."

York: Columbia University Press, 2008), 4, traces the earliest characterization of "wonder" back to Socrates, for whom wonder springs when "an everyday assumption has suddenly become untenable: the familiar has become strange, throwing even the unquestionable into question."

4. Malcolm Margolin, "Indian Pedagogy," in *Ecological Literacy*, 78.

5. C. S. Lewis, *The Weight of Glory* (New York: HarperCollins, 2001 [1949]), 42.

"Grandpa, see that pinecone? It looks like a little tree on the grass. Can I touch it?"

"It does look like a tree, Kenley. Let's not pick it up now. I want to show you something."

We pass a few more houses, and she yells excitedly, "Wait, Grandpa. Look at these yellow flowers. I can smell them. Do you want to smell them?"

"Sure." Sniff. "Come on, honey."

Soon she stopped still in her tracks. "Grandpa, wait. Stop. Listen. Do you hear them? Can you hear all the birds?"

What biologist E. O. Wilson calls "biophilia"—the love of life or living things—is acutely strong in children, particularly when they are young, as Rachel Carson has pointed out.[6] Their natural sense of wonder is nourished through direct experience in Creation and requires consistent support from adults. However in today's world children are more likely to play video games than they are to climb trees, to watch a nature DVD than to spend time in nature itself. Richard Louv describes this phenomenon as "nature-deficit disorder."[7] In screen-stimulated environments, the unstructured play of children—and their corresponding connection with Creation—is little more than nostalgia. The physical, psychological, and spiritual well-being of a whole generation is at stake. Children know little about the songbirds, trees, waterways, soil, and plants in their neighborhoods. And yet, in the West, they can instantly recognize scores of corporate logos. Shockingly one inner-city adolescent was even able to identify *by their sounds* six sundry automatic weapons used on the streets.[8] In contrast, to teach children to love their local ecosystems will empower them to "grow into engaged, effective citizens committed to preserving those places."[9]

From Object to Subject

Is it even possible for adults to recapture the naïve wonder of childhood? Maybe not. But maybe so. The wonder of a four-year-old girl is innocent and pure, filled with trust, immediacy, and joy. A seminary professor in his late fifties cannot return to the same innocence; he is too aware of the breadth and depth of environmental degradation and has seen too much pain and alienation in the created order. And yet it is important for adults to nourish a

6. Rachel Carson, *A Sense of Wonder* (New York: Harper & Row, 1965).
7. Richard Louv, *Last Child in the Woods* (Chapel Hill, NC: Algonquin Books of Chapel Hill, 2005), 74.
8. Gary Paul Nabhan and Stephen Trimble, *The Geography of Childhood* (Boston: Beacon, 1994), xiii.
9. Pamela Michael, "Helping Children Fall in Love with the Earth," in *Ecological Literacy*, 121.

"second naïveté," a love of Creation that is informed, firsthand, and responsible.[10] Jesus himself highlights this second naïveté: "Truly I tell you, unless
you change and become like children, you will never enter the kingdom of
heaven" (Matt. 18:3). This childlikeness marks the beginning of a Christian
ecological worldview.

To cultivate such a worldview, it is imperative that we move from knowing
the natural world as object to knowing it as subject.[11] To objectify Creation,
as modern Western culture has done, is to see it in the abstract, disembodied,
with the human as the only significant subject. Objectification allows us to stay
in control and hold the created world at a distance; we observe the Earth, but
seldom do we see ourselves as part of the Earth. Most experiences of nature
today, for both children and adults, are secondhand. This subject-object dualism
fosters a sense that human subjects are independent of the rest of Creation,
denying our interdependence; it focuses on, and even obsesses over, those things
that make us different from the Other, resulting in stereotyping and exclusivism.

A subject-subject model is embodied, rooted in touching and being touched.
It "rests on the assumption that the world is composed of living, changing,
growing, mutually related, interdependent entities, of which human beings are
one."[12] The subject-subject perspective is profoundly relational, and signifies
that the other subject has value, in and of itself. To be clear, this model does
not mean that rivers and bees "are conscious, purposive subjects, but only
that their raison d'être is not to be objects for us."[13] The process of adopting
a subject-subject mentality demands maturity, fearlessness, and discipline.
In love, it takes the Other seriously and strives to know it as it really is "in
itself." In humility, it opens itself to learn from the Other those realities only
the Other can teach. Far from romantic sentimentality, it requires us to pay
loving, detailed attention to the Other within its unique world.

Experiencing Creation

It takes me (Jen) forty-five minutes to ride my bike down my cul-de-sac, across
the local soccer field and neighborhood park, and down a country road devoid
of humanity. The goats and the hawk live there; in the summer, a flock of sheep
is in charge. Once I saw a bedraggled alpaca by the creek. I am most certain
of the existence of the Creator down that dead-end road. The other day, I let
my bike rest on the slope of the steep ditch. The alfalfa stood tall and green,

10. Sallie McFague, *Super, Natural Christians* (Minneapolis: Fortress, 1997), 116.
11. On what follows, see ibid., 67–90.
12. Ibid., 96.
13. Ibid., 111.

rippling and rolling in the wind—brilliant green waves that stretched out for acres. The rare Oregon winter sun warmed my cheeks, and I became aware of the stillness. No creature made a sound. Perhaps, like me, they were enraptured. In moments like these, the only thing that seems right is to bear silent witness. There are a hundred other such encounters I could narrate—standing by the waves of the Pacific Ocean, driving into the Grand Ronde Valley where farmland unfurls like a patchwork quilt—moments where I connect with something so rooted within me that it feels like coming home. I am just beginning to learn to wrap words around what is an encounter with God, the natural world, *and* myself. It is a rare moment in which I escape into liminal space.

An ecotone is just such a liminal space; it is a transitional zone between two different biological communities.[14] Salmon, on their arduous journey to the ocean, are converted from fingerling to smolt in the transitional waters of an estuary, where fresh waters from river deltas intermix with the briny tides of the sea. In one of God's natural miracles, the brackish water of the estuary provides an ideal environment for "smoltification," the physiological alteration of juvenile salmon from freshwater fish to saltwater, and indeed an unmatched place for adult salmon to "re-convert" on their way home. Ecotones, such as estuaries and riparian fringes, are biologically defined spaces, but ecotones can be "spiritual" spaces as well: areas in which a city bumps up against a wildlife refuge; places of worship, where our physical life is integrated with our spiritual communal life; supper tables with friends sharing their lives. In these places we have the possibility of intermixing with what is utterly Other.

On this journey to experience Creation, we must ask ourselves if we will be able to see the space we inhabit as holy, if we will allow ourselves to learn from and understand the landscapes around us, if we can be swept up into them.[15] When we find ourselves in these places of encounter, boundaries get thin. Our vision of what is "holy" expands. Like Moses, it is as we approach the mysterious God of Creation resident within a desert bush that we remove our sandals, feeling the soil underfoot invade the space between our toes (Exod. 3:5). Our "relatability" to God as subject opens us up to relate to Creation as subject; as we approach God we will approach Creation. When we risk relating with the natural world, we will discover similar kinds of wonder and pain that we experience in relationships with each other and with God. But such is the essence of relationship, of communion, of the experience of entering into the life of the Other and receiving life in return.

14. Barry Lopez, *Arctic Dreams* (New York: Vintage, 2001 [1986]), 123.
15. Douglas Burton-Christie, "Into the Body of Another: *Eros*, Embodiment and Intimacy with the Natural World," *Anglican Theological Review* 81, no. 1 (1999): 14–15.

On Darkness and Wildness

In his study of darkness and night in preindustrial society, historian Roger Ekirch has explored what it was like in society before the lightbulb, when only the wealthy could afford the luxury of a candle. People developed a language surrounding each phase of night: there was candlelight (the first phase of night), then the dead of night, then first cock crow, then second cock crow. Folks slept differently—they usually slept twice. After about four hours of uneasy sleep, they would wake up for an hour or so. They might meditate or pray or talk to bedmates or even visit neighbors. Then they would go back to sleep for another four-hour stretch. People referred to these as their first and second sleeps. Accidents were common at night: people fell into ditches, ponds, rivers, or off bridges. Crime rates rose during the night; laws became fuzzy and rules shifted. Night's darkness filled our ancestors with fear.[16]

Darkness is connected in our symbolic consciousness with foreboding, fear, and even death. Likewise we have inherited the deep-seated impression that nature is constantly renewable and practically inexhaustible and impervious.[17] We can call to mind the numerous stories we tell (historical and fictional) that perpetuate these symbolic partial-truths: from Hansel and Gretel's terror of the dark forest to Francis Bacon's scientific theory that nature is limitless. Just as humans stereotype one another, so we stereotype the natural world. To grasp the whole picture of "darkness," we need to revise our symbolism and embrace "both-and" imagery. Darkness is not only death and destruction; Larry Rasmussen reminds us that it is also a place of dreaming, a time for stars: "New life always begins in darkness, in dark wombs or dark soil, even dark tombs. New life is the gift of darkness."[18]

What is true of darkness is true of wildness: our symbolism must take on a "both-and" character. The natural world is certainly at times violent and brutally survivalist—Tennyson pronounced it "red in tooth and claw." But, paradoxically, Creation's wildness is also holy and sacred, something for which our souls long. God confronted Job with the inscrutable wonder of the created world (Job 38–41), while Jesus sought solace and perspective in the wilderness where the wild beasts kept him company (Mark 1:13). How many of us would dare a similar journey into the wild? Perhaps we avoid the wilderness out of fear. Or maybe it is unfamiliarity because wild spaces are disappearing. Terry Tempest Williams calls it "simply lack of land, no natural corridors to

16. Joyce and Richard Wolkomir, "When Bandogs Howle and Spirits Walk," *Smithsonian* 31, no. 10 (January 2001): 38–44; see also A. Roger Ekirch, *At Day's Close* (New York: W. W. Norton, 2005).

17. Larry R. Rasmussen, *Earth Community, Earth Ethics* (Maryknoll, NY: Orbis, 1996), 220.

18. Ibid., 226.

reconnect the wild, the continuous world we have lost." And what we have lost contributes to our fear: "We raise clenched fists to the wind. We are still afraid of wildness: wild places, wild acts, wild thoughts."[19]

In reconnecting with the wild, we must reconsider our definition of wilderness. Rather than a relationship of fear, what would it mean to think of ourselves in a relationship with nature? To be in love means rejecting any orientation that "seduces us into believing that our only place in the wild is as spectator, onlooker."[20] It is possible to visualize a world in which boundaries are more permeable, and we become less separated from each other, God, and the whole community of life.[21] In risking relationality with the natural world we will find ourselves rejecting definitions of darkness only as death or of nature only as romantic or violent. We will remember, as Annie Dillard encouraged us, that Creation is simultaneously lovely—"My God what a world. There is no accounting for one second of it"[22]—*and* terrible—"We wake in terror, eat in hunger, sleep with a mouthful of blood."[23] At times, theologian Belden Lane states, "Nature's ferocity unnerves us."[24] At the same time, it is a place of compassion and wonder, in which elephants slow their travel pace to adjust to the needs of a crippled member.[25]

It is only in accepting the complexity of definitions, embracing both the darkness and the light, the violence and compassion of the natural world, that we will see reality and the holiness of the wild.

Creation and Suffering

Christian philosopher Holmes Rolston III writes, "If God watches the sparrow fall, God must do so from a very great distance."[26] Rolston uses the white pelican to illustrate his struggle reconciling a benevolent God with the violent suffering of sentient creatures in the natural world. The female white pelican typically lays two eggs, the second a few days after the first. Pelicans usually only parent one chick at a time; the second pelican is insurance—a "backup chick"—in case something goes wrong with the first. As the first chick develops she (or he) grabs most of the food, attacks her sibling, and eventually

---

19. Terry Tempest Williams, *Red* (New York: Pantheon, 2001), 102–3.
20. Ibid., 106.
21. Burton-Christie, "Into the Body of Another," 16.
22. Annie Dillard, *Pilgrim at Tinker Creek* (New York: HarperCollins, 2007 [1974]), 267.
23. Ibid., 177.
24. Belden Lane, *Ravished by Beauty* (New York: Oxford University Press, 2011), 218.
25. Mark Bekoff, *The Emotional Lives of Animals* (Novato, CA: New World Library, 2007), 3.
26. Holmes Rolston III, *Science and Religion* (New York: Random House, 1987), 140; see also Jay B. McDaniel, *Of Gods and Pelicans* (Louisville: Westminster John Knox, 1989), 19–21.

pushes it out of the nest. The parents refuse to take the second chick back into the nest, and he (or she) dies of starvation or neglect. It is "natural" for the parents and first chick to behave as they do. The second chick's death serves the posterity of the species. Yet what are we to say about the suffering of the second chick? Is he a "subject"? Does God see his plight?

Christopher Southgate describes three traditional "solutions" and counter-points to the question of why there is "great suffering" in the natural world. A Thomist would answer that the white pelicans need to reject one chick in order to be what God created them to be; conversely, suffering (and the dis-posal of the feeble) seems to be necessary to the natural selection of God's ongoing creation. Others believe that the world was harmonious and absent of violence until humanity sinned; however we have evidence of disease and brutality in the created order before humans appeared on the scene. And still others hold that animals do not experience pain; alternatively investigations show that the nervous systems and biochemistry of sentient creatures are such that they experience pleasure and suffer pain. Southgate concludes that we live in a "profoundly ambiguous world": the creation is "very good" (Gen. 1:31) *and* it is "groaning in labor pains" (Rom. 8:22).[27]

Navigating our way through the thorny question of suffering is demand-ing. Luther's theology of the cross accentuates that (human) suffering is an inevitable aspect of being Christian and that God is hidden (*Deus absconditus*) in suffering. Yet, frequently, to focus on finding "spiritual" meaning in suffer-ing results in ignoring the systemic nature of suffering and sin. As Holocaust survivor Elie Wiesel remarked: "A religion that glorifies suffering will always find someone to suffer."[28] Nevertheless it is possible to address suffering both spiritually and systemically. Korean theologian Chung Hyun Kyung empha-sizes that to be human is both to suffer and to combat any oppression that causes suffering.[29]

Creation teaches us that not all suffering is destructive, that suffering is part of the struggle as finite creatures change and grow—to suffer, as Carl Jung writes, is to carry "the legitimate pain of being human." Yet, there is also a suffering that is disintegrative, that, in the words of Rasmussen, "negates life and destroys the realization of creation."[30] As Christians we follow a God who seeks out that which is shattered by sin, both personal and systemic, and

27. Christopher Southgate, "How Could a Good God Create Nature Red in Tooth and Claw?" (Earth Day lecture at St. John's University, Collegeville, MN, April 22, 2013); see also Christopher Southgate, *The Groaning of Creation* (London: Westminster John Knox, 2008), 3–6.
28. Cited in Deanna A. Thompson, *Crossing the Divide* (Minneapolis: Fortress, 2004), 128.
29. Chung Hyun Kyung, *Struggle to Be the Sun Again* (Maryknoll, NY: Orbis, 1990), 39, 54.
30. Rasmussen, *Earth Community, Earth Ethics*, 289.

re-creates what is beautiful and good. We cannot evade the degenerative "suffering" of rain forests and mountaintops as they surrender to the bulldozers of human greed. When the Creation suffers degradation, God suffers. For the sake of life, discipleship calls us to love God's Creation "fiercely" *in* its suffering: if we as Christians "were present only in a redeeming way to creation's beauty and not in its plunder and rape, then broken creation would never be healed."[31] Love entreats us to be in solidarity with everyone and everything suffering disintegratively.[32]

■ ■ ■

Creation's grandeur has the power to awaken childlike wonder at its beauty and to evoke trepidation at its wildness and brutality. By reconsidering those symbols (such as darkness, natural, and wildness) that objectify nature, we gain fresh insight into our own createdness and a renewed experience with the natural world. We can engage Earth's suffering, knowing that we serve a God who suffers with Creation, that in the cross God began the healing of all things, and that becoming fully human means loving fiercely all that God loves.

The Scientist as Prophet

> As long as slavery was discussed in economic terms, there was not much progress toward abolishing it. Abolition came after it reached the pulpits of this nation as a moral issue. We need to see ecological issues in moral terms also.
>
> —Fred Krueger[33]

To explore and experience the grandeur of Creation—beautiful, dark, and wild as it is—makes its groaning and suffering that much more apparent.

The Cries of the Earth

The first murder recorded in the Bible is fratricide, the account of Cain slaughtering his brother Abel in a crop field (Gen. 4). The sons of Adam and Eve had been bringing sacrifices to God. God had "no regard" for Cain's offering, though the text does not explicitly reveal why. Because God accepted

---

31. Ibid., 287–88.
32. Cynthia Moe-Lobeda, "A Theology of the Cross for the 'Uncreators,'" in *Cross Examinations*, ed. Marit Trelstad (Minneapolis: Augsburg Fortress, 2006), 193.
33. Frederick W. Krueger, executive coordinator, National Religious Coalition on Creation Care. The source of the quote is unknown, nor does Krueger remember when he first used it. Personal email, Aug. 7, 2013. Used by permission.

Abel's sacrifice but rejected Cain's, Cain killed his brother in a jealous rage. So God issued divine punishment: "What have you done? Listen; your brother's blood is crying out to me from the ground! And now you are cursed from the ground, which has opened its mouth to receive your brother's blood from your hand. When you till the ground, it will no longer yield to you its strength; you will be a fugitive and a wanderer on the earth" (vv. 10–12). In spilling blood upon the land, Cain betrayed his own vocation to the earth. A caretaker of the land would provide for it, yet Cain had brought death rather than life to it. The earth itself resisted the betrayal—in action, by ceasing to yield, and in voice, as the spilled blood cried out.

The Hebrew "crying out" (*tsaʿaq*) is a violent verb, similar to the cry for help one might utter when encountering physical violation (see Deut. 22:24). Thus the land experienced profound desecration through the act of Cain. In the Bible, Creation has a voice that demands to be heard. For as long as the Earth has been groaning, there have been prophets speaking on its behalf. Hosea offers a thought-provoking variation on the land: the land mourns for us (Hos. 4:3). The prophet Isaiah declared: "The earth lies polluted / under its inhabitants; / for they have transgressed laws, / violated the statutes, / broken the everlasting covenant. / Therefore a curse devours the earth, / and its inhabitants suffer for their guilt" (Isa. 24:5–6). Human action (and inaction) has been contributing to the destruction of the planet for a very long time.

Scripture and many scientists agree on this point: the earth is "crying out." In our day the scientist often plays the role of prophet. "More than any other single segment of the general public today—certainly more than government leaders, lawyers, philosophers, and educators—more, even, than most mainline preachers, it is the scientists who are telling us that our world is in critical shape and that the human element is chiefly to blame for it," writes Douglas John Hall.[34] The scientific community has concluded, with considerable consensus, that there are major ecological changes taking place, and that the causes are primarily anthropogenic. Increasingly Christian theologians, biblical scholars, and leaders have become more willing to take note of, discuss, and engage these modern-day prophets.

Faith and Science

The interactions between the ecological movement and Christianity, between science and religion, are often cautious, suspicious, and even antagonistic. Wendell Berry once told a seminary audience "that the culpability of Christianity

---

34. Douglas John Hall, *Imaging God* (Grand Rapids: Eerdmans, 1986), 8.

in the destruction of the natural world and uselessness of Christianity in any effort to correct that destruction are now established clichés of the conservation movement."[35] But as the ecocrisis and our awareness of it deepen, scientists and conservationists are acknowledging the important role faith and religion have to play in tackling the problem. Aldo Leopold recognized this vital truth well over fifty years ago: "No important change in ethics was ever accomplished without an internal change in our intellectual emphasis, loyalties, affections, and convictions. The proof that conversation has not yet touched these foundations of conduct lies in the fact that philosophy and religion have not yet heard of it. In our attempt to make conservation easy, we have made it trivial."[36] While science does not exist as a discipline to answer questions of faith, and religion is not a matrix for scientific formulas, the two can and ought to engage in conversation, especially when the survival of the planet is at stake.

So how are we to investigate the controversial relationship between faith and science? To begin with, Fuller Seminary's Nancey Murphy points out "that the warfare of science and religion is now conclusively shown to have been a myth." The uproar surrounding Galileo and Darwin has been overplayed, while other friendly and productive exchanges between science and religion tend to be ignored.[37] Ian Barbour outlines four options for how religion and science relate to each other.[38] The first option, *conflict*, involves a clash between "scientific materialism" and "biblical literalism." Both make dogmatic claims about the source of truth or epistemology—logical data versus infallible Scripture—forcing choices, such as between evolution and God, and demonizing the opposing view. In the second option, *independence*, each endeavor is autonomous, with its own language, jurisdiction, and turf; with this option a person can be a scientist *and* a Christian but sees no need to reconcile those worlds. A third option is *dialogue*, in which both worldviews converse in a spirit of hospitality, humility, and teachability. The last option, *integration*, holds that a synthesis or intermingling is possible between theology and science, with a common, recognized language.

Our goal in this text is to honor both science and religion in the hope of furthering hospitable dialogue. If science by itself has failed to motivate the kind of expansive change needed to make a significant impact on the

35. Wendell Berry, "Christianity and the Survival of Creation," in *The Art of the Commonplace*, ed. Norman Wirzba (Berkeley: Counterpoint, 2002), 305.

36. Aldo Leopold, *The Sand County Almanac* (New York: Oxford University Press, 1949), 174.

37. "Can We Believe in Both Science and Religion?," transcript of episode with participants Nancey Murphy, Muzaffar Iqbal, and Michael Shermer, *Closer to Truth*, PBS, episode 2 (2013), Robert Lawrence Kuhn, executive producer, http://www.pbs.org/program/closer-to-truth/.

38. Ian Barbour, *Religion and Science* (New York: HarperCollins, 1997), 77–105.

ecocrisis and if Western Christianity bears substantial responsibility for this moment of crisis, then science and faith need each other. We must invite both to the table, acknowledging where they may inform each other, and where their traditional answers are insufficient. Both *can* make room for the other. Christianity, too often, has turned the Bible into something its authors never intended: a science textbook. Galileo Galilei once quoted an eminent cardinal who said that the intention of the Holy Spirit in Scripture is "to teach us how one goes to heaven, not how heaven goes."[39] Likewise science has not proven itself very capable of dealing with moral questions, nor of answering "ultimate" questions, such as, "Why is there something rather than nothing?" or "What are we all here for?"[40] Pope John Paul II once said, "Science can purify religion from error and superstition. Religion can purify science from idolatry and false absolutes."[41]

The relationship between religion and science has, in part, revived interest in natural theology.[42] Natural theology, especially as elucidated by Thomas Aquinas, is the degree to which we can know God by natural reason through an investigation of nature and without special revelation. Theologians have (famously) debated the sufficiency of natural theology for a true knowledge of God that leads to faith.[43] Today a number of Christian thinkers are no longer trying to "prove" the existence of a Creator through nature; rather, more unassumingly, they begin with a belief in God's existence as revealed in Scripture and tradition and then ask what we can know about this God through an investigation of Creation.[44] Interestingly a number of scientists, especially among those researching fundamental physics, are directing attention to natural theology.[45] A physicist not normally favorable toward religion writes: "It may seem bizarre, but in my opinion science offers a surer path

39. Galileo Galilei, "Letter to the Grand Duchess Christina (1615)," in *Discoveries and Opinions of Galileo*, trans. Stillman Drake (Garden City, NY: Doubleday, 1957), 186.

40. For an example of a scientist who acknowledges the limits of scientific logic for answering "ultimate" questions, see Peter Medawar, *The Limits of Science* (Oxford: Oxford University Press, 1984), 66.

41. Cited in Tadeusz Pacholczyk, "Are Science and Religion Really Enemies?," *Making Sense Out of Bioethics* (October 2008), *Catholic Education Resource Center* (website), http://www.catholiceducation.org/articles/apologetics/ap0273.htm.

42. On the broad array of definitions and approaches to natural theology, see *The Oxford Handbook of Natural Theology*, ed. Russell Re Manning (Oxford: Oxford University Press, 2013). David Fergusson outlines five types of natural theology in "Types of Natural Theology," in *The Evolution of Rationality*, ed. F. LeRon Shults (Grand Rapids: Eerdmans, 2006), 380–93.

43. See *Natural Theology: Comprising "Nature and Grace" by Professor Dr. Emil Brunner and the Reply "No!" by Dr. Karl Barth*, trans. Peter Fraenkel (Eugene, OR: Wipf & Stock, 2002 [1946]).

44. Christopher Southgate, "Natural Theology and Ecology," in *Oxford Handbook of Natural Theology*, 459; R. J. Berry, *God's Book of Works* (London: T&T Clark, 2003), xiii.

45. John Polkinghorne, *Science and Creation* (London: SPCK, 1988), 15.

to God than religion."[46] Nonetheless natural theology is most useful when it avoids a "God of the Gaps"—simply plugging God in whenever science has unanswered questions—and focuses on how God can offer insights on cosmology and "ultimate" questions.

In order to enter into fruitful dialogue, both scientists and theologians must be willing to leave the comfort of their silos, their professional fields, and, in the words of Wendell Berry, to "feel the emotions and take the risks of amateurism."[47] Over the last centuries, a lot of water has passed under the bridge of the relationship between faith and science. Emotions on both sides run deep and are easily riled. Yet the Earth is waiting for us to face our fears and take the risk of vulnerable dialogue.

The Groaning of Creation

> I am concerned about the wounds and bleeding sores on the naked body of the earth. Have we not seen the long-term effects of these bleeding sores? The famine? The poverty? The chemical and nuclear accidents? . . .
> We are responsible directly or indirectly. We are, all of us, strangling the earth.
>
> —Wangari Maathai[48]

Halfway between North America and Asia lies Midway Atoll—a 2.4-square-mile island in the North Pacific Ocean. It is home to the Midway Atoll Wildlife Refuge and is the natural habitat for millions of seabirds. Today hundreds of thousands of albatross chicks lie dead on the island, bodies stacked in mountainous piles. They have been choked to death by bits of plastic gathered as "nourishment" by their parents from the ocean. Bird carcasses reveal stomachs full of cigarette lighters, bottle caps, and tampon applicators. Photographer Chris Jordan comments, "Like the albatross, we first-world humans find ourselves lacking the ability to discern anymore what is nourishing from what is toxic to our lives and our spirits."[49]

The ecocrisis is as toxic to humans as it is to the rest of Creation, yet we in the first-world remain comfortably insulated, while those in the majority

46. Paul Davies, *God and the New Physics* (New York: Simon & Schuster, 1983), ix.

47. Wendell Berry, *Citizenship Papers* (Washington, DC: Shoemaker & Hoard, 2003), 39.

48. Wangari Maathai, cited in Baboucarr Mbye, "Gambia: What is KMC Doing about the Bakoteh Dump Site?" *The Independent*, Banjul, Gambia, May 16, 2003, http://allafrica.com /stories/200305160041.html.

49. Jon Bowermaster, "Ocean Horror Show: Dead Sea Birds with Bellies Full of Plastic Garbage," *Take Part*, August 29, 2012, http://www.takepart.com/article/2012/08/28/plastic -waste-killing-birds-tens-thousands?cmpid=tp-ptnr-hufpo.

world suffer the devastating effects of this human-made apocalypse. If the scientist is a modern-day prophet, we must pay attention and listen. What follows is a departure from our safe silo of theology and biblical studies and is an amateur venture into scientific inquiry. Our goal is not necessarily to speak with expert authority, but, risking amateurism, to raise critical matters worthy of engagement and dialogue. In this broad overview, we will leave many issues undiscussed or underdiscussed, such as air pollution, genetically modified foods, or the use of pesticides and chemicals. What follows is a sampling; the issues of ecological degradation are widespread, constantly shifting, and multiplying.

"Hockey Stick" Graphs

When the Intergovernmental Panel on Climate Change (IPCC) issued its 2001 report on global climate change, it highlighted the "Hockey Stick," a chart that demonstrates how temperatures around the planet over 1,000 years have increased disproportionately with the advent of industrialization and employment of fossil fuels. The graph gives a striking visualization of the impact of elevated carbon dioxide (CO_2) levels on global warming and proposes that the decade of the 1990s was the hottest in the last 600 years. Because of the dramatic nature of the hockey stick graph, it engendered sharp controversy and opposition. One observer claims, "The hockey stick graph has become one of the most iconic and politically charged images in the history of science."[50]

While the IPCC used the original hockey stick graph (see fig. 3.1) to address global climate change, Rasmussen has found hockey stick graphs everywhere.[51] Using a common date range of 1750–2000, he offers 24 different graphs, all of the hockey stick variety. They include graphs of problems we will attend to in this section—population, water use, CO_2 atmospheric concentrations, and loss of biodiversity and tropical rain forests—and other ecologically related issues, such as coastal zone biogeochemisty, total real gross domestic product, paper consumption, and McDonald's restaurants. His point is to show the interrelatedness of a wide range of predicaments, that global warming and climate change, though they may be the most pressing concerns today, are really just the tip of the (shrinking) iceberg. Unprecedented "hockey stick" growth is taking the whole planet and its human population into uncharted waters.

---

50. Shawn Lawrence Otto, "Review: *The Hockey Stick and the Climate Wars*," *Huffington Post*, February 27, 2012, http://www.huffingtonpost.com/shawn-lawrence-otto/the-hockey-stick -and-the-_b_1304399.html, accessed Jan. 4, 2014. See also Michael E. Mann, *The Hockey Stick and the Climate Wars* (New York: Columbia University Press, 2012), 147–48.
51. Larry L. Rasmussen, *Earth-honoring Faith* (New York: Oxford University Press, 2012), 132–33.

Fig. 3.1 Northern Hemisphere

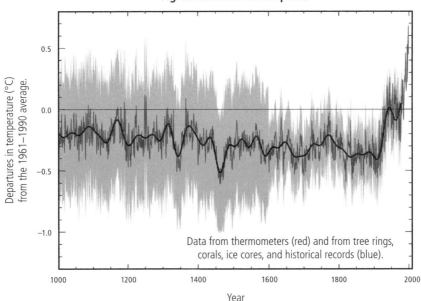

Source: IPCC Third Assessment Report, "Climate Change 2001: Waking Group 1: The Scientific Basis," GRID-Arendal, http://www.grida.no/publications/other/ipcc_tar/wg1/005.htm

Climate Change

On July 10, 2013, over 200 scientists and academicians who identify as evangelicals released an urgent letter imploring the United States Congress to take concrete action on climate change. Their letter begins:

> As evangelical scientists and academics, we understand climate change is real and action is urgently needed. All of God's Creation—humans and our environment—is groaning under the weight of our uncontrolled use of fossil fuels, bringing on a warming planet, melting ice, and rising seas. The negative consequences and burdens of a changing climate will fall disproportionately on those whom Jesus called "the least of these": the poor, vulnerable, and oppressed.[52]

Some might express surprise that such a large number of evangelicals would come together on this issue, but it should not be alarming. They are in line with widespread scientific opinion. Addressing climate change, Donald Kennedy, executive editor-in-chief of *Science* magazine, remarked, "Consensus as strong as

52. For a copy of the letter and its signatories, see http://sojo.net/sites/default/files/Evangelical%20Scientists%20Initiative%20Letter.pdf, accessed July 15, 2013; see also Janelle Tupper, "Evangelical Scientists Call for Climate Action," *God's Politics* (blog), Sojourners website, July 10, 2013, http://sojo.net/blogs/2013/07/10/evangelical-scientists-call-climate-action.

the one that has developed around this topic is rare in science."[53] Mark Maslin, in his helpful introduction to global warming, notes that the 2007 report by the IPCC, "amounting to nearly 3,000 pages of detailed review and analysis of published research, declares that the scientific uncertainties of global warming are essentially resolved."[54] Organizations from all over the globe, like the IPCC, have provided strong substantiation that these atmospheric changes are global rather than regional and that they are a result of its human inhabitants. And yet in a 2013 poll, while over two-thirds of Americans are convinced of the reality of global warming, only 42 percent attribute it to human activity.[55]

Global warming is driven by the phenomenon of more greenhouse gases being released into the atmosphere than are trapped by the ocean, forest, and soil, resulting in a changed climate. Since the Industrial Revolution, greenhouse gases have proliferated and the planet has been warming. Those gases (including CO_2, methane, nitrous oxide, ozone, and CFCs) reflect infrared radiation and warm the planet. The buildup of greenhouse gases trapped in the atmosphere has been exacerbated by human action—burning vast amounts of ancient carbon deposits (fossil fuels), the release of methane from livestock, emissions from vehicles, and deforestation. The level of CO_2 currently in the air is 40 percent more than in preindustrial times, where it had remained relatively stable at 280 parts per million for 1,000 years. As of 2013 it had reached 400 parts per million.

As a result of increased CO_2 concentrations, the global average surface temperature in the twentieth century increased 0.75°C (1.3°F), resulting in the sea level rising approximately 22 centimeters over the same period.[56] Polar ice caps are melting at exponential rates. Climate models project additional warming of 1.1°C –6.4°C (2.0°F –11.5°F) and a sea-level rise of 18–59 centimeters by the end of the century, if not sooner. Climate change is not linear, and *feedback loops* and *tipping points* make predictions complicated. A feedback loop, which

53. Donald Kennedy, "An Unfortunate U-Turn on Carbon," *Science* 291, no. 5513 (March 30, 2001): 2515.

54. Mark Maslin, *Global Warming: A Very Short Introduction*, 2nd ed. (Oxford: Oxford University Press, 2009), Kindle locations 359–61. See also Douglas Allen, "Is the Sky Falling: A Brief Introduction to Climate Change Science," in *Christians, the Care of Creation, and Global Climate Change*, ed. Lindy Scott (Eugene, OR: Pickwick, 2008); John T. Houghton, *Global Warming* (Cambridge: Cambridge University Press, 2004); Intergovernmental Panel of Climate Change, Martin L. Parry et al., eds., *Climate Change 2007: Impacts, Adaptations, and Vulnerability* (Cambridge: Cambridge University Press, 2007).

55. From a Pew Research Center survey conducted March 13–17, 2013, on 1,501 adults nationwide, PollingReport.com (website), http://www.pollingreport.com/enviro.htm, accessed July 12, 2013; see also Peter T. Doran and Maggie Kendall Zimmerman, "Examining the Scientific Consensus on Climate Change," *Eos, Transactions American Geophysical Union* 90, no. 3 (January 20, 2009): 22–23.

56. Maslin, *Global Warming*, Kindle locations 361–62.

Fig. 3.2 Global Atmospheric Concentration of CO_2 (ppm)

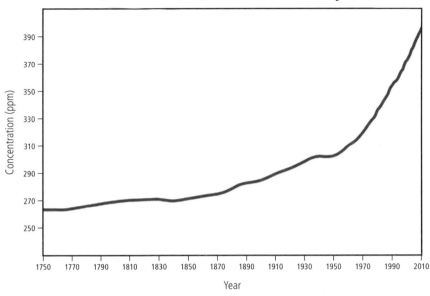

Source: National Oceanic and Atmospheric Administration (NOAA), cited in "Atmospheric concentration of Carbon Dioxide (ppm)," European Environment Agency, January 10, 2013, http://www.eea.europa.eu/data-and-maps/figures/atmospheric-concentration-of-co2-ppm-1, accessed July 15, 2013.

can be negative or positive, is when an ecosystem is affected by something it initially caused. Scientists are concerned, for example, about the northern boreal forests, where changes in the vegetation because of climate change is prompting even more warming.[57] A tipping point is "a critical threshold at which a tiny perturbation can qualitatively alter the state or development of a system."[58] When a tipping point is reached in the earth's system, it cannot be undone or reversed. Maslin states, "Scientists feel that 2°C is the tipping point when almost all people in the world become losers from climate change."[59]

Short-term economic perspectives impede long-term solutions. It is estimated that reducing global carbon emissions today would cost 1 percent of world gross domestic product (GDP), while the consequences of not doing so could cost up to 20 percent of world GDP.[60] Many scientists predict that the effects of global warming may start slowly but will become severe, especially

57. Douglas Fischer, "Shift in boreal forest has wide impact," *The Daily Climate*, March 28, 2011, http://www.dailyclimate.org/tdc-newsroom/2011/03/boreal-shift, accessed Jan. 4, 2014.
58. Timothy M. Lenton et al., "Tipping Elements in the Earth's Climate System," *Proceedings of the National Academy of Science* 105, no. 6 (February 12, 2008): 1786.
59. Maslin, *Global Warming*, Kindle locations 1804–5.
60. Ibid., Kindle Locations 377–78.

if a tipping point is reached: desertification, drought, and famine will be widespread; heat waves and forest fires will be more common; higher temperatures will reduce crop yields; water will become scarce; fish populations will decline; natural disasters like hurricanes and flooding will increase; biodiversity will decrease.[61] And, needless to say, it will be the vulnerable who will suffer the greatest. The United Nations Development Programme states:

> Climate change is the defining human development challenge of the 21st Century. Failure to respond to that challenge will stall and then reverse international efforts to reduce poverty. The poorest countries and most vulnerable citizens will suffer the earliest and most damaging setbacks, even though they have contributed least to the problem. Looking to the future, no country—however wealthy or powerful—will be immune to the impact of global warming.[62]

In short, humanity is "conducting an unintended, uncontrolled, globally pervasive experiment," by which "Earth's atmosphere is being changed at an unprecedented rate."[63] Truly "in the twentieth century, the glory of the human has become the desolation of the Earth."[64]

Water Degradation

On the evening of April 20, 2010, the Deepwater Horizon oil spill in the Gulf of Mexico became the largest accidental marine oil spill in the history of the oil industry. Eleven people aboard the rig lost their lives, and an estimated 53,000 barrels of oil a day poured from the well before it was capped. In total, over 5 million barrels of crude oil and more than 1.9 million gallons of toxic Corexit dispersants used to sink the oil were spilled into the gulf. Oceanographer Ian R. MacDonald stated: "These things reverberate through the ecosystem. It is an ecological echo chamber, and I think we'll be hearing the echoes of this, ecologically, for the rest of my life."[65] Indeed two years

---

61. Ernest Callenbach, *Ecology: A Pocket Guide* (Berkeley: University of California Press, 2008), 71–75.

62. Maslin, *Global Warming*, Kindle locations 388–89.

63. World Meteorological Organization, "The Changing Atmosphere: Implications for Global Security" (1988), 292, http://www.cmos.ca/ChangingAtmosphere1988e.pdf, accessed July 27, 2013.

64. Thomas Berry, *The Christian Future and the Fate of the Earth*, ed. Mary Evelyn Tucker and John Grim (Maryknoll, NY: Orbis, 2009), 117.

65. Quoted in Campbell Robertson and Clifford Krauss, "Gulf Spill Is the Largest of Its Kind, Scientists Say," *New York Times*, August 2, 2010, http://www.nytimes.com/2010/08/03/us/03spill.html?_r=0.

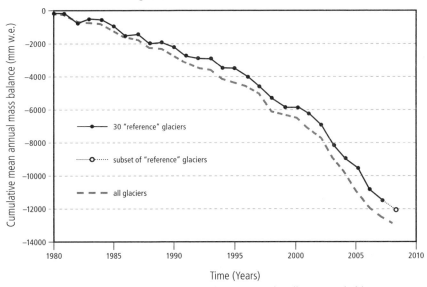

Fig. 3.3 Glacier Mass Balance 1980–2008

Source: World Glacier Monitoring Service, June 10, 2011, http://www.geo.uzh.ch/microsite
/wgms/mbb/sum09.html.

later those reverberations were showing up as mutated sea creatures in the gulf waters.[66]

Three-quarters of the globe is covered by water, yet the oceans are not as infinite as our "blue planet" terminology might indicate. Three major issues threaten the health of the world's oceans: global warming, overfishing, and pollution. Ocean water is a major absorber of greenhouse gases; an overabundance of CO_2 due to global warming reacts in the water to form carbonic acid, which endangers marine life, causes significant harm to coral reefs, and has effectively collapsed the oyster industry in the Pacific Northwest.[67] Consumption of seafood worldwide has tripled since the 1950s, pushing innumerable ocean species toward extinction. Scientists project that many species of wild seafood will be 90 percent depleted by 2050. The fishing industry has significantly altered the marine ecosystem. Some estimate that as the world's oceans are "strip-mined," thousands of marine mammals are killed per day "along with millions of non-target sea animals."[68]

66. Dahr Jamail, "Gulf Seafood Deformities Alarm Scientists," *Al Jazeera*, April 20, 2012, http://www.aljazeera.com/indepth/features/2012/04/201241682318260912.html.
67. Jude Wait et al., ed., *Sustainable World Sourcebook* (Berkeley: Sustainable World Coalition, 2010), 10.
68. Zoe Weil, "Most Good, Least Harm: A Simple Principle for a Better World and Meaningful Life," in *Hungry for Change*, ed. Northwest Earth Institute (Portland, OR: NWEI, 2011), 28.

Places like the Mississippi Delta are *dead zones*, areas that are uninhabitable for fish because of pollutants and contaminants dumped into the water that feed uncontrolled algae blooms. There are at least 200 dead zones around the world: from the Baltic Sea to Chesapeake Bay, from the Black Sea to the Bohai Sea, and they are rapidly increasing.[69]

Freshwater, like ocean water, is far from an infinite resource. Earth has a closed water system, so that there is the same amount of water today as at the planet's creation, and it is the same water. Only 2.5 percent of the water on the planet is fresh. In addition, only 1.3 percent of freshwater is surface water, which supports most life systems; the rest is locked up in polar ice caps, glaciers, and groundwater.[70] Of the freshwater available globally, 70 percent is used for irrigation, 20 percent is earmarked for industrial purposes, and 10 percent goes to households and municipalities.[71] In 2010, 89 percent of people in the world had access to improved drinking water sources, a significant step forward. However, due primarily to the lack of water and decent sanitation, diarrhea remains the leading cause of illness and death around the world. The United Nations estimates that 1.5 million children die each year from diseases like diarrhea that could be eradicated through clean water. On a typical day, patients suffering from diarrhea and related diseases occupy over one-half the hospital beds in sub-Saharan Africa.[72]

The water crisis is one of the most pressing issues facing our planet today. We have options regarding the depletion of many resources, but water is not one of them because "unlike oil and coal, water is much more than a commodity: it is the basis of life."[73] With so much stress on the system and an overburdened population, the next world war may be waged over this precarious resource.

Deforestation and Land Degradation

> Stand still. The trees ahead and bushes beside you
> Are not lost. Wherever you are is called Here,
> And you must treat it as a powerful stranger,
> Must ask permission to know it and be known.
> The forest breathes. Listen. It answers,

69. Wait et al., *Sustainable World Sourcebook*, 11.

70. "The World's Water," USGS Water Science School, http://water.usgs.gov/edu/earth wherewater.html, accessed July 15, 2013.

71. UN-Water, "Water Use," http://www.unwater.org, accessed July 15, 2013.

72. UN-Water, "Drinking Water, Sanitation, and Hygiene," http://www.unwater.org, accessed July 15, 2013.

73. Sandra Postel, "Water: Will There Be Enough?," in *Hungry for Change*, 96.

I have made this place around you.
If you leave it, you may come back again, saying Here.
No two trees are the same to Raven.
No two branches are the same to Wren.
If what a tree or a bush does is lost on you,
You are surely lost. Stand still. The forest knows
Where you are. You must let it find you.
—David Wagoner[74]

No one can guarantee that our grandchildren will read Wagoner's poetry and resonate with the experience of being found by the natural world, with only 7 percent of forestland in the United States made up of century-old stands.[75]

In the Pentateuch we read these surprising words: "If you besiege a town for a long time, making war against it in order to take it, you must not destroy its trees by wielding an ax against them. Although you may take food from them, you must not cut them down. Are trees in the field human beings that they should come under siege from you?" (Deut. 20:19). Today, tragically, we make war against both human beings and trees. Rain forests are vanishing at a rate of 100,000 acres a day.[76] High rates of deforestation are removing the earth's lungs, since trees capture greenhouse gases from the air. The Amazon rain forest encompasses one-half of the world's remaining rain forests, captures one-tenth of its carbon, and is home to one-tenth of its species. Yet scientists forecast that a 4°C rise in temperature over the century could shrink it by 85 percent; even a less dramatic rise in temperature could result in a loss of 20–40 percent of the rain forest.[77]

Agribusinesses and our economic support of them are largely responsible for the destruction of forests worldwide. The driving force for converting forested land to agriculture is that there are more people on the planet *and* more of those people are eating more meat *and* more land is needed to feed people on meat than on plants. Twenty-eight percent of the Earth's surface is now being used for crop and livestock production, and vast areas of Amazonia have been burned to establish industrial soybean plantations to produce feed.[78]

74. David Wagoner, "Lost," in *Collected Poems, 1956–1976* (Bloomington: Indiana University Press, 1976), 182.

75. Wait et al., *Sustainable World Sourcebook*, 14.

76. Ibid., 15.

77. David Adam, "Amazon could shrink by 85% due to climate change, scientists say," *The Guardian*, March 11, 2009, http://www.theguardian.com/environment/2009/mar/11/amazon-global-warming-trees.

78. George Wuerthner, "Assault on Nature: C.F.A.O.S. and Biodiversity Loss," in *Hungry for Change*, 92.

Palm oil is the most widely traded vegetable oil in the world, used in everything from cosmetics and food to biofuel. North Americans rarely (if ever) see these realities because they take place in developing nations. Consider what might happen if the giant redwoods of California—the oldest living organism in the world at about 4,000 years—disappeared overnight, removed for meat production space.

The loss of green space inevitably means a loss of place for indigenous peoples. Kenyan environmentalist Wangari Maathai, winner of the Nobel Peace Prize, writes about coming back home to an altered landscape: "When I went home to visit my family in Nyeri, I had another indication of the changes under way around us. I saw rivers silted with topsoil, much of which was coming from the forests where plantations of commercial trees had replaced indigenous forest. I noticed that much of the land that had been covered by trees, bushes, and grasses when I was growing up had been replaced by tea and coffee."[79]

Closely related to deforestation is land degradation. The Dust Bowl of the 1930s and its consequences on farmers and their land are firmly fixed in memories of Depression-era America. John Steinbeck's words ring out as the Dust Bowl is being replayed around the globe:

> And then the dispossessed were drawn west—from Kansas, Oklahoma, Texas, New Mexico; from Nevada and Arkansas, families, tribes, dusted out, tractored out. Carloads, caravans, homeless and hungry; twenty thousand and fifty thousand and a hundred thousand and two hundred thousand. They streamed over the mountains, hungry and restless—restless as ants, scurrying to find work to do—to lift, to push, to pull, to pick, to cut—anything, any burden to bear, for food. The kids are hungry. We got no place to live. Like ants scurrying for work, for food, and most of all for land.[80]

Soil is a dynamic layer on the earth's surface, capable of supporting a vegetative cover and composed primarily of weathered materials along with mineral nutrients, water, air, and billions of microscopic organisms. The process of making soil is exceedingly slow; in normal conditions it can take hundreds of years to produce one inch of topsoil.[81] The major causes of soil degradation include overgrazing by livestock, erosion through over-tilling, deforestation (such as for firewood or charcoal), overuse of agricultural chemicals, and improper irrigation.[82] Wendell Berry warns that as topsoil is stripped from

79. Wangari Maathai, *Unbowed* (London: Arrow, 2008), 121.

80. John Steinbeck, *The Grapes of Wrath* (New York: Penguin, 2002 [1939]), 233.

81. G. Tyler Miller Jr., *Essentials of Ecology*, 4th ed. (Belmont, CA: Brooks/Cole, 2007), 67.

82. Jeanne Roy, ed., *Ten Stresses on the Planet* (Portland, OR: Center for Earth Leadership, 2008), 11–13.

the land, "the fertility of the soil will become a limited, unrenewable resource like coal or oil."[83]

The primary sufferers from land degradation are underprivileged farmers, just like in the Dust Bowl of the 1930s. In the developing (majority) world, a brutal cycle takes place: the degradation of the land means declining productivity, which leads to increased food insecurity, which in turn causes people to take unhealthy risks with the land. Land degradation, declining productivity, and food insecurity are ruthlessly connected.

Loss of Biodiversity

Creation in its splendor was made to teem with yellowtail birds, rainbow trout, Asian elephants, crickets, and those little houseflies that buzz around our kitchens in the summer. The Creator's abounding diversity is exemplified in the Hebrew notion of "swarming": "Let the waters bring forth swarms of living creatures" (Gen. 1:20). Holmes Rolston III suggests that "swarms" contains the intention of biodiversity, a plentiful Creation of multiple kinds of species that co-exist in one large, created environment: "'Swarms' is, we can say, the prescientific word for biodiversity. Earth speciates."[84]

This biodiversity is being threatened, and the primary causes are anthropogenic.[85] Species extinction is occurring at rates of three to four orders of magnitude above historic averages and unseen since the last global mass-extinction event. The Millennium Ecosystem Assessment (MA) of 2005 reports: "The current rate of biodiversity loss, in aggregate and at a global scale, gives no indication of slowing, although there have been local successes in some groups of species. The momentum of the underlying drivers of biodiversity loss, and the consequences of this loss, will extend many millennia into the future."[86] A study published in 2013 states that many land species are facing extinction because they are unable to adapt to the rapid pace of climate change expected over the twenty-first century.[87] Polar bears hunt on sea ice and depend on it to

83. Wendell Berry, *The Unsettling of America* (San Francisco: Sierra Club, 1977), 10.

84. Holmes Rolston III, "The Bible and Ecology," *Interpretation* 50, no. 1 (1996): 23.

85. See Anantha Kumar Duraiappah and Shahid Naeem et al., *Ecosystems and Human Well-Being: Biodiversity Synthesis* (Washington, DC: World Resources Institute, 2005); J. Emmett Duffy et al., "Forecasting decline in ecosystem services under realistic scenarios of extinction," in *Biodiversity, Ecosystem Functioning, and Human Wellbeing*, ed. Shahid Naeem et al. (Oxford: Oxford University Press, 2009), 60.

86. Rashid Hassan, Robert Scholes, and Neville Ash, eds., *Ecosystems and Human Well-Being: Current State and Trends*, vol. 1 (Washington, DC: Island Press, 2005), 3.

87. Robin McKie, "Climate change is happening too quickly for species to adapt," *The Guardian*, July 14, 2013, http://www.theguardian.com/environment/2013/jul/14/climate-change -evolution-species-adapt.

live. Some loss in biodiversity is a part of the fabric of the created order, but species loss of this magnitude and at this speed is problematic and is damaging, possibly irrevocably, the integrity of the Earth's ecosystems.

Current agricultural practices contribute extensively to loss of biodiversity. Even though more arable land is being converted to agriculture, industrial monocultural farming (growing only one type of crop or plant variety for many years on the same land) makes use of ever fewer species. Since 1900 some 75 percent of plant genetic diversity has been lost, and 30 percent of livestock breeds are at risk of extinction. Only twelve plant and five animal species provide 75 percent of our total food supply.[88] Because the same few species are so widely grown and are planted repeatedly in the same space, the conditions they require must be replicated, often requiring significant inputs of nutrients, water, and energy. This reduces available resources for native species, shifts the conditions for the growth of those native species, and introduces pollutants that they may find toxic. With little genetic diversity, outbreaks of disease or pests are more likely, resulting in the use of larger quantities of agricultural toxins.[89] The MA states: "The global extent of farming and the specific trade-offs it entails imply that agriculture is the single largest threat to biodiversity and ecosystem function of any single human activity."[90]

Loss of biodiversity affects ecosystems, oceans, lands, animals, indigenous plants, *and* people. But perhaps most unfortunate is the loss of a small voice from God. When all is told, writes Thomas Berry, there is a latent theological problem with species loss: "To wantonly destroy a living species is to silence forever a divine voice."[91] When a species is destroyed, whether through human inaction or action, one of God's forms of revelation is unalterably lost.

Population Growth

God's opening command to Adam and Eve was, "Be fruitful and multiply, and fill the earth" (Gen. 1:28). Not unlike the rest of God's living creatures, God blessed humankind and directed them to multiply and enjoy abundant offspring. Of all the imperatives found in the pages of Scripture, the one to be fruitful and multiply is the single most obeyed and is the only one we have actually managed to fulfill. It is hard to know what to do with God's initial

88. United Nations Food and Agriculture Organization, Economic and Social Development Department, "What is Agrobiodiversity?" (2004), http://www.fao.org/docrep/007/y5609e/y5609e01.htm#TopOfPage, accessed July 27, 2013.

89. Thanks to Julie Firman for her expertise on agrobiodiversity.

90. Kenneth G. Cassmann and Stanley Wood et al., "Cultivated Systems," in *Ecosystems and Human Well-Being: Current State and Trends*, 777.

91. Thomas Berry, *The Dream of the Earth* (San Francisco: Sierra Club, 1990), 46.

edict to humankind when we are becoming increasingly aware of the global impact of a growing population. Garrett Hardin, who wrote tellingly (and controversially) on the interconnection of population growth and ecology, said, "A finite world can support only a finite population; therefore, population growth must eventually equal zero."[92]

Certainly we have been warned before that the world would reach (or had reached) its capacity, especially with the human population exploding from 1 billion in 1850 to 2.5 billion in 1950 to 7 billion in 2012 to a projected 9–10 billion in 2050 (ten times the number 200 years earlier). Rev. Robert Malthus in 1798 famously proposed that the world's population would outstrip food supplies and our ability to secure resources. More recently, Paul Ehrlich in 1968 highlighted (in a stridently alarmist tone) that at this level of growth it is getting increasingly problematic to provide food for the world's inhabitants.[93] A team of scientists in 1972 suggested that our views of limitless economic and ecological expansion are not only inaccurate but also toxic to healthy living. Industrial, mechanistic perspectives will fail us, they said; the Earth can only support a certain amount of human life.[94]

Again we return to the marginalized. There is a close connection between the population explosion, global warming, and food security. Lester Brown points out that corn is an integral commodity in the world food economy, especially for developing countries.[95] Corn is cheap, moveable, and does not require refrigeration. The United States is the leading producer of corn in the world today. In fact, American corn producers planted 96 million acres in 2012, the most in 75 years. However, that same year a heat wave swept through middle-America corn country. The heat and accompanying drought destroyed countless crops and careers. The 2012 crop went down as one of the worst in history.

Whenever a food shortage hits, the poor disproportionately experience its wrath. As the price of corn rises, the poor and the destitute eat less. Indeed there is less food to feed more people, who have less money to buy other necessities. The cycle perpetuates itself. While people in the West had the wherewithal to delay the impact of this food shortage, those in the global South and East began to experience it almost immediately. Henry I. Miller describes the effects of the ecocrisis on the poor using a vivid analogy: "Like the sinking of the Titanic, catastrophes are not democratic. A much higher fraction of passengers from the cheaper decks were lost. We'll see the same

92. Garrett Hardin, *Exploring New Ethics for Survival* (New York: Viking, 1972), 252.
93. Paul R. Ehrlich, *The Population Bomb* (New York: Ballantine, 1968).
94. Donella H. Meadows et al., *The Limits to Growth* (London: Earth Island, 1972).
95. Lester Brown, *Full Planet, Empty Plates* (London: W. W. Norton, 2012).

phenomenon with global warming."[96] And with food security. For First World people, it is hard to see this connection when we can peruse the full shelves of the grocery store.

With population explosion comes an upswing in waste and toxicity. Human waste—be it garbage, sewer water, plastics, broken cars—must go somewhere. The laws of physics have long told us that the universe is a closed system; there is no creation or destruction of actual matter. All matter comes from somewhere and must go somewhere. Thus when we stockpile nuclear waste, pollute a river, or create smog, those pollutants will eventually go somewhere. And somewhere is often everywhere. We eat them. We swim in them. We breathe them. Coal is the main driver of economic development in China. The average life span of a Chinese citizen living in the rural southern part of the country is more than five years longer than that of a citizen living in the urban north, due to air pollution from burning coal. In effect, those 500 million northern Chinese are losing 2.5 billion years of life expectancy because of the dark cloud of smog.[97] As we destroy the Earth, we ultimately destroy ourselves, for we are part of the Earth.

■ ▓ ▪

Old Testament scholar Ellen Davis speaks of the charge to humanity— "Be fruitful and multiply, and fill the earth and subdue it; and have dominion over . . ." (Gen. 1:28)—as the commandment to practice skilled mastery. In her exegesis, practicing skilled mastery among the creatures is tethered to the prior blessing of the animals (Gen. 1:22) and is exercised by paying attention to the gift of the land—the fruitfulness God provided to both humans and creatures (Gen. 1:29–30). She suggests that the first example of the craft of being human is making sure that there is enough for all, that resources are shared and justice is practiced. Today it seems that if global warming, the loss of freshwater, deforestation, land degradation, species extinction, and overpopulation are any indication, practicing skilled mastery is a craft we have almost certainly lost.

Romans 8 affirms that the Creation is anticipating the day when humans live into their vocation: "For the creation waits with eager longing for the revealing of the children of God" (v. 19). The apostle's reference to the suffering of

96. Quoted in Andrew Revkin, "Poorest Nations Will Bear Brunt as World Warms," *New York Times*, April 1, 2007, 6.

97. Edward Wong, "Pollution Leads to Drop in Life Span in Northern China, Research Finds," *New York Times*, July 8, 2013, http://www.nytimes.com/2013/07/09/world/asia/pollution -leads-to-drop-in-life-span-in-northern-china-study-finds.html?ref=environment&_r=0&gwh =0DC8CF30290F7A2B75D87FCDE13FA30A&gwt=pay.

Creation is clear: "for the creation was subjected to futility" (v. 20). The future well-being of humanity and the planet are inextricably connected: "in hope that the creation itself will be set free from its bondage to decay and will obtain the freedom of the glory of the children of God" (v. 21). Some see the groaning of Creation as hopeful because it signals the coming of Christ, the redemption of our bodies. But eschatological escapism is not faithful to the context, or to the planet. Acknowledging humanity's interconnection with Creation resists seeing the degradation of the earth as a signal of Christ's coming. Instead it places degradation in the sin narrative—linking harm of the earth with humanity's failure to live into the commandment to practice skilled mastery. Perhaps Creation is waiting for us to remember who we are, to relocate ourselves as thoroughly earth-bound creatures, to embrace our calling to practice skilled mastery, and to find ways to bring healing and hope to the Earth. Such a perspective reminds us of the hope we have, located in our very identity as children of God.

Soon after the Boston Marathon tragedy in 2013, an earlier quote from Fred Rogers (of Mr. Rogers's Neighborhood) went viral: "When I was a boy and I would see scary things in the news, my mother would say to me, 'Look for the helpers. You will always find people who are helping.'" Planetary degradation is a scary thing. It is so frightening that many of us react to it like we react to grief: we ignore it, pretend it is not happening, medicate ourselves to sleep at night, and go on with life as best we can. But the truth is, as bad as the situation gets, there are helpers everywhere. Across the globe individuals, churches, and organizations are working to heal the planet. There are people and places we can connect with as we live into our vocation as people of hope—as children of God.

Part II

Exploring Ecotheology

4

Voices in the Wilderness

Christianity's History with Creation

When the Jews were threatened with genocide under the rule of the Persians, the book of Esther records Mordecai exhorting the Jewish Queen: "Who knows? Perhaps you have come to royal dignity for just such a time as this" (Esther 4:14). Thomas Berry, pondering the unrivaled devastation of the planet in our day, wrote: "All indications suggest that we are, in a sense, a chosen group, a chosen generation, or a chosen human community. . . . We are not asked whether we wish to live at this particular time. We are here. The inescapable is before us."[1] Today we are confronted by an unparalleled ecological crisis. At times like this, how has the Christian community responded?

In the minds of many, both inside and outside the church, there remains deep-seated doubt that the Christian community can or will respond to today's Earth-threatening issues. In his 1967 article in *Science* magazine—still the most oft-quoted article in the magazine's history—historian Lynn White Jr. claimed that "Christianity bears a huge burden of guilt" for the current ecological crisis. White indicted the Judeo-Christian heritage for being "the most anthropocentric religion the world has seen" and argued that this religious heritage provided the major impulse in the West for the conquest of nature through technology: "Both our present science and our present technology are so tinctured with orthodox Christian arrogance toward nature that no solution for our ecologic crisis can be

1. Thomas Berry, *Befriending the Earth* (Mystic, CT: Twenty-Third Publications, 1991), 5.

67

expected from them alone."[2] While White's historical analysis can be nuanced, his conclusion has had a deep impact on scientists and ethicists.[3] Wendell Berry's observation bears repeating, "The culpability of Christianity in the destruction of the natural world and uselessness of Christianity in any effort to correct that destruction are now established clichés of the conservation movement."[4]

White presumes that throughout its history, Christianity has reinforced a despotic domination of humanity over Creation, rooted in an anthropocentric reading of Genesis 1. This premise should be amended.[5] The modern ideology that humanity has the God-given right to conquer and oppress nature solely for its own absolute purposes gained prominence with the rise of Western scientific modernity during the Renaissance and had deep roots in ancient Greek thought and classic philosophers like Plato and Aristotle. While it may be impossible and unfair to attach anthropocentrism to any one particular influence or ideology, Western Christianity has undoubtedly played a key role in the formation of the social and cultural worldview of the modern West, including the West's "ecological" attitude and conduct toward nature. And yet Paul Santmire, one of the earliest and most respected writers on the history of ecology within Christianity, writes, "The theological tradition in the West is neither ecologically bankrupt . . . nor replete with immediately accessible, albeit long-forgotten, ecological riches hidden everywhere in its deeper vaults."[6]

Without having to rewrite history, reject orthodoxy, or engage in theological gymnastics, we can recover threads of ecological concern buried, and often overlooked, in Christian history. Such historical reflection is unapologetically "revisionist" while striving to remain faithful. According to Santmire, it differs noticeably from "reconstructionists" who "insist that a totally new theological word about nature must be spoken in our time."[7] Rather revisionists "work within the milieu of classical Christian thought as defined by the ecumenical creeds."[8] In

2. Lynn White Jr., "The Historical Roots of Our Ecologic Crisis," *Science* 155 (March 10, 1967): 1203–7.

3. Ben A. Minteer and Robert E. Manning, "An Appraisal of the Critique of Anthropocentrism and Three Lesser Known Themes in Lynn White's 'The Historical Roots of Our Ecologic Crisis,'" *Organization and Environment* 18, no. 2 (June 2005): 171. Max Oelschlaeger, *Caring for Creation* (New Haven: Yale University Press, 1994), 1, begins his book with a "confession." Because of the bias he developed through reading Lynn White's thesis, "for most of my adult life I believed, as many environmentalists do, that religion was the primary cause of ecological crisis."

4. Wendell Berry, "Christianity and the Survival of Creation" (1992), in *The Art of the Commonplace*, ed. Norman Wirzba (Washington, DC: Shoemaker & Hoard, 2002), 305.

5. For a summary of critiques of White's thesis, see Steven Bouma-Prediger, *For the Beauty of the Earth*, 2nd ed. (Grand Rapids: Baker Academic, 2010), 66–68.

6. H. Paul Santmire, *The Travail of Nature* (Philadelphia: Fortress, 1985), 8.

7. H. Paul Santmire, "In God's Ecology: A Revisionist Theology of Nature," *Christian Century* 117, no. 35 (December 13, 2000): 1300.

8. Ibid., 1301.

this chapter we approach Christian history through a revisionist lens, believing that we need not reconstruct or reject our heritage to find a historical precedent for an ecotheological framework.

Our conviction is that the worldview of the modern West, Christian and otherwise, is constantly evolving. Newly revised ideas and practices—including those spiritual, theological, and Christian—*can* affect new directions in society and culture, and Christian ecological theology *can* serve as a catalyst in reimagining a greener perspective.

Early Christianity

> The whole creation prays. Cattle and wild beasts pray, and bend their knees, and in coming forth from their stalls and lairs look up to heaven, their mouth not idle, making the spirit move in their own fashion. Moreover the birds now arising are lifting themselves up to heaven and instead of hands are spreading out the cross of their wings, while saying something which may be supposed to be a prayer.
>
> —Tertullian (c. 160–c. 225)[9]

The early Latin theologian Tertullian epitomizes the difficulty in revising Christian history. With numerous writers in the early church, like Tertullian, we can uncover texts like the one above in which they exhibit an appreciation for nature and the goodness of the Creator. Tertullian sees in the natural world images and reminders of God's call to prayer. At the same time, Tertullian's eschatology foresaw the ultimate annihilation of Earth and heaven: "The fact that everything sprang from nothing will ultimately be made plausible by the dispensation of God which is to return all things to nothing. For *the heaven shall be rolled together as a scroll*, nay, it will disappear along with the earth itself, with which it was made in the beginning."[10] The problem is not in turning up Earth-affirming texts; the predicament is that in the church, by and large, a faith disengaged from Creation overshadowed other perspectives. As we will see, there are important exceptions, such as Irenaeus and Francis of Assisi. Revisionist history chooses, because of the crisis of our historical moment, to highlight those "exceptions."

Gnosticism and Irenaeus

Investigating the rise and threat of gnosticism is vital to an exploration of historic Christian conduct toward nature, in part because vestiges of it remain

9. *Tertullian's Tract on the Prayer*, trans. Ernest Evans (London: SPCK, 1953), no. 29, p. 41.
10. Tertullian, *The Treatise Against Hermogenes*, trans. J. H. Waszink (Westminster, MD: Newman, 1956), chap. 34.1–2, p. 71.

in Christianity today. According to Roger Olson, gnosticism emerged in the first centuries following Christ and held that "matter, including the body, is an inherently limiting prison or even evil drag on the good soul or spirit of the human person and that the spirit is essentially divine—a 'spark of God' dwelling in the tomb of the body."[11] Essential to gnostic thinking is its "radical dualism," in which God (the spiritual) is utterly other than the created world (the material).[12] In gnosticism a transcendent deity prevailed over an immanent Christ; God could not have become incarnate on earth in fully human form because material is evil. Salvation was understood as rising above or escaping the imprisonment of the material and nature. A gnostic worldview helped to create division among Christians, fostering "spiritual elitism, secrecy and division within the budding young Christian church."[13]

Irenaeus (c. 130–202) opposed gnostic philosophy in the second century, becoming a key figure in the development of Christian theology. He spoke and wrote of God as Creator of a good world, bringing all of Creation toward a final, eschatological fulfillment. His anti-gnostic understanding of redemption is called *anakephalaiosis*, or "recapitulation." In *Against the Heresies*, he wrote, "When [the Son of God] became incarnate and was made man, He recapitulated in Himself the long unfolding of humankind, granting salvation by way of compendium, that in Christ Jesus we might receive what we had lost in Adam, namely, to be according to the image and likeness of God."[14] Irenaeus saw the incarnation itself as soteriological. As the second Adam, Christ moved through the full extent of human existence and reversed the sin and disobedience that originated in the garden. Christ saves by unraveling the knot of sin that Adam tied. A critical moment in the process of redemption occurred at the temptation, when Christ (fully human) conquered Satan and overturned the fall; the cross and resurrection are then the culmination of recapitulation. In opposition to gnosticism, Irenaeus argued that redemption was not about fleeing from what God had created.[15] Christ and Adam cannot be separated, neither can salvation and the whole Creation. His thinking affirmed a comprehensive view of salvation through which all Creation—human and other-than-human—is restored. Ecclesiastically, Irenaeus's theology was embodied in the sacraments, and the Eucharist

11. Roger E. Olson, *The Story of Christian Theology* (Downers Grove, IL: InterVarsity, 1999), 29.

12. Hans Jonas, *The Gnostic Religion* (Boston: Beacon, 1958), 42.

13. Olson, *Story of Christian Theology*, 29.

14. Irenaeus of Lyons, *Against the Heresies*, trans. Dominic J. Unger, OFM (New York: Newman, 2012), III.18.1, pp. 87–88.

15. Olson, *Story of Christian Theology*, 76.

became a celebration of the communion humanity shares with Creation and of God's messianic blessings.[16]

Irenaeus is a vital figure for constructing an ecotheology from our own history that focuses on the interrelated nature of God and humanity with the natural world, and on the cosmological dimension of Christ's healing work.

Dualism and the "Great Chain of Being"

The perspective of Irenaeus did not rise to prominence. Christianity grew up in an age when the human person was becoming increasingly alienated from nature and the physical self. Such an intellectual environment would eventually lead to the adoption of Neoplatonism's "great chain of being." This plan and structure of the world, which would hold sway in the West with little resistance well into the eighteenth century, conceived of the universe as an infinite number of hierarchical connections, from the most meager particle up to the One most perfect absolute Being.[17] In the logic of the great chain of being, through a kind of reverse evolution, the "lower" derives from the "higher." The closer a creature is to the One, through intellect and spirituality, the more perfect that being is. Those creatures that are lower in the hierarchy, the natural world, animate and inanimate, are more removed from God.[18] God and the soul were of similar type; to reach its created purpose, the soul must then forsake the body to pursue God.

With enduring consequences, the great chain of being "became the cognitive matrix for Christian theology during its formative, postbiblical centuries."[19] The dominant patristic emphasis on the "ascent of the soul" resulted in a corresponding disaffection from nature. Origen (c. 185–254), like his predecessor Clement, was immersed in the Platonism and Stoicism of Philo of Alexandria, Jewish scholar of the first century, and is a significant example of a hierarchical view of the world.[20] His belief in the primacy of rationality

16. Rosemary Radford Ruether, "Theological Resources for Earth-Healing: Covenant and Sacrament," in *The Challenge of Global Stewardship*, ed. Maura A. Ryan and Todd David Whitmore (Notre Dame, IN: University of Notre Dame Press, 1997), 62; Santmire, *Travail of Nature*, 43–44.

17. Arthur O. Lovejoy, *The Great Chain of Being* (Cambridge, MA: Harvard University Press, 1964 [1936]), 59.

18. See, for example, *Origen on First Principles*, trans. G. W. Butterworth (London: SPCK, 1936), II.9.3, p. 132: "As for dumb animals and birds and creatures that live in water, it seems superfluous to inquire about them, since it is certain that they should be regarded as of contingent and not primary importance."

19. Santmire, *Travail of Nature*, 47.

20. Hilary Marlow, *Biblical Prophets and Contemporary Environmental Ethics* (Oxford: Oxford University Press, 2009), 27–30. Marlow claims that despite efforts to nuance Origen's thought, his "functional anthropocentrism" remains.

Tension Point: History

Our team did not reach consensus on how we should engage Christian history and its ambiguity toward Creation. We acknowledged that there were many aspects of Christian history that made room for love of Creation; we also agreed that other aspects of our heritage led to disengagement from the Earth.

What we didn't agree on was whether or not we had the right to critique or challenge the parts of those histories unfavorable to a healthy ecotheological worldview today. We were torn. We felt that to critique those in the past for their lack of Creation care was anachronistic and unfair to them in their own time. However we also felt as though it was our duty to criticize and confront systemic problems in our history, for only in dealing with the historical problems head-on could we forge a new path.

- What is your response to the ambiguity of Christian history toward care of Creation?
- By what means do we believe we are "right" today and that Christians in ages past were "wrong"? How do we engage the changing nature of what issues Christ-followers need to address?
- Should Christians today repent on behalf of the damage our forebears might have done to Creation, even if they were unaware of the long-term effects? Why or why not?

---

is evidenced in his apologetic, *Against Celsus*: "The Creator, then, has made everything to serve the rational being and his natural intelligence."[21] This prioritization of the rational soul over the material had ramifications for Origen's understanding of salvation; in his comments on Romans 8:21, he refers to the eschaton, "when at the end and consummation of the world souls and rational creatures have been released as it were from their bars and prisons by the Lord."[22] Those aspects of Origen's theology that are Earth-denying stand in contrast to Irenaeus. Origen's God and spirituality were more detached from this world, while Irenaeus embodied salvation and renewal in the experience of humanity and Creation.

As our early faith tradition was forming, so was the Greco-Roman understanding of the human person, which was rooted in hierarchical thinking. A dualism that prioritized soul over body—and by extension certain humans over others and humanity over nature—was deeply engrained in

---

21. *Origen: Contra Celsum*, trans. Henry Chadwick (Cambridge: Cambridge University Press, 1953), IV.78, p. 246.
22. *Origen on First Principles*, I.7.5, p. 65.

that formation.[23] Plato, Cicero, and Seneca were instrumental in shaping the philosophical underpinning of class structure, the idea that some occupations (and therefore people) are less than human, that the other-than-human world was associated with sin and evil, and that the body was associated with sordid nature. The construct of soul and body, rooted in the *Phaedo* of early Plato and its Neoplatonic heritage, has unquestionably taken root in Christianity's collective consciousness. Today dualism has declining loyalty and influence, yet its entrenchment in Western theology cannot be underestimated.[24]

Talking Animals and Anthropocentrism

Historical revision focuses primarily on Christian theology within creedal orthodoxy, but early Christian apocryphal literature provides a fascinating and important excursus for the modern reader. In the *Acts of Peter*, written in the last half of the second century, the apostle Peter confronts a false teacher, ironically named Simon (Peter's name before Jesus changed it), by enlisting a large dog. The obedient animal enters Simon's house, stands up on its hind legs, and delivers Peter's directive. When Simon tells the dog to tell Peter that he is not available, the dog reprimands him: "You most wicked and shameless man, you enemy of all that live and believe in Jesus Christ, here is a dumb animal sent to you and taking a human voice to convict you and prove you a cheat and deceiver" (*Acts of Peter*, 12).

Elsewhere in the *Apocryphal Acts of the Apostles* animals figure prominently: the apostle Paul's death in the Roman arena is averted when the fierce lion released to maul him turns out to be the very lion Paul had previously baptized; an ass's colt bids the apostle Thomas sit on its back and ride into Jerusalem with these words: "I am of that race that served Balaam and thy Lord and teacher also sat upon one that belonged to me by race"; a leopard and a lamb follow the apostle Philip on his missionary journey after coming to faith in the wilderness and praying, "We glorify and bless you who have visited and remembered us in the desert."[25] Charming stories, but surely, in spite of their apostolic star power, they are of little worth for an *orthodox* Christian ecotheology.

23. Judith Perkins, "Fictional Narratives and Social Critique," in *Late Ancient Christianity*, ed. Virginia Burrus (Minneapolis: Fortress, 2005), 62.

24. Rosemary Radford Ruether, "Ecofeminism: The Challenge to Theology," in *Christianity and Ecology*, ed. Dieter T. Hessel and Rosemary Radford Ruether (Cambridge, MA: Harvard University Press, 2000), 103. We discuss this more extensively in chap. 7.

25. Christopher R. Matthews, "Articulate Animals: A Multivalent Motif in the Apocryphal Acts of the Apostles," in *The Apocryphal Acts of the Apostles*, ed. François Bovon, Ann Graham Brock, and Christopher R. Matthews (Cambridge, MA: Harvard University Press, 1999), 205–32.

Just because certain ancient writings were excluded from the canon for doc-trinal reasons does not mean they should be rendered inconsequential *histori-cally*. These documents, writes Judith Perkins, provide "valuable testimony for the kinds of self-understandings, beliefs, and attitudes motivating Christians in an earlier period." Their value, in ways not dissimilar to the hagiographies of the saints, goes beyond their "historicity." To dismiss apocryphal texts out of hand denies the importance they had in "engaging Christian imaginations" and in offering narratives "whose stories long continued to shape Christian thinking."[26] They are essential for constructing a "people's history." History is not monolithic. It shifts depending on who is telling (or not telling) the story; things like social location, class, gender, age, and race impact it. To see his-tory "from below" requires paying attention to stories previously overlooked.[27] This practice is critical to our particular endeavor, since Creation has almost always been disregarded as meaningful subject matter.

Some of these ancient Christian texts are subversive in nature. Ancient Rome was an "intensely hierarchical" society where "relationships were most frequently defined on a vertical axis of patronage rather than on a horizontal axis of class solidarity."[28] Ultimately the Christian tradition would not prove immune to hierarchies of its own. Nevertheless resistance to social norms was sometimes "hidden" in early Christian apocryphal works, disrupting the system through the use of literary devices like talking animals. Aristotle's definition of slaves as "the lower sort" unquestionably influenced the Roman understanding of class distinction.[29] So according to some recent scholarship, when animals speak they are standing in for the voiceless and have-nots of so-ciety, subverting Aristotle's definition of status establishing identity.[30] But while talking animals say something about the status of underprivileged humans, they also say something about the animals themselves: they are not just objects but subjects . . . with voice. These stories of talking animals give evidence, claims Perkins, "that Jesus by his saving action has effected the integration and community of all living creatures. All have entered into a new partnership."[31]

26. Perkins, "Fictional Narratives and Social Critique," 47.
27. Virginia Burrus and Rebecca Lyman, "Shifting the Focus of History," in *Late Ancient Christianity*, 5.
28. Ibid., 7.
29. Aristotle, *Politics*, trans. Benjamin Jowett, bk. 1, part V, The Internet Classics Archive, http://classics.mit.edu/Aristotle/politics.1.one.html, accessed April 20, 2013: "Where then there is such a difference as that between soul and body, or between men and animals . . . the lower sort are by nature slaves, and it is better for them as for all inferiors that they should be under the rule of a master."
30. Judith Perkins, "Animal Voices," *Religion and Theology* 12, no. 3–4 (2005): 389–91.
31. Perkins, "Fictional Narratives and Social Critique," 61.

St. Augustine

Augustine (354–430) remains both a widely influential and disputed theologian. Eastern Orthodoxy finds aspects of his theology unpalatable; moreover, his "ecological" heritage is dubious at best. While it may be impossible to appease Orthodox misgivings, significant pieces of Augustine's thinking regarding the Earth can be retrieved. Before his conversion to Christianity, Augustine spent nine years as a Manichean, a dualistic religion that saw the physical realm as evil. Later he came under the influence of Plotinus and Neoplatonism. But as his theology matured we can discern numerous Creation-friendly themes; his "most lyrical writing about nature" comes toward the end of *City of God*, penned just a few years before his death.[32]

In his later years Augustine's theology was profoundly formed by his awareness of the overwhelming grace and goodness of God. God is more than Aristotle's unmoved mover, but One who is actively creating and sustaining goodness in the world. For Augustine, the goodness and beauty of nature is nothing short of miraculous: "Is there anybody, after all, who can reflect on the works of God by which the whole of this universe is governed and administered and not be stunned and overwhelmed by the miracles? Just reflect on the force in a single grain of any seed you like; it is something tremendous, enough to set you trembling as you think about it."[33] While Augustine held to a hierarchy in nature consistent with the great chain of being, it was one in which even the lowliest creature has "God as its Author and Creator," and it is "with respect to their own nature, that created things give glory to their Maker."[34] In Augustine's matured thinking, love of God gave rise to love of nature. Through love we come to see the world's goodness as God views its goodness, and "God is loved in what he had made."[35] Augustine did not shy away from the idea that humans have dominion over the rest of nature, but his is a theocentric dominion of generous love, one "that allows all things to be and to function in ways appropriate to their natures."[36] Before the fall, humans were in a communal relationship with the rest of nature; domination, greed, and covetousness, for Augustine, appeared with the fall. Commenting

32. Arthur O. Ledoux, "A Green Augustine: On Learning to Love Nature Well," *Theology and Science* 3, no. 3 (2005): 333.

33. Augustine, *Homilies of the Gospel of John 1–40*, trans. Edmund Hill, OP, ed. Allan D. Fitzgerald, OSA (Hyde Park, NY: New City Press, 2009), 8.1, p. 168. Santmire, *Travail of Nature*, 71, refers to the "omni-miraculous character" of Augustine's view of nature.

34. Augustine, *The City of God*, trans. R. W. Dyson (Cambridge: Cambridge University Press, 1998), XII.4, p. 503.

35. Augustine, *The Confessions*, trans. Maria Boulding, OSB, ed. John E. Rotelle, OSA (Hyde Park, NY: New City Press, 1997), XIII.31.46, p. 376; see also Ledoux, "A Green Augustine," 335.

36. Santmire, *Travail of Nature*, 69–70.

on the implications of Augustine's vision of dominion, Scott Dunham writes: "Human beings, which are some of the creatures that God has created in a universe of creatures, are called to love God and love the way that God loves, which they can know and do through the providential and redemptive work of God."[37] Through reading both of God's books we learn what it means to love both Creator and creature. For Augustine, if "that love is related to the creator it will no longer be covetousness but charity."[38]

The last highlighted theme involves Augustine's eschatological convictions. Early in his theological thinking he held to the Neoplatonic notion of the immortality of the soul, but by the end of his career he was integrating the resurrection of the body as a key aspect of his theology.[39] Even though he rejected chiliastic (millennial) theories about end times, he envisioned the renewal of all things at the final consummation: "It may well be, then—indeed, this is entirely credible—that, in the world to come, we shall see the bodily forms of the new heaven and the new earth in such a way as to perceive God with total clarity and distinctness, everywhere present and governing all things, both material and spiritual."[40] Significantly, Augustine, like Irenaeus, viewed human salvation history as something that happens within the scope of God's universal history for all things.

■ ■ ■

In the end, the ecological legacy of early Christianity remains ambiguous. On one hand, the belief arose that humans are fundamentally alienated from nature, that God is a matter-transcending deity, and that salvation is otherworldly and indifferent to nature. On the other hand, Christians could have faith in the goodness of God's Creation and in salvation as the restoration of nature. Every generation is convinced it is facing uncharted territory—but the crossroads at which the church finds itself in this particular historical moment is not unlike the place Irenaeus stood with his contemporaries under gnostic threat. Santmire writes, "Christian theology must surely be prepared once again to become an advocate of the goodness of the material order."[41] Perhaps the way Christians truncate the gift of abundant life to mean abundance at the expense of the rest of Creation rather than abundance for the planet as

37. Scott A. Dunham, *The Trinity and Creation in Augustine: An Ecological Analysis* (Albany, NY: State University of New York Press, 2008), 133.
38. Augustine, *The Trinity*, trans. Edmund Hill, OP, ed. John E. Rotelle, OSA (Brooklyn, NY: New City Press, 1991), IX.2.13, p. 278.
39. Santmire, *Travail of Nature*, 64–71.
40. Augustine, *City of God*, XXII.29, p. 1177.
41. Santmire, *Travail of Nature*, 8.

a whole is the gnostic threat of our time. Our devotion to Christ as Creator, Redeemer, Sustainer, and Reconciler ought to motivate our practices of caring for the Earth, as well as revising theological perspectives that are no longer life-giving and remembering those perspectives that have always been with us.

Eastern Orthodox Christianity

The day of resurrection!
Earth, tell it out abroad;
the passover of gladness,
the passover of God.
From death to life eternal,
from earth unto the sky,
our Christ hath brought us over,
with hymns of victory.

Now let the heavens be joyful!
Let earth the song begin!
Let the round world keep triumph,
and all that is therein!
Let all things seen and unseen
their notes in gladness blend,
for Christ the Lord hath risen,
our joy that hath no end.
—John of Damascus
(676–749)[42]

My (A. J.'s) urban home, nestled in a neighborhood of century-old spruce and oak trees, is baptized in color every Oregon autumn. A certain electricity fills the air. Most magnificent are the polyphonic voices of diversely painted leaves announcing to the world the bluster to come. Red, bright orange, and sometimes purple, Creation shouts its praise to its Maker. (I shout too in frustration over how much raking they require.) But their lively colors actually signal the preparation of life giving way to something new. An ecologist friend once reminded me that when we walk in the fallen leaves, rake them, and make piles that our kids roll around in, we unwittingly embrace death. Now, as I walk among the fall leaves with my little boy, I am awakened to a side of Creation I often forget: in order for Creation to live, it must also die. Within the cold

42. John of Damascus, "'Tis the Day of Resurrection," trans. J. M. Neale, The Hymn Society, Hymnary.org, http://www.hymnary.org/text/the_day_of_resurrection_earth_tell_it, accessed May 8, 2013.

tomb of winter waits a spring resurrection when vibrant leaves will return to woody branches.

The Eastern Orthodox tradition embraces both/and theology: a transcendent God immanent in the Creation; the tree of Adam's disobedience in the tree of Christ's crucifixion; the sanctification of the material; the goodness of nature honored through simple living. Orthodoxy lends us a unique vision of the Earth and makes key contributions to contemporary ecotheology.

Transcendence and Immanence

Eastern Orthodox writers have long held distinctive ways of understanding God's relationship to the created world: the Creator is ontologically other than the Creation (transcendence) *and* God is omnipresent within the Creation (immanence). One of the Cappadocian fathers, Basil the Great (c. 330–379), spoke in terms of God's transcendent essence (*ousia*) *and* God's immanent or present operations (*energeiai*): "We say that we know our God from His operations [*energeiai*], but do not undertake to approach near to His essence [*ousia*]. His operations come down to us, but His essence remains beyond our reach."[43] Gregory Palamas (1296–1359), a later Byzantine theologian, reiterated that all of Creation was made by the energies (*energeiai*) of the Trinity. Maximus the Confessor (c. 580–662) spoke of *Logos-logoi* as a way to conceptualize the transcendence and immanence of God. Christ the Word (*Logos*) has planted in each created thing a characteristic word or thought about its inner essence (*logoi*). As a thing becomes truer to its purpose or being, it is drawn into the divine realm. Every living bug, dead leaf, moving cloud, and careening astroid is a *logoi* from the mind of Christ, who thereby serves as a unifying presence throughout the cosmos.[44] Each being is a subject, not an object that can be instrumentalized for its goods, value, or usefulness to humans.

Basil and Palamas employed language of *energeia* to describe immanence, and Maximus used *logoi*. Elsewhere Orthodox writers spoke of the immanent presence of the Holy Spirit. In various places, they described the Spirit as a flood, dew, a cloud, light, lightning, a fiery furnace, an enlivening breeze blowing within the garden of Christ, a hovering or descending dove, and a warmth that thaws all that is frozen, ripens all things, and brings springtime to God's

---

43. Basil of Caesarea, "Letter 234," New Advent (website), ed. Kevin Knight, http://www.newadvent.org/fathers/3202234.htm, accessed July 22, 2013.

44. Kallistos Ware, "God Immanent Yet Transcendent: The Divine Energies according to Saint Gregory of Palamas," in *In Whom We Live and Move and Have Our Being: Panentheistic Reflections on God's Presence in a Scientific World*, ed. Philip Clayton and Arthur Peacock (Grand Rapids: Eerdmans, 2004), 160.

people.[45] Furthermore the Spirit would sometimes even change human senses to supernatural ones. John Cassian (c. 365–435) writes of being overwhelmed ecstatically by the *smell* of the Spirit: "We are often suddenly filled in these visitations with odors that go beyond the sweetness of human making, such that a mind which has been relaxed by this delightful sensation is seized with a certain spiritual ecstasy and forgets that it is dwelling in the flesh."[46]

God's essence is transcendent, past human understanding; as Creator, God's nature is utterly beyond the nature of Creation. Bishop Kallistos Ware writes that, on the other hand, "God is inexhaustibly immanent, maintaining all things in being, animating them, making each of them a sacrament of his dynamic presence."[47] Truly this is "a God who hides himself" (Isa. 45:15), and yet the Lord is "near by," filling "heaven and earth" (Jer. 23:23–24). God is the beginning (*arche*) of all things, above Creation, yet hidden *within* Creation and close enough to smell, taste, and even touch. Jaroslav Pelikan writes that within Orthodoxy there is "immanence without pantheistic identification, transcendence without deistic isolation."[48]

Salvation and Deification

One of the most important contributions Orthodoxy has to make to a comprehensive ecotheology is its understanding of salvation. The Orthodox perspective can be disconcerting to Protestants centered solely on conversion of the individual. Orthodoxy rejects the Augustinian concept of depraved humanity and emphasizes instead humanity's creation in the image of God. Restoration of that image takes priority over a penitential theology. To that end, salvation is more than the forgiveness of a person's sin and brokenness; salvation is a process by which people are formed into the fullness of Jesus Christ (Eph. 4:13).[49] To become one with God is to discover our original nature fulfilled.[50] Becoming like Christ is not only the purpose of the Christian life, it is salvation itself.

The Orthodox speak of the process of salvation that restores God's image and transforms people into the likeness of Christ as "deification," or *theōsis*.

---

45. Stanley M. Burgess, *The Holy Spirit: Eastern Christian Traditions* (Peabody, MA: Hendrickson, 1989), 7–8.

46. John Cassian, *The Conferences*, trans. Boniface Ramsey, OP (Mahwah, NJ: Paulist Press, 1997), IV.V, p. 157.

47. Ware, "God Immanent Yet Transcendent," 160.

48. Jaroslav Pelikan, *The Spirit of Eastern Christendom (600–1700)* (Chicago: University of Chicago Press, 1974), 248.

49. Elizabeth Theokritoff, "The Salvation of the World and Saving the Earth: An Orthodox Christian Approach," *Worldviews* 14 (2010): 142–43.

50. Monk Melchisedec, "St. Maximus the Confessor: An Initiation," *Sobornost* 28, no. 2 (2006): 48.

The key biblical image for grasping deification is Jesus's transfiguration (Mark 9:2–9). In that event, writes Orthodox theologian Elizabeth Theokritoff, we catch "a vision not only of Christ's divine glory but also of the glory of his humanity, of the nature that he shares with us."[51] And this transfiguration, importantly, directs our attention to the transfiguration of the whole created order. Christ's salvific work always has the entire Creation in its scope: "To speak of the created world *is* to speak of the creation that Christ has taken up and potentially transfigured in himself."[52] Because Adam's sin undermined the harmony established between God, humanity, and Creation, Creation is healed along with humanity. Bishop Ware writes, "Human beings are not saved *from* but *with* the material world; through humankind the material world is itself to be redeemed and transfigured."[53] Orthodoxy envisions a Creation that is reconciled to God as humanity is healed to reflect the image of God.[54]

Icons and Sacramentality

Another area of Orthodox faith and practice that is often bewildering to Protestants is iconography, and yet icons provide an excellent resource for constructing an ecotheology. A reverence for the created is central to Orthodox spirituality. Entering any Eastern Orthodox church will likely surprise a Western Christian unacquainted with the theology of icons. Brightly colored, intensely stylistic, and brilliantly written—icons are "written" not painted—icons depict the life of Christ, the saints, and Scripture. In this way, the fashioned Creation becomes a gateway to the Creator. However for many Western Christians, icons smack of idolatry. But at the seventh ecumenical council of Nicea (787) the church affirmed icons and gave clear theological demarcations for their use. Sacred (material) things such as icons could be venerated (*douleia*, *proskunēsis*, or *schetikē timē*), but only God could be worshiped (*latreia*).

John of Damascus, perhaps the most brilliant iconodule or iconophile ("lover of icons"), argued that icons were an essential part of the life of the church. Referencing the incarnation—"And the Word became flesh and lived among us" (John 1:14)—he wrote, "I reverence therefore matter and I hold in respect and venerate that through which my salvation has come about. I

---

51. Theokritoff, "Salvation of the World," 143.
52. Ibid., 142.
53. Kallistos Ware, "The Spirituality of the Icon," in *The Study of Spirituality*, ed. Cheslyn Jones, Geoffery Wainright, and Edward Yarnold (Oxford: Oxford University Press, 1986), 197.
54. Leonid Ouspensky, "The Meaning and Content of the Icon," in *Eastern Orthodox Theology*, ed. Daniel B. Clendenin (Grand Rapids: Baker, 1995), 59.

reverence it not as God, but as filled with divine energy and grace."[55] John believed that the most venerable part of matter was Christ's body, the wood of his cross, the rock of his tomb, even the ink and parchment of Scripture. Matter was a vehicle of adoration, divine revelation, and salvation. Bishop Ware comments, "Icons safeguard not only the authenticity of Christ's material body, but also the Spirit-bearing potentialities of all material things."[56] Icons remind us that the whole material Creation can be redeemed in Christ.[57]

Ephrem the Syrian (306–373) was a theologian, poet, hospital entrepreneur, and lover of the sick, who died of the plague while ministering to its victims. He envisioned the way of salvation within the entire scope of Creation, running "from the Tree right to the Cross; it extended from the Wood to the Wood and from Eden to Zion, from Zion to the Holy Church and from the Church to the kingdom."[58] All Creation is a liturgy of grace, an icon of the Creator. The same Spirit who brooded over the waters of Creation to bring forth sea creatures and fish hovers over the baptismal waters.[59] Ephrem's reference to baptism demonstrates the significance of sacramentality to Orthodoxy. The Eucharist also speaks to an underlying unity, not just with other believers but also with our Creator who is immanent in an inimitable way in everyone *and* everything. Theokritoff emphasizes that "all the sacraments of the Church are predicated on the belief that God's presence has permanently transformed his creation, but in ways that are still for the most part hidden: our task is to make them manifest." Making the sacramental mystery concrete in the world is part of Orthodox ecological activism, what some writers call the "human priesthood" of Creation. To that end, many Orthodox writers refer to a "Eucharistic ethos" as an essential attitude for addressing the ecocrisis.[60]

Asceticism

It is striking and significant that a number of writers, both Orthodox and Protestant, are calling Christ-followers to a new "asceticism" in our lifestyles as

55. John of Damascus, *Three Treatises on the Divine Images*, trans. Andrew Louth (Crestwood, NY: St. Vladimir's Seminary Press, 2003), II.14, p. 71–72.

56. Ware, "The Spirituality of the Icon," 196.

57. Burgess, *The Holy Spirit: Eastern Christian Traditions*, 12.

58. *Des heiligen Ephraem des Syrers Hymnen Contra Haereses*, ed. Edmund Beck, Corpus Scriptorum Christianorum Orientalium (hereafter, CSCO) 169 (Louvain: R. Draguet, 1957), 26.4, cited in Seely Joseph Beggiani, "The Typological Approach of Syriac Sacramental Theology," *Theological Studies* 64, no. 3 (2003): 551.

59. *Des heiligen Ephraem des Syrers Hymnen de Nativitate (Ephiphania)*, trans. Edmund Beck, CSCO 187 (Louvain: Secrétariat du CSCO, 1959), Epiph. 8.15, p. 160.

60. Theokritoff, "Salvation of the World," 154.

we adopt further levels of personal responsibility for the healing of Creation.[61] Certainly asceticism carries negative implications whenever it denigrates the body or is imposed involuntarily on the poor or underprivileged. For example, some early fathers taught that after Adam and Eve sinned, sex became a necessary evil; living a life free from the need of sex became the mark of a *true* ascetic. But there is another side to asceticism. Epiphanius of Salamis (c. 310–403) believed that when the Spirit rested upon a saint, the wild beasts would live in harmony with her or him as in Eden. And today, in a world and culture enslaved to terminal ways of life, the silent reflection and the "Jesus Prayer" of Orthodox Hesychast spirituality—from *hesychia*, meaning "stillness, rest, silence"—could restore simplicity and communion with God and Creation.[62]

At its healthiest and most practical, asceticism derives from *askesis*, which simply means "exercise" or "training." One intentionally adopts an ascetic lifestyle, through what the Orthodox call *enkrateia* or "self-control," in order to discipline one's life, abstain from certain indulgences, and reduce consumption of resources. Patriarch Bartholomew I, noted for his ecological commitment, addressed the ascetic way:

> Asceticism is not a flight from society and the world but a communal attitude of mind and way of life that leads to the respectful use, not abuse, of material goods. Excessive consumption may be understood to issue from a worldview estranged from self, from land, from life, and from God. Consuming the fruits of the earth in an unrestrained manner, we become consumed ourselves by avarice and greed. Excessive consumption leaves us emptied, out-of-touch with our deepest self. *Asceticism is a corrective practice, a way of* metanoia, *a vision of repentance.*[63]

In Orthodox spirituality, asceticism helps Christians develop discernment around what is life-giving and what is not, around an aesthetic, judicious sharing in the goodness of Creation and an arbitrary, self-gratifying abuse of God's gifts. Anestis Keselopoulos, in his work on Symeon the New Theologian (949–1022), describes the value of an "ascetic and non-consumerist ethos." When we restrain our possessiveness toward the natural world, we find ourselves

61. For example, Joachim G. Persoon, "Towards an Ethiopian Eco-Theology with Inspiration from Monastic Spirituality," *Swedish Missiological Themes* 98, no. 2 (2010): 220–25; Larry L. Rasmussen, "Earth-Honoring Asceticism and Consumption," *CrossCurrents* 57, no. 4 (Winter 2008): 498–513.

62. Boris Brobinsky, "Nicholas Cabasilas and Hesychast Spirituality," *Sobornost* 7 (1968): 483–510.

63. Patriarch Bartholomew I, "A Rich Heritage," address during environmental symposium, Santa Barbara, California, November 8, 1997, in *Cosmic Grace, Humble Prayer*, ed. John Chryssavigis (Grand Rapids: Eerdmans, 2003), 219–20.

"more truly and organically connected with it," as God created us to be. Our external actions lead to internal, personal transformation. Moreover a new asceticism aims to bring about justice in our world and "the restitution of goods to people to whom they equally belong," rooted in God's common provision. For the sake of the Earth and those suffering unduly from its deterioration, the Christian life should be marked by "temperance" and not by lavishness, consumerism, or "superfluous pseudo-needs."[64]

■ ■ ■

Orthodox Christianity, though often misunderstood by the Western church, has much to offer a holistic ecotheology. Its profound grasp of the incarnation undergirds a healthy perspective on God's immanence and transcendence; its doctrines of salvation, deification, and iconography are grounded in the goodness of Creation; and an asceticism of restraint can undergird a non-consumerist lifestyle.

Western Christianity

All the elements and all creatures cry aloud at the blaspheming of nature and at wretched humankind's devotion of so much of its short life to the rebellion against God; whereas unthinking nature submissively carries out the divine laws. This is why nature complains so bitterly about humanity.

—Hildegard of Bingen (1098–1179)[65]

In 1620 "the God of Heaven" brought William Bradford and the *Mayflower* pilgrims safely over "the vast and furious ocean" to "a good harbor." Almost three decades later he reminisced on their first impressions of the new land. The landscape was "a hideous and desolate wilderness, full of wild beasts and wild men."[66] The Nigerian novelist Chimamanda Adichie warns of "single stories" like this one. A single story is the power of the narrator to describe a people or culture or place in a way that makes it *the* definitive story. Single stories and myths dehumanize or stereotype, often resulting in oppressive paradigms. Adichie tells the story of a London merchant named John Locke who made a record of his journey to West Africa in 1561. After referring to Africans as beasts that had no houses, he wrote "they are also people without

---

64. Anestis G. Keselopoulos, *Man and the Environment*, trans. Elizabeth Theokritoff (Crestwood, NY: St. Vladimir's Seminary Press, 2001), 124–26.

65. Hildegard of Bingen, *Liber Vitae Meritoram* III, 13, cited in Heinrich Schipperges, *Hildegard of Bingen*, trans. John A. Broadwin (Princeton: Markus Wiener, 1997), 57.

66. William Bradford, "A Hideous and Desolate Wilderness" (1647), in Chris J. Madoc, *So Glorious a Landscape* (Lanham, MD: Rowman & Littlefield, 2001), 24–25.

heads having their mouths and eyes in their breasts." Adichie says, "What is important about John Locke is that it represented the beginning of telling African stories in the West, a tradition of sub-Saharan Africa as a place of negatives and darkness."[67] What story informed Bradford and the pilgrims' attitude toward the created order in 1620? How do their stories inform us?

In this section we turn to the Western church in our review of Christianity's historical and theologically diverse relationship to God's Creation. In premodern times much of the presumed anthropocentrism should be qualified. And, importantly for our purposes, throughout this period there are significant alternative voices that deserve highlighting. Nonetheless the change in worldview that came with the Renaissance and modernity would have sweeping ramifications for how the church visualized its relationship to nature.

Western Medieval Christianity

Viewing medieval Christianity through a *theological* lens, we observe that the Western church took important steps to affirm the goodness and wonder of God's Creation; nonetheless, it also reinforced many anthropocentric, dualistic traditions.[68] Most of theology continued to find its intellectual pattern in the great chain of being, drawing on the widespread influence of Pseudo-Dionysius the Areopagite. Thomas Aquinas (1225–1274), the towering theological figure of this period, gives evidence of some of the theological tensions surrounding nature. Aquinas affirmed the Creator's immanence—"Therefore God must be in all things"—while simultaneously developing a matter-denying theology: bodies serving souls, nature as lower than and subservient to humankind, and material as secondary to the intellectual and spiritual.[69] His view maintained the dominant hierarchical interpretation of the Greek world.

However, this theological tradition is not representative of all medieval Christianity. For the peasant, life was severe and primitive; the vast, dark forests produced fear rather than a sense of mastery over environment: "The immensity of an untamed nature made it appear that people, far from controlling the world around them, were in fact held in thrall by it."[70] Nature may have been subservient in Thomas's hierarchy but not in life's realities. Medieval religious art gave a prominent place to nature and ecology. In Irish monasticism both high crosses, such as those at Ahenny in County Tipperary, and illustrated

67. Chimamanda Adichie, "The Danger of a Single Story," October 2009, Ted Talk, http://www.ted.com/talks/chimamanda_adichie_the_danger_of_a_single_story.

68. On what follows, see Santmire, *Travail of Nature*, 75–95.

69. Thomas Aquinas, *Compendium of Theology*, trans. Cyril Vollert (St. Louis: B. Herder, 1947), chap. 130, p. 139.

70. Charles T. Wood, *The Age of Chivalry* (New York: Universe Books, 1970), 38.

manuscripts, like the *Book of Kells*, celebrate the natural world.[71] Benedictine monasticism, with its ideal of *ora et labora*, to pray and to work, helped monks foster a close relationship with the natural world through ritual and by rolling up their sleeves and getting dirt under their fingernails.[72] A number of mystics provide an alternative voice to the dominant theological view.[73] Hildegard of Bingen was a woman at peace with the created world around her, so much so that she could speak of the "complaint of the elements" (*querela elementorum*) against people. In Hildegard's understanding, the elements of nature and humanity were mutually interrelated. Confused by human restlessness, cruelty, and rebelliousness, nature responded with pestilences, pollution, weather disasters, and crop failures.[74] Hildegard had a remarkable awareness of how the whole human person—body *and* soul—was united with God's Creation.

Unquestionably, the shining figure of this period is Francis of Assisi (1182–1226), whom one biographer calls "a model of gentleness and care."[75] Francis has rightly received widespread recognition as an "ecological" saint, even from many outside the Christian faith.[76] Modern Christians can take a cue from Francis's witness as we seek a more holistic way of knowing and relating to Creation. In fact, it may be more illuminating to read his life than his theology. Francis perceived that "all creatures of our God and King"—together with burning sun, silver moon, rushing wind, sailing clouds, rising morn, flowing water, masterful fire, mother earth, flowers and fruits, those of tender heart, pain and sorrow, and death itself—lift up their voices to sing, bless, and worship their Creator.[77] This praise was not simply humanity praising God *for* Creation, but the whole Creation joining in praising God—"All your works shall give thanks to you, O LORD" (Ps. 145:10). This point is critical: Francis did not appreciate Creation because of its beauty or because it drew him to God; Francis loved and cared for even the lowliest creature as a brother or sister because God did.[78] Richard

71. Susan Power Bratton, *Environmental Values in Christian Art* (Albany: State University of New York Press, 2008), 65–77.

72. René Dubos, "Franciscan Conservation versus Benedictine Stewardship," in *Environmental Stewardship*, ed. R. J. Berry (New York: T&T Clark, 2006), 57–58.

73. On Meister Eckhart (1260–1328) and Creation, see Richard J. Woods, *Meister Eckhart* (New York: Continuum, 2011), 49–64.

74. Schipperges, *Hildegard of Bingen*, 54–59.

75. Leonardo Boff, *Francis of Assisi*, trans. John W. Diercksmeier (Maryknoll, NY: Orbis, 1982), 3.

76. Although calling Francis "ecological" is anachronistic, historian Lynn White, "Historical Roots of Our Ecologic Crisis," 1207, proposes Francis as "a patron saint for ecologists."

77. Francis of Assisi, "All Creatures of Our God and King," hymn paraphrased from "Canticle of the Sun," Oremus (website), http://www.oremus.org/hymnal/a/a100.html, accessed March 10, 2013.

78. Santmire, *Travail of Nature*, 108.

Bauckham sees Francis as vitally important for reimagining our vision of stewardship because in his life he realized "mutuality, interdependence, friendliness and confraternity between human beings and other creatures of God."[79]

Francis's life was christocentric and cruciform. He identified with the kenotic Christ who emptied himself and descended to earth out of humility and love: "The kenotic Christ brought Francis's piety 'down to earth.'"[80] Furthermore, in his eschatology Francis longed to live at peace with the whole Creation, as if the new heavens and the new earth, and "the freedom of the glory of the children of God" (Rom. 8:21), were already a reality.[81] In sum, Santmire calls Francis "an embodiment of the ecological promise of classical Christianity."[82]

The Reformers and Nature

Christianity inherits numerous theological insights from the Reformation that can inform ecotheology. While the final "ecological" verdict on the Reformers' theology is debated, there remain key Creation-affirming aspects of Reformation theology.

Martin Luther's (1483–1546) theology of the cross (*theologia crucis*) provides an excellent resource for a developing ecotheology.[83] Luther's is an earthbound theology of descent. In contradistinction to inherited "ascent" theologies, he stressed that God has descended to this earth and became incarnate as a human being *and* a created being. Luther rejected the "great chain of being" and any dualistic severance of the spiritual from the material.[84] God is embodied in Jesus; therefore, in Jesus's humanity we meet God's divinity. In the finite we discover the infinite (*finitum capax infiniti*); in the immanent we encounter the transcendent. Luther writes, "For how can reason tolerate it that the Divine majesty is so small that it can be substantially present in a grain, on a grain, over a grain, through a grain, within and without, and that, although it is a single Majesty, it nevertheless is entirely in each grain separately, no matter how immeasurably

79. Richard Bauckham, "Modern Domination of Nature—Historical Origins and Biblical Critique," in *Environmental Stewardship*, 45.

80. Santmire, *Travail of Nature*, 113.

81. Thomas of Celano, *Vita prima S. Francisci Assisiensis*, 81, cited in Edward A. Armstrong, *St. Francis* (Berkeley: University of California Press, 1973), 9.

82. Santmire, *Travail of Nature*, 118.

83. See Paul S. Chung, "Discovering the Relevance of Martin Luther for Asian Theology," *Dialog: A Journal of Theology* 44, no.1 (Spring 2005): 38–49; Cynthia Moe-Lobeda, "A Theology of the Cross for the 'Uncreators,'" in *Cross Examinations*, ed. Marit Trelstad (Minneapolis: Augsburg Fortress, 2006), 181–95; Larry Rasmussen, "Returning to Our Senses: The Theology of the Cross as a Theology for Eco-Justice," in *After Nature's Revolt*, ed. Dieter T. Hessel (Philadelphia: Fortress, 1992), 40–56.

84. Larry Rasmussen, *Earth Community, Earth Ethics* (Maryknoll, NY: Orbis, 1996), 274.

numerous these grains may be?"[85] Luther held to a far-ranging doctrine of the ubiquity, or real earthly presence, of Christ. At the same time, his vision of God's immanence was tethered by an equal belief in God's transcendence:

> God is substantially present everywhere, in and through all creatures, in all their parts and places, so that the world is full of God and He fills all, but without His being encompassed and surrounded by it. He is at the same time outside and above all creatures. . . . His own divine essence can be in all creatures collectively and in each one individually more profoundly, more intimately, more present than the creature is in itself; yet it can be encompassed nowhere and by no one.[86]

Another way to approach Luther is through his image of Creation as the "mask of God," behind which God is hidden (*Deus absconditus*).[87] Nature is not God, but in Creation the hidden God is revealed. Luther's spirituality was grounded in a deep appreciation for God's created world. Because of the incarnation, Luther gained a new connection with the natural world: "All creatures will appear a hundred times more beautiful to me than before."[88] Not surprisingly, he would often speak of "reverence in the face of life." In a manner reminiscent of Francis of Assisi, Luther envisioned the earthliness of humanity as something that brought it into solidarity with the rest of Creation.[89] Indeed, through our redemption in Christ, humanity's relationship with the created world was renewed: "We are now living in the dawn of the future life; for we are beginning to regain a knowledge of the creation, a knowledge we had forfeited by the fall of Adam. Now we have a correct view of the creatures."[90]

John Calvin's (1509–1564) theological work on Creation represents, according to Anna Case-Winters, "a rich and too seldom consulted resource for any who work at a Christian theology of nature. . . . In Calvin's theology, God has a relation to *all* of creation not just to human beings."[91] Calvin's doctrine of Creation was rooted firmly in his understanding of God's providence: God is

85. Martin Luther, "Daß diese Worte Christi . . . (1527)," in *D. Martin Luther's Werke (Weimarer Ausgabe)* (hereafter, *WA*) (Weimar, Germany: Hermann Böhlau, 1906–1961), 23.134.34–136.36, cited in Rasmussen, *Earth Community, Earth Ethics*, 273.

86. Luther, "Daß diese Worte Christi . . . (1527)," *WA*, 23.134.34–136.36, cited in Heinrich Bornkamm, *Luther's World of Thought*, trans. Martin H. Bertram (St. Louis: Concordia, 1958), 189.

87. Luther, *WA*, 40.1.94.

88. Luther, *WA*, *Tischreden*, 1.1160, cited in H. Paul Santmire and John B. Cobb Jr., "The World of Nature according to the Protestant Tradition," in *The Oxford Handbook of Religion and Ecology*, ed. Roger S. Gottlieb (Oxford: Oxford University Press, 2006), 119.

89. Santmire, *Travail of Nature*, 130.

90. Luther, *WA*, *Tischreden*, 1.1160, cited in Bornkamm, *Luther's World of Thought*, 184.

91. Anna Case-Winters, *Reconstructing a Christian Theology of Nature* (Burlington, VT: Ashgate, 2007), 51.

wholly faithful to the created order of the universe. An anxious relationship between Creation and providence was an increasingly prominent theme in Calvin's writing.[92] To Calvin, God's natural order is fragile and fearful: "All the fierce animals you see are armed for your destruction. But if you try to shut yourself up in a walled garden, seemingly delightful, there a serpent sometimes lies hidden. . . . Amid these tribulations must not man be most miserable, since, but half alive in life, he weakly draws his anxious and languid breath, as if he had a sword perpetually hanging over his neck?"[93] Reading these words from his *Institutes* one gains a sense of why providence was so central to Calvin's theology. Only reliance on divine providence can set a person free from the chaos and angst of the created world.

Creation might be terrifying, but it is also "the theater of God's glory." Calvin zealously scorned any human-made image of God, and yet his love for the created wonders of God's hand has led one interpreter to refer to him as "the creation-intoxicated theologian."[94] In a striking passage, Calvin writes that "this skillful ordering of the universe is for us a sort of mirror in which we can contemplate God, who is the otherwise invisible."[95] For Calvin, Christians are invited to look into the mirror of the natural world and reflect on the providence, attributes, vastness, and purposes of God. Contemplating God through nature reveals more of who God is than does mere philosophical speculation.[96] By opening our eyes of faith we see that the created order bears witness to its Creator:

> In every part of the world, in heaven and on earth, [God] has written and as it were engraven the glory of his power, goodness, wisdom and eternity. . . . For all creatures, from the firmament even to the centre of the earth, could be witnesses and messengers of his glory. . . . For the little singing birds sang of God, the animals acclaimed him, the elements feared and the mountains resounded with him, the rivers and springs threw glances toward him, the grasses and the flowers smiled. So that in truth there was no need to seek him from afar.[97]

Both Luther and Calvin offer valuable resources for constructing ecotheology. Luther spoke to the descent and earthiness of God in the incarnation, to God's neglected immanence, and to the hiddenness of God in Creation.

92. See Susan Schreiner, *The Theater of His Glory* (Durham, NC: Labyrinth, 1991), 7–37.
93. John Calvin, *Institutes of the Christian Religion*, 2 vols., ed. John T. McNeill, trans. Ford Lewis Battles (Philadelphia: Westminster, 1960), I.17.10 (i.223).
94. Peter Wyatt, *Jesus Christ and Creation* (Alison Park, PA: Pickwick, 1996), 91.
95. Calvin, *Institutes*, I.5.1 (i.52–53).
96. Case-Winters, *Reconstructing a Christian Theology of Nature*, 53.
97. John Calvin, *Opera omnia quae supersunt* (*Corpus Reformatorem*), 9.793, 795, cited in François Wendel, *Calvin*, trans. Philip Mairet (New York: Harper & Row, 1963 [1950]), 161.

Calvin lifted up God's providential care for the Creation and humanity's calling to contemplate the theater of God's glory. Given these Creation themes,
why does the Reformers' ecological heritage remain ambiguous? Because, in
spite of these ecologically friendly elements, their primary emphasis was on
God and humanity. In their soteriology (doctrine of salvation), God's grace
was chiefly oriented toward human salvation and only secondarily toward the
redemption of Creation.[98] Santmire's conviction that the Reformers' theology
is "theanthropocentric"—Karl Barth's term emphasizing that God's Word is
primarily addressed to *humanity* in Jesus Christ—is certainly debated.[99] It
is fair to say that both an incarnational christocentrism and a deeply rooted
theocentric theology of nature curtailed the anthropocentrism of Luther
and Calvin.[100] In their historical and social context, the Reformers' stress on
the individual's relationship with God through grace by faith was met with
widespread resonance. Nonetheless in the centuries that followed, whatever
Creation-affirming beliefs the Reformers held faded away, and their attention
to personal salvation primed Protestants to secularize and disregard nature.

Modern Western Christianity

In modern Western Christianity, we arrive at the crux of how an anthropocentric worldview (by which humanity exercised despotic dominion over
God's Creation) came to the fore as the narrative that superseded all others.
Some argue that up until this time, a "horizontal" perspective that humans
were related to other creatures because of their common Creator tempered
any understanding of dominion as "vertical" or hierarchical.[101] Others see a
distinct foreshadowing of anthropocentrism in the ancient world. The tragedy
of anthropocentrism becoming the overarching narrative is complicated and
disputed, so here we can only highlight a few of the major story lines.

During the period of the European Renaissance, the works of Italian hu-
manist writers privileged a "vertical" worldview, overpowering and subduing

---

98. It should be noted that both Luther and Calvin held to a final eschatological transformation or renewal of all things, a new heaven and a new Earth. See also Santmire, *Travail of
Nature*, 132; Case-Winters, *Reconstructing a Christian Theology of Nature*, 54–55.

99. Santmire, *Travail of Nature*, 148–49. However, Case-Winters, *Reconstructing a Christian Theology of Nature*, 45–46, argues that too many people have inaccurately read Calvin
because they have depended too much on Karl Barth's theanthropocentric lens. See also Peter A.
Huff, "Calvin and the Beasts: Animals in John Calvin's Theological Discourse," *Journal of the
Evangelical Theological Society* 42, no. 1 (March 1999): 67–68.

100. Santmire, *Travail of Nature*, 132–33; Santmire and Cobb, "World of Nature according
to the Protestant Tradition," 122; Wyatt, *Jesus Christ and Creation*, 158–59.

101. See Richard Bauckham, *God and the Crisis of Freedom* (Louisville: Westminster John
Knox, 2002), 138–41.

anything "horizontal," since God had designated humanity (in Gen. 1:26) to take up the mantle of power, ingenuity, and creativity. Bauckham comments, "Human creatureliness is forgotten in the intoxication with human godlikeness."[102] To exercise sovereignty over the world is to attribute to humanity godlike qualities. One of the Italian humanists, Marsilio Ficino (1433–1499), wrote:

> In these industrial arts it may be observed how man everywhere utilises all the materials of the universe as though all were subject to man. . . . He acts as the vicar of God, since he inhabits all the elements and cultivates all. . . . He does not only rule the animals cruelly, but he also governs, fosters and teaches them. Universal providence is proper to God who is the universal cause. Therefore man who universally provides for all things living is a certain god. He is the god without doubt of the animals since he uses all of them, rules them, and teaches some of them. He is established also as god of the elements since he inhabits and cultivates them all.[103]

It is this fundamental belief that humanity has divine power and authority to alter and re-create the natural world that furnished modernity with its prevailing worldview.

Francis Bacon (1561–1626) translated the Renaissance vision into a system that gave rise to the modern scientific endeavor. Although Bacon's project was more nuanced than is often represented, he offered a utilitarian perspective rooted in Genesis 1:28: "For by the Fall man declined from the state of innocence and from his kingdom over the creatures. Both things can be repaired even in this life to some extent, the former by religion and faith, the latter by the arts and sciences."[104] Note that the recovery of dominion over the created order is to be accomplished through science, as distinct from faith. Bacon stripped the Creation of its aliveness and turned it into mere inert, dead matter, which humanity could then manipulate through science and technology. Because humanity no longer saw itself as sharing createdness with the rest of the natural world, it could objectify, devalue, and detach itself from Creation. In fact Bacon espoused that the "more sensible and more majestic" of human ambition was to attempt "to renew and extend the power and empire

102. Richard Bauckham, "Modern Domination of Nature—Historical Origins and Biblical Critique," in *Environmental Stewardship*, 34.

103. Marsilio Ficino, *Theologia Platonica de immortalitate animorum*, in Marsile Ficin, *Théologie Platonicienne de l'immortalité des âmes*, ed. and trans. Raymond Marcel (Paris, 1964), ii.224–25, cited in Charles Trinkaus, *In Our Image and Likeness* (London: Constable, 1970), ii.483–84; see also Bauckham, "Modern Domination of Nature," 33–37.

104. Francis Bacon, *The New Organon*, ed. Lisa Jardine and Michael Silversthorne (Cambridge: Cambridge University Press, 2000), bk. II, LII, p. 221.

of the human race itself over the universe of things, . . . [to] recover the right over nature which belongs to him by God's gift."[105] This development marks a major turning point in Earth's history: anthropocentrism utterly dethrones theocentrism, and a mechanistic, scientific framework becomes the model of modernity. Thomas Carlyle, writing in the nineteenth century, exemplifies the fallout from this worldview: "We war with rude nature; and, by our resistless engines, come off always victorious, and loaded with spoils."[106]

The Reformation provided impetus to scientific modernism in two ways. Through their understanding of Christian vocation, the Reformers, especially Calvin, empowered laity to forgo monastic withdrawal and to move actively into the world. Because of their chosenness by God, Christians had a divine vocation "to work for new social forms and new configurations of the human environment."[107] One historian writes that for Calvin, the Christian believer was "given immense creative authority and sent into an 'open' world to remold it to God's glory."[108] In addition, the Reformers forwarded a new hermeneutic that prioritized a literal or historical sense of Scripture over an allegorical reading. This "hermeneutical revolution" had far-reaching ramifications. Previously it was presumed that the primary purpose of the Bible *and* the natural world was fundamentally allegorical or symbolic. After the Reformation, one could address the Bible and the natural world more directly, less symbolically, including God's command to exercise dominion.[109] Philosophically, Immanuel Kant (1724–1804) accepted a scientific, mechanistic view of the natural world. Taking this perspective for granted allowed him in turn to spiritualize (and moralize) God and humanity and thereby isolate both from nature. Kant viewed God and humanity as transcendent to nature.[110] With few exceptions, Kant's presuppositions were uncritically incorporated into Protestantism. Thereafter, the personalization of religion and salvation became the driving force of Protestant theology. Theanthropocentrism and soteriology moved toward the center, and Creation was squarely upstaged.

■ ▓ ▪

In sum, Western Christianity leaves yet another ambiguous ecological legacy. In both the medieval and Reformation periods, there are observable paradigms

105. Ibid. bk. I, CXXIX, pp. 100–101.
106. Cited in Trevor Blackwell and Jeremy Seabrook, *The Revolt against Change* (London: Vintage, 1993), 24.
107. Santmire, *Travail of Nature*, 127.
108. Langdon Gilkey, *Reaping the Whirlwind* (New York: Seabury, 1976), 185.
109. Peter Harrison, "Having Dominion: Genesis and the Mastery of Nature," in *Environmental Stewardship*, 23.
110. Santmire, *Travail of Nature*, 134–37.

of a theocentric worldview and appreciation for the created world and Creator, to say nothing of clarion models, like Francis of Assisi and Hildegard of Bingen. Ultimately, though, religion succumbed to a scientific worldview in which humanity stood hierarchically in dominion over nature. Scholars like Laurel Kearns agree that the shift of worldview from 1500 to 1700 was the "disintegration of a more immanent and organic view of nature, and the ascendancy of the modern, mechanistic worldview that sees nature as dead, or inert, and atomized."[111]

The Birth of Contemporary Christian Ecotheology

> The doctrine of creation has been made a devout datum of past time. The mathematization of meaning in technology and its reduction to operational terms in philosophy has left no mental space wherein to declare that nature, as well as history, is the theater of grace and the scope of redemption.
>
> —Joseph Sittler[112]

In 1961 Lutheran theologian Joseph Sittler gave a prophetic address, "Called to Unity," to the World Council of Churches gathering at New Delhi. His message, quoted in part above, emphasized "cosmic Christology" and sought to bring the whole of Creation within the compass of God's grace and Christ's redemption. Although Christianity still struggles under the shadow of the modern scientific worldview, it does so with increasing uneasiness. The last fifty years have seen significant biblical, theological, and ethical revisions and changes within a broad range of Christian traditions, all of which make a holistic ecotheology more viable and accessible. The brief outline of key figures that follows makes no claim to comprehensiveness; our primary purpose is to name just a few of the writers who have influenced this work. It is exciting that any attempt to be inclusive is beyond our capacity because of the sheer amount of ecotheological writing currently accessible.[113]

Europeans did not consider preservation or conservation until, in the words of Wallace Stegner, "generations of living in America and 'breaking' its wilderness

---

111. Laurel Kearns, "The Context of Eco-Theology," in *The Blackwell Companion to Modern Theology*, ed. Gareth Jones (New York: Blackwell, 2004), 469.

112. Joseph Sittler, "Called to Unity," in *Evocations of Grace*, ed. Steven Bouma-Prediger and Peter Bakken (Grand Rapids: Eerdmans, 2000), 45.

113. On what follows, see Anne Marie Dalton and Henry C. Simmons, *Ecotheology and the Practice of Hope* (Albany: State University of New York Press, 2010), 19–37; Kearns, "Context of Eco-theology," 466–84; Santmire and Cobb, "World of Nature according to the Protestant Tradition," 132–46; Wallace Stegner, "A Capsule History of Conservation," in *Where the Bluebird Sings to the Lemonade Springs* (New York: Random House, 1992), 117–32.

had taught us to know it, and knowing it had taught us to love it, and loving it had taught us to question what we were doing to it."[114] Authors such as James Fenimore Cooper (1789–1851)—"What will the axemen do, when they have cut their way from sea to sea?"—and Henry David Thoreau (1817–1862)—"In wildness is the preservation of the world"—and John Muir (1838–1914)—"The mountains seemed to kindle to a rapt, religious consciousness, and stood hushed like devout worshippers waiting to be blessed"—prepared the conservationist platform for contemporary authors of "place," like Annie Dillard, Wendell Berry, Ellen Davis, Barry Lopez, Terry Tempest Williams, and David James Duncan. In the twentieth century, Aldo Leopold's *Sand County Almanac* and Rachel Carson's *Silent Spring* deserve their epoch-making reputations.[115]

Within mainstream Protestantism, Catholicism, and Eastern Orthodoxy, a number of authors rise to the surface. Lutheran pastor Paul Santmire has been writing broadly on ecotheology for over forty years. Within the Reformed tradition, Jürgen Moltmann and Wesley Granberg-Michaelson have been addressing ecotheological issues since the 1980s. William Gibson, Dieter Hessel, and Benjamin Chavis have provided leadership in ecojustice and the fight against eco-racism. Writing from Latin America, Leonardo Boff has shown convincingly the interconnection between ecology and liberation theology. Douglas John Hall, James Gustafson, and Larry Rasmussen have explored topics related to stewardship and ethics. Sallie McFague, Rosemary Radford Ruether, and Catherine Keller have made vital feminist contributions to the ecotheological dialogue. Representatives from Eastern Orthodoxy, including Bishop Kallistos Ware, Elizabeth Theokritoff, and Patriarch Bartholomew I, are making a unique and indispensible impact on a far-reaching ecotheology. Holmes Rolston III, Bill McKibben, R. J. Berry, and Susan Bratten are Christians who have articulately and passionately engaged the scientific community and broader culture. Many Roman Catholics have been active in driving the ecotheological conversation forward, including Thomas Berry, Denis Edwards, Elizabeth Johnson, and Celia Deane-Drummond. Ernst Conradie and Wangari Maathai have offered distinctive and fundamental perspectives from Africa, while Chung Hyun Kyung and Paul S. Chung have spoken challengingly from their Asian context. Andrea Smith and Randy Woodley embody an indigenous worldview in their writing and praxis.

With notable exceptions, evangelical and Pentecostal voices have been curiously missing from the broader ecotheological conversation. In large part,

---

114. Stegner, "A Capsule History of Conservation," 118.
115. Aldo Leopold, *A Sand County Almanac* (Oxford: Oxford University Press, 1949); Rachel Carson, *Silent Spring* (New York: Houghton, 1962), dedicated her work to a personal hero, Albert Schweitzer, who himself had championed a Christian "reverence for life."

this book is attempting to invite the diverse range of evangelical Christians to bring their hearts, souls, minds, and strengths to the ecological table. In doing so, they will be joining an expanding array of leaders committed to the love and care of Creation. As authors we acknowledge our indebtedness to evangelical forerunners, such as Calvin DeWitt, Loren Wilkinson, and Steven Bouma-Prediger, writers who have paved the way by their theological insights and engaged lifestyles. Richard Bauckham, N. T. Wright, and Douglas Moo Jr. have given biblical and hermeneutical undergirding to an evangelical perspective. The evangelical faith of John Houghton, cochair of the Intergovernmental Panel on Climate Change (IPCC) that won a Nobel Peace Prize, underlies his contribution to the scientific community, as does that of Katherine Hayhoe. Matthew and Nancy Sleeth, and their work at Blessed Earth, continue to make valuable inroads with the evangelical community through writing and speaking. It is exciting to see Pentecostals becoming increasingly involved in green Christianity, with theologians like Amos Yong, Matthew Tallman, and Marthinus Daneel leading the way.

To reiterate, this survey of individuals who have laid the groundwork for the rise of modern Christian ecotheology is fragmentary. With gratitude we recognize all those upon whose shoulders we stand; with regret we apologize to those whose names deserve acknowledgment but are unmentioned here.

■ ■ ■

As Christians our history, though undeniably ambiguous, does offer theological, biblical, and real-world resources for engaging the unparalleled realities of the ecocrisis. Throughout its history, as it has faced new and demanding challenges, the church has turned afresh to the Bible and to its forebears to discern the call of Jesus at any given moment. Sometimes the Christian community hears that call swiftly and finds itself in the vanguard of the struggle, with "clenched teeth and trembling fists" (Dietrich Bonhoeffer).[116] At other times the church holds back cautiously, waiting to see how the winds will blow before taking unnecessary risks. Our conviction is that time is limited for engaging the predicament in which our planet is immersed, that we cannot flee the "inescapable," and that God has situated us in this place "for just such a time as this" (Esther 4:14). In memory and honor of those who have gone before us, and in love for Creation and for those inexorably affected by our decisions, both now and in the future, the time has come for Christ-followers to "re-vision" their history, study reflectively, think imaginatively, pray humbly, and act boldly.

---

116. Dietrich Bonhoeffer, *Berlin: 1932–1933*, trans. Isabel Best, David Higgins, and Douglas W. Stott, ed. Larry L. Rasmussen (Minneapolis: Fortress, 2009), 269.

5

The God of Burning Bushes

Trinity and Ecology

In Numbers 20 the congregation of Israel quarreled with Moses in the wilderness because they had no grain, figs, grapevines, pomegranates, or water. So Moses and Aaron went to the tent of meeting; there the Lord spoke to Moses: "Take the staff, and assemble the congregation, you and your brother Aaron, and command the rock before their eyes to yield its water. Thus you shall bring water out of the rock for them; thus you shall provide drink for the congregation and their livestock" (v. 8). Moses and Aaron gathered the congregation before the rock, where Moses twice struck it with his staff. Water poured out abundantly, and the people and livestock drank. But the Lord reprimanded Aaron and Moses and barred them from entering the Promised Land, and said it was "because you did not trust in me, to show my holiness before the eyes of the Israelites" (v. 12).

When I (Jen) was in Sunday school, I remember being disturbed by what this story seemed to be saying about God. In my mind, this story moved quickly from a cheerful rhapsody to a dark fugue in a minor key, similar to God calling all of Creation good then destroying the Earth in a great flood. In some ways, refusing Moses and Aaron access to the Promised Land fit right in with the portrait of an angry God that was being etched in my mind. Many years later in seminary, William Brown's writing helped me see the possibility of a less retaliatory God. Brown asserts that striking the rock could be seen as a transgression of both divine and ecological boundaries: "The human task of subduing the earth does not pit humanity against nature, but reflects a working with nature through cultivation and occupation, through promoting and harnessing creation's integrity."[1]

Numbers 20 depicts the people of God as exhausted, anxious, and hopeless, cursing the desert for their thirst. In the same way that God provided manna in the wilderness, God was prepared to give the people water. But just as there were boundaries around a sacred tree in the Creation story and around the sustainable consumption of manna, so there were boundaries around how Moses was to interact with the rock. God never told Moses to strike it—God told Moses to speak to it. Striking the rock—demonstrating power and dominance over the created world—was a sin against God and the created world. Perhaps not entering the Promised Land was about breaking trust with God as well as breaking a boundary with Creation. This is certainly not the version of the story—or the God—that I had learned about in Sunday school. *That* God was angry with Moses for not following instructions. But is it possible that God was also angry on behalf of the Other, because humanity had once again trespassed against Creation?

It is not hard to imagine what striking the rock might look like today. Hydraulic fracturing—the process of pumping water, sand, and chemicals in enormous quantities and at high pressures into the earth to fracture layers of shale and release oil or natural gas—does not seem that far removed from the Israelites' seeking a natural resource in the desert, nor from Moses beating the rock. The consequences of modern-day rock striking are destructive: massive amounts of carbon dioxide are released into the air, millions of gallons of water (a highly threatened resource) are used while producing equal amounts of wastewater, and toxic chemicals are leached into drinking water.

Who is this God who cares about all Creation—even rocks? It is the same God who tended the garden alongside humanity, who chose to become incarnate and to dwell among us on Earth and not just in the heavenly realm. The Scriptures bear witness to a God who has consistently called attention to the importance of our relationship to the Earth. But, as has persistently been our nature, we seem only to pay attention when we are in crisis, when we are dying of thirst in the wilderness. Only then do we notice what has been there all along—a divine command to be caretakers and a divine consequence for failing to live into that vocation. The God who cares about the whole community of life is the one eternal God. An investigation into the nature of *that* God shows how fundamental a coherent theology is to a coherent ecotheology.[2]

1. William P. Brown, *The Ethos of the Cosmos* (Grand Rapids: Eerdmans, 1999), 126.
2. James M. Gustafson, *Ethics from a Theocentric Perspective* (Chicago: University of Chicago Press, 1981), 23–24.

In fact, a thoughtful inquiry into the doctrines of Trinity, Christology, and pneumatology (the theology of the Holy Spirit) leads to a discipleship that encompasses the nurture and stewardship of all our relationships with God.

Trinity

> My idea of God is not a divine idea. It has to be shattered time after time. He shatters it Himself. He is the great iconoclast. Could we not say that this shattering is one of the marks of His presence?
>
> —C. S. Lewis[3]

Dorothy L. Sayers, English novelist and theologian, takes issue with the church's bias against doctrine, expressing tongue-in-cheek frustration with a widespread reliance on rudimentary, uninformed theological thinking. If people were to take a brief exam about God, Sayers suggests that most answers would generally sound something like this: God the Father[4] is "always ready to pounce on anybody who trips up over a difficulty in the Law, or is having a bit of fun"; God the Son "has a good deal of influence with God, and if you want anything done, it is best to apply to Him"; as far as God the Holy Spirit, "there is a sin against Him which damns you forever, but nobody knows what it is." And what of the Trinity, asks Sayers? "'The Father incomprehensible, the Son incomprehensible, and the whole thing incomprehensible.' It's something put in by theologians to make it more difficult—and it's got nothing to do with daily life or ethics."[5]

As we will see, the doctrine of the Trinity, because it is rooted in relationship and mission, has a great deal to do with both daily life and ethics, and with humanity and the rest of Creation.

God's "Nature"

The sixth-century Athanasian Creed, one of the church's clearest articulations of the Trinity, declares, "Nothing in this trinity is before or after, nothing is greater or smaller; in their entirety the three persons are coeternal

3. C. S. Lewis, *A Grief Observed* (New York: HarperOne, 2001 [1961]), 78.
4. Whether we use "Creator" or "Father" to describe this person of the Godhead, what we mean is "Unoriginate Origin," in the words of Catherine Mowry LaCugna, "The Practical Trinity," in *Exploring Christian Spirituality*, ed. Kenneth J. Collins (Grand Rapids: Baker, 2000), 280. She further writes, "It is not as though there is first a God, then there are divine persons. The doctrine of the Trinity insists that God does not exist *except* as Father, Son, Spirit."
5. Dorothy L. Sayers, *Creed or Chaos?* (Manchester, NH: Sophia Institute, 1974 [1949]), 21–22.

and coequal with each other. So in everything, as was said earlier, we must worship their trinity in their unity and their unity in their trinity."[6] Trinitarian doctrine is not an arrogant attempt to define, grasp, or control God; rather it stands at the very heart of Christian belief, practice, and worship. Years before leaders gathered in church councils to debate and delineate doctrine and dogma, Christ-followers were already worshiping and declaring their Trinitarian beliefs through liturgy. Trinitarian worship came before Trinitarian formulations; the practices of the church gave rise to theological formulations.[7] It is no exaggeration to state that the doctrine of the Trinity arose out of a longing by the church more fully to know in truth the One it was already worshiping in spirit.

To speak of doctrines and dogmas arising out of worship is to acknowledge that our yearning to understand the Trinity arises out of relationship. The last several decades of Trinitarian scholarship have predominately revolved around relationality and love.[8] Such an emphasis is not to declare the language of the early church—*ousia* and *hypostasis*—unimportant. Rather it is to highlight that numerous early theologians also envisioned God's nature in the framework of an ontology of relationship.[9] Perhaps the term that best conveys this relationality in God is *perichōrēsis*, a word that describes how substances can mix without losing their distinct properties. It might be translated as "mutual indwelling" or "coinherence." Originally the word was used to describe the relationship of the human and the divine in the second person of the Trinity.[10] John of Damascus then used *perichōrēsis* to describe the intimate fellowship

6. "The Athanasian Creed," Christian Reformed Church, http://www.crcna.org/welcome/beliefs/creeds/athanasian-creed, accessed January 4, 2014.

7. Jaroslav Pelikan, *The Christian Tradition: A History of the Development of Doctrine*, vol. 1, *The Emergence of the Catholic Tradition (100–600)* (Chicago: University of Chicago Press, 1975), 173–74, states: "The oldest surviving liturgical prayer of the church was a prayer address to Christ: 'Our Lord, come!' [1 Cor. 16:22] Clearly it was the message of what the church believed and taught that 'God' was an appropriate name for Jesus Christ. But before this belief and teaching developed into the confession of the Trinity and the dogma of the person of Christ, centuries of clarification and controversy had to intervene, and the relation of this belief to the full range of Christian doctrine had to be defined."

8. For example, Leonardo Boff, *Trinity and Society* (Maryknoll, NY: Orbis, 1988); Stanley J. Grenz, *The Social God and the Relational Self* (Grand Rapids: Eerdmans, 2001); Catherine Mowry LaCugna, *God for Us* (New York: HarperOne, 1993); Jürgen Moltmann, *The Trinity and the Kingdom*, trans. Margaret Kohl (Norwich: SCM, 1981); Amos Yong, *Spirit—Word—Community* (Burlington, VT: Ashgate, 2003); John D. Zizioulas, *Being as Communion* (Yonkers, NY: St. Vladimir's Seminary Press, 1997).

9. Roger E. Olson, *The Story of Christian Theology* (Downers Grove, IL: InterVarsity, 1999), 187, states that Gregory of Nazianzus (c. 329–390) "gave ontological status to relations."

10. Verna Harrison, "*Perichōrēsis* in the Greek Fathers," *St. Vladimir's Theological Quarterly* 35, no. 1 (1991): 55–59.

within the godhead.[11] Likewise, contemporary theologian John Zizioulas uses the phrase "being as communion" to emphasize relationality in the Trinity.

If the essence of Trinitarian theology is relationality, then it makes complete sense to state with St. John, "God is love" (1 John 4:8). Love is not simply an attribute *of* God; God *is* love. Fourteenth-century mystic John Ruusbroec wrote, "Here the Persons give way and lose themselves in the maelstrom of essential love, that is, in the blissful Unity, and nevertheless remain active as Persons in the work of the Trinity."[12] It is vital to note the tension here: to "lose oneself" is not fusion but selfless love, for the "Persons" remain active. An ontology of relationship means an ontology of love. Since love is situated in the center of Trinitarian existence, love is also at the heart of human beings created in God's image. David Benner writes, "Born out of the love of God, our very being is being-in-Love, for our being is in the God who is love."[13] When framed in this way, to love—whether God, other persons, or the Creation—is an eternal reflection of the Trinity and therefore an imperative for Christians who worship the Three-in-One.

The Paradox of God's Presence

A critical issue for constructing a sound ecotheology is how to understand God's "relationship" to the other-than-human part of Creation. In what ways might an ontology of love be extended to all that God has created? Colossians 1:19–20 says, "For in him [Christ] all the fullness of God was pleased to dwell, and through him God was pleased to reconcile to himself all things, whether on earth or in heaven, by making peace through the blood of his cross." If all things on earth and in heaven are to be "reconciled" to God through Christ's death on the cross, it implies at the very least that there must be some kind of relationship to be restored. The phrase "making peace" points to the idea of shalom in the Hebrew Scriptures.[14] Indigenous theologian Randy Woodley, in

---

11. John of Damascus, *De fide contra Nestorianos* 36, cited in ibid., 61, wrote: "As in the Holy Trinity the three hypostases, through natural identity and coinherence [*perichōrēsis*] in each other, are and are called one God, so in our Lord Jesus Christ the two natures, through hypostatic identity and coinherence [*perichōrēsis*] in each other, are one Son."

12. John Ruusbroec, "The Little Book of Clarification," in *The Spiritual Espousals and Other Works*, trans. James A Wiseman, OSB (New York: Paulist Press, 1985), 262.

13. David G. Benner, *Spirituality and the Awakening Self* (Grand Rapids: Brazos, 2012), 74. Roman Catholic theologian Catherine LaCugna, *God for Us*, 273, extends this perichoretic love into our relationships with others in the human community: "*Perichōrēsis*, embodied in inclusiveness, community and freedom, is thus the 'form of life' for God and the idea of human beings whose communion with each other reflects the life of the Trinity."

14. Douglas J. Moo, "Nature in the New Creation: New Testament Eschatology and the Environment," *Journal of the Evangelical Theological Society* 49, no. 3 (2006): 472–73.

addressing this particular text, calls attention to the "community of creation" and the far-reaching impact of shalom that Christ brought through his death on the cross: "Justice and equality, provision and freedom, salvation and healing of creation are found in Christ."[15]

But to speak of the relationship between God and the created order is to raise the question of God's transcendence vis-à-vis God's immanence. Langdon Gilkey summarizes the traditional Christian position: "God transcends the world as distinct from it, and yet God is immanent within the world as the source of its being, as the principle of its life and order, and as the ground of its hope for fulfillment."[16] In Christian history, though, this tension of "both-and" has proved difficult to maintain. Erring too far on either side can lead to opposite errors. On the one side, to overemphasize God's transcendence and distinction *from* nature can lead to dualism and deism, by which both God *and* humanity stand over against nature. On the other side, to dismiss transcendence in favor of immanence can result in a monism or pantheism, which views everything as part of God.[17]

The scales have tipped toward transcendence within the traditions of Western Christianity. As the pendulum swings back, it is no great surprise that many writers are seeking to envision God's immanence in creative and engaging ways, using concepts like *panentheism* (from "all," "in," and "God"—the belief that God is present in all of Creation). Panentheism is appealing because it raises the viability and co-creative activity of God's presence in the world beyond traditional (omnipotent) providence. Respected scholars, such as Rosemary Radford Ruether and Jürgen Moltmann, have argued for particular versions of panentheism—and it should be noted that there is much diversity among those who espouse panentheism.[18] However the slippery slope of panentheism leads to monism (all of reality is of one substance), by which there is no actual difference between pan*en*theism and pantheism. Again, we must affirm any effort to accentuate God's relatedness to Creation, but it does little good to dissolve the mystery in favor of immanence. In his helpful summary of some of the issues at stake, Steven Bouma-Prediger underscores that a healthy

15. Randy S. Woodley, *Shalom and the Community of Creation* (Grand Rapids: Eerdmans, 2012), 40.

16. Langdon Gilkey, "Creation, Being, and Non-Being," in *God and Creation*, ed. David B. Burrell and Bernard McGinn (Notre Dame, IN: University of Notre Dame Press, 1990), 229.

17. Ibid. See also Steven Bouma-Prediger, *The Greening of Theology* (Atlanta: Scholars Press, 1995), 284–301.

18. John W. Cooper, *Panentheism: The Other God of the Philosophers* (Grand Rapids: Baker Academic, 2006), 237–58 and 291–94. For a brief evaluation of the "contested concept" of panentheism, see Roger E. Olson, review of *In Whom We Live and Move and Have Our Being*, ed. Philip Clayton and Arthur Peacock, *Christian Century* 122, no. 24 (November 29, 2005): 44–45.

ecotheology emphasizes both transcendence and immanence *and* affirms "that God's relatedness actually *depends* upon God's otherness."[19]

Trinitarian Implications for Ecological Mission

Out of this discussion, we can draw two implications for missional, ecological living. First, the more deeply we reflect on the Trinity the more we are led to mystery. When it comes to divine transcendence, the Cappadocian father Gregory of Nyssa (c. 335–395) reminds us to remain humble in the face of the incomprehensible nature of God: "We . . . have learned that that nature is unnameable and unspeakable, and we say that every term either invented by the custom of men, or handed down to us by the Scriptures, is indeed explanatory of our conceptions of the Divine Nature, but does not include the signification of that nature itself."[20] Our images of God must not become gods in themselves, for in so doing we become idolaters. Language cannot fully comprehend the divine. No single word communicates a vision of God that is broad enough to encompass divine truth. As has been said: if God wanted just to speak to our minds, Mary would have written a book instead of bearing a child. For this reason, we can speak of God as Father, Mother, Creator, Vivifier, Redeemer, etc.[21] We need a multiplicity of images and metaphors—particularly coming from those unlike us—in our descriptions of God; otherwise we have little to restrain us from creating God in our own image. The Trinity's diverse nature drives us to a love of mystery. Henry Bugbee links this mystery to wilderness: "The world does not become less 'unknown' . . . in proportion to the increase of our knowledge about it. . . . Our experience of the world involves us in a mystery which can be intelligible to us only as mystery. The more we experience things in depth, the more we participate in a mystery intelligible to us only as such; and the more we understand our world to be an unknown world."[22]

Secondly, the propensity of the Western church to overemphasize the transcendence of God at the expense of immanence has had profound implications for formation and discipleship. Too often the goal of "spiritual" formation has

---

19. Bouma-Prediger, *Greening of Theology*, 286.

20. Gregory of Nyssa, "On 'Not Three Gods,'" The Fathers of the Church, New Advent, http://www.newadvent.org/fathers/2905.htm, accessed January 9, 2014.

21. Bouma-Prediger, *Greening of Theology*, 290, addresses the language of the "fatherhood" of God: "An adequate Christian ecological theology must re-envision God as mother as well as father. To attend to models of the relationship between God and creation is implicitly if not explicitly to attend to models of God. And for much too long the predominant if not exclusive model of God has imaged God as male."

22. Henry Bugbee, *The Inward Morning* (Athens: University of Georgia Press, 1999 [1958]), 76; see also David James Duncan, *My Story as Told by Water* (San Francisco: Sierra Club, 2001), chap. 6.

been to escape this earthly existence, to let "the things of earth . . . grow strangely dim."[23] But as Benner stresses, spirituality "invites us to find the transcendent in the mundane, the sacred in the shadow."[24] A balanced sense of the immanence of God calls us to a "spirituality" that loves earthly things more passionately, not less. A transforming Christian discipleship rejects an exclusivist dichotomy between the present and the eternal, between immanence and transcendence.

Christology

> If he [Christ] is so exclusively God that He was never in any real sense an ordinary human being with human limitations like our own, then it is clearly meaningless for us to try and follow in His steps. . . . If Jesus Christ is God of God, and made the world to His own pattern, then . . . by disregarding Christ we shall come into collision with the very nature of the universe.
>
> —Dorothy L. Sayers[25]

An indigenous Christ-follower named Afua Kuma depicts Jesus as the Lord of the Obo-Kwahu forests in Eastern Ghana.[26] For Kuma, Jesus is the God of the African destitute, a feeder and advocate of the orphan, and a fighter of the dark powers of *Kakae*—the monster who rules the forest with his oppressive powers. In the Liberator's destruction of evil, the forest becomes safe once again for travelers, hunters, and Creation. Jesus is the 'Osagyefo, who, like Moses, leads God's people *and* Creation to freedom. Kuma's praise of the "Jesus of the deep forest" speaks to her rich African theology and profound identification with the natural world. Kuma speaks of a Jesus whose liberating actions are as much about the forest as about humans.

Sadly it seems vastly more difficult for the Western church to make a similar connection between Christology and ecology. Even with the upsurge in ecotheological scholarship in the last half century, the work on the relationship between ecology and Christology is proportionately lacking.[27] Since the resurrected Jesus Christ is at the heart of Christianity, that deficiency is striking. The number of ways in which Christology can inform our ecotheology and ecopractice is significant.

---

23. Helen H. Lemmel, "Turn Your Eyes upon Jesus," Timeless Truths (website), http://library.timelesstruths.org/music/Turn_Your_Eyes_upon_Jesus/, accessed November 15, 2012.
24. Benner, *Spirituality and the Awakening Self*, 122.
25. Cited in Laura K. Simmons, *Creed without Chaos* (Grand Rapids: Baker Academic, 2005), 84.
26. Kwame Bediako, *Jesus and the Gospel in Africa* (Maryknoll, NY: Orbis, 2004), 8–15.
27. Celia Deane-Drummond, *Eco-Theology* (Winona, MN: Anselm Academic, 2008), 99.

The initial sentence of the Chalcedonian Definition (451) reads:

> Following the holy Fathers we teach with one voice that the Son [of God] and
> our Lord Jesus Christ is to be confessed as one and the same [Person], that he
> is perfect in Godhead and perfect in manhood, very God and very man, of a
> reasonable soul and [human] body consisting, consubstantial [*homoousios*] with
> the Father as touching his Godhead, and consubstantial with us as touching his
> manhood; made in all things like unto us, sin only excepted.[28]

Orthodox Christology confesses the full humanity and full divinity of our
Lord Jesus Christ. While it can be dangerous to assign certain attributes to his
humanity and others to his divinity, for the sake of our work we will look first
at his "humanity" and then at his "divinity" as we seek to draw christological
implications for a holistic ecotheology.[29]

The Humanity of Jesus

In examining the humanity of Jesus as revealed in the Gospels, three things
deserve mentioning insofar as they relate to ecotheology. First, Jesus exhibited
a *unique relationship to the land*. In his parables and teaching, Jesus was much
more nature-based than we usually recognize. He spoke of sparrows, sheep,
wolves, goats, oxen, donkeys, foxes, fish, snakes, sea monsters, worms, scorpi-
ons, moths, swine, dogs, birds, cocks, salt, figs, grapes, eggs, fruit, oil, wheat,
mustard seeds, yeast, nests, fig trees, trees, branches, wood, logs, specks, lilies,
grass, grain, shrubs, bramble bushes, thorns, thistles, weeds, soils, land, rocky
ground, mountains, deserts, dust, gardens, fields, vineyards, light, fire, earth,
wind, water, seas, lakes, rivers, rain, floods, stones, rocks, pearls, sand, sun,
moon, stars, sky, heavens, clouds, weather, and more. East Asian theologian Kwok
Pui-lan observes Jesus's use of nature and says: "I do not think these natural
images are just rhetorical devices or embellishments of Jesus' teaching because
I think they are an inseparable part of his message."[30] The Earth lamented the

28. "The Definition of Faith of the Council of Chalcedon," in *Medieval Sourcebook: Council of Chalcedon, 451*, Internet History Sourcebooks Project, Fordham University (website),
1996–2006, ed. Paul Halsall, sec. 264, http://www.fordham.edu/halsall/basis/chalcedon.asp.
29. Cyril of Alexandria in 430 CE argued strongly for the idea of *communicatio idiomatum*,
"a term applied to the person of Christ by those in the early church who believed that although
the human and divine natures remained separate, the attributes of the one could be applied
to the other." Karen J. Torjesen and Gawdat Gabra, eds., *Claremont Coptic Encyclopedia*,
Claremont Colleges Digital Library, http://ccdl.libraries.claremont.edu/cdm/ref/collection/cce
/id/492, accessed November 15, 2012.
30. Kwok Pui-lan, "Response to Sallie McFague," in *Christianity and Ecology*, ed. Dieter T.
Hessel and Rosemary Radford Ruether (Cambridge, MA: Harvard University Press, 2000), 48.

crucifixion of the second Adam, its Creator: "From noon on, darkness came over the whole land until three in the afternoon" (Matt. 27:45); and at the moment of his death, "The earth shook, and the rocks were split" (v. 51).

While Jesus's compassion for the real, earthly circumstances of people, especially the underprivileged, is manifest in his miracles of healing and feeding, is there evidence of his bringing healing to nature? Recent scholarship has shown that, far from being an act of ecological indifference, the cursing of the fig tree (Mark 11:12–24) was a prophetic critique of the temple and its lack of fruitfulness.[31] Richard Bauckham remarks that Jesus's nature miracles, such as when he quieted the storm (Mark 4:35–41), demonstrate that the healing of human and other-than-human relationships "belongs to the holistic salvation that the kingdom of God means in the Gospels."[32] During his wilderness temptation, Jesus was "with the wild beasts" (Mark 1:13). Here we catch a glimpse of a renewed peace or shalom between "wild" nature and humanity, fulfilling Isaiah's messianic vision—"The wolf shall live with the lamb, / the leopard shall lie down with the kid, / the calf and the lion and the fatling together, / and a little child shall lead them" (Isa. 11:6).

Secondly Jesus filled the role of Hebrew *prophet*. Like Elijah and Isaiah, Amos and Jeremiah, he fearlessly exposed how the dominant powers were oppressing the forgotten and the poor. Jesus initiated his prophetic ministry in his hometown of Nazareth (Luke 4:16–19). Aligning himself with Isaiah's messianic portrait, he made clear that his missional priorities were on behalf of the poor, the captives, the blind, and the oppressed. If Jesus consistently prioritized the forgotten people of his world, and if it is becoming increasing clear that the well-being of all people on this planet—especially the poor and those on the margins—is inextricably entangled with the health of the whole created order, it is not a stretch to imagine Jesus calling Earthcare a central aspect of discipleship today. As Kwok comments, "Social ecology cannot be separated from natural ecology."[33]

Jesus's prophetic ministry to the poor can be extended to the entire Creation. Insisting that this extrapolation is more than sentimentality or novelty, Sallie McFague suggests a theocosmocentric ("God-creation-centered") point of view: if God is both Creator and Redeemer, then surely God cares for the whole Creation and not just the portion that is human. She points toward a prophetic Christology

31. Ched Myers, *Binding the Strong Man* (Maryknoll, NY: Orbis, 1988), 297–99, gives a helpful summary of the cursing in its context. He writes that the narrative function of the cursing of the fig tree is "to begin Jesus' ideological project of subverting the temple-centered social order" (299).

32. Richard Bauckham, "Jesus, God and Nature in the Gospels," in *Creation in Crisis*, ed. Robert S. White (London: SPCK, 2009), 211; see also Richard Bauckham, *Living with Other Creatures* (Waco: Baylor University Press, 2011), 63–78; Mark Bredin, *The Ecology of the New Testament* (Colorado Springs: Biblica, 2010), 41–46.

33. Kwok, "Response to Sallie McFague," 49.

rooted in Jesus's life and teaching: "The *principle* that Jesus' ministry is focused on God's oppressed creatures must, in our day, include the deteriorating planet."[34]

Thirdly Jesus modeled *cruciformity*. Douglas John Hall emphasizes Jesus's cruciform life in his analysis of *imago Dei*.[35] In Colossians we read this fundamental christological statement: "He is the image [*eikon*] of the invisible God" (Col. 1:15). Paul tells his readers in Rome that God predestined them "to be conformed to the image [*eikon*] of his Son" (Rom. 8:29). Since Jesus is the image of God, we are able to discover in him God's original intention for humankind. When creating humankind "in the image of God" (Gen. 1:27), God told them to "fill the earth and subdue it" (v. 28). In Hebrew, the word "subdue" is *kabash*; in the Septuagint, the Greek word is *katakurieuo*. Strikingly, Jesus says to his bickering disciples: "You know that among the Gentiles those whom they recognize as their rulers lord it over them, and their great ones are tyrants over them" (Mark 10:42). The word used for "lord it over" is *katakurieuo*, drawing from the Creation narrative. The way of Empire, Jesus insists, is to misuse power to subdue the weak: "But it is not so among you; but whoever wishes to become great among you must be your servant, and whoever wishes to be first among you must be slave of all. For the Son of Man came not to be served but to serve, and to give his life a ransom for many" (Mark 10:43–45). Hall comments, "Jesus' perfection as the divine *imago*, which is at the same time perfect humanity, is embodied in a lordship that serves."[36] From an ecotheological perspective, humanity's relationship to the Earth does not involve "subduing," if that refers to a destructive power differential.

Jesus revealed a life of taking up the cross, servanthood, and subverting the traditional view of dominion.[37] McFague stresses putting genuine Christology into practice: "For affluent Christians, it demands a different view of the abundant life, one that includes *cruciform living*, the practice of restraint, diminishment, the death of unlimited desire, and control of ecological selfishness."[38] Cruciform living was not only Jesus's practice, it revealed and still reveals the nature and character of God.[39] To be clear, when we speak of the cruciform life, we are speaking of a servanthood *chosen* out of freedom, not an abusive, enforced servility. The model of Jesus directs us away from suffering that is unjustifiable, negative, and disintegrative, and toward actions that oppose such suffering.

34. Sallie McFague, "An Ecological Christology: Does Christianity Have It?," in *Christianity and Ecology*, 35–36.

35. Douglas John Hall, *Imaging God* (Grand Rapids: Eerdmans, 1986), especially 76–87.

36. Ibid., 79.

37. See Joseph Sittler, "The Cruciform Character of Human Existence," *Chicago Lutheran Seminary Record* 54, no. 3–4 (Oct. 1949): 18–21.

38. McFague, "An Ecological Christology," 41 (emphasis added).

39. N. T. Wright, *The Challenge of Jesus* (Downers Grove, IL: InterVarsity, 1999), 94–95.

Jesus's humanity—defined and expressed in relationship to the land, as a prophet, and as an exemplar of cruciform living—becomes a paradigm of discipleship for the modern follower of Christ.

The Divinity of Christ

Looking through the lens of Christ's divinity, we can discern three additional themes that impact a Christian ecotheology. The first revolves around the ramifications of a *cosmic Christology*. The primary text for outlining a cosmic Christology is Colossians 1:15–20:

> He is the image of the invisible God, the firstborn of all creation; for in him all things in heaven and on earth were created, things visible and invisible, whether thrones or dominions or rulers or powers—all things have been created through him and for him. He himself is before all things, and in him all things hold together. He is the head of the body, the church; he is the beginning, the firstborn from the dead, so that he might come to have first place in everything. For in him all the fullness of God was pleased to dwell, and through him God was pleased to reconcile to himself all things, whether on earth or in heaven, by making peace through the blood of his cross.

The first section of this text conveys the centrality of Jesus Christ for the whole of Creation; not only is the Creation in Christ, through Christ, and for Christ, but, in some mysterious way, Christ is the One who holds all things together. The second half of the hymn points to cosmic reconciliation and to the fact that Christ is head of the new Creation, including the church and all things "on earth or in heaven." The word *eirenopoiesas* ("making peace") reflects the Old Testament expectation that God would one day establish universal restoration, renewal, and peace—shalom.[40] Including the whole Creation within the scope of Christ's work on the cross in no way diminishes the reconciliation that Christ's death and resurrection make possible between humanity and God. In Jesus Christ, creation and redemption are given their proper place. He is both the "mediator of creation" and the "mediator of reconciliation" for all things.[41]

Secondly Paul tells us that Jesus Christ is the *wisdom of God* (1 Cor. 1:24). The depiction of wisdom or "sophia" is rooted in the Old Testament; in fact, Elizabeth Johnson asserts, "Overall, there is no other personification of

40. Moo, "Nature in the New Creation," 472–73. See also Douglas J. Moo, "Creation and New Creation: Transforming Christian Perspectives," in *Creation in Crisis*, 248. Moo does *not* see this cosmic work as a kind of universal salvation.

41. Moo, "Nature in the New Creation," 473; see also Ernst M. Conradie, ed., *Creation and Salvation*, 2 vols. (London: LIT Verlag, 2012).

such depth and magnitude in the entire scriptures of Israel."[42] The Book of Wisdom (a deuterocanonical text) describes Sophia as "a reflection of eternal light, a spotless mirror of the working of God"; furthermore, "she renews all things. . . . She reaches mightily from one end of the earth to the other, and she orders all things well" (Wisdom of Solomon 7:26–8:1). Wisdom Christology had vital connections with Logos Christology, which came to full fruition in the Gospel of John.[43] The Word (*logos*) of John 1:1–3 echoes the representation of wisdom as the agent and partner of Creation in Proverbs 8:22–31. Wisdom has built her house and invited all people to eat the food and drink the wine at her table (Prov. 9:1–6). Jesus, the personification of wisdom in John's Gospel, invites all people to himself: "I am the bread of life. Whoever comes to me will never be hungry, and whoever believes in me will never be thirsty" (John 6:35).

Wisdom Christology informs our developing ecotheology by reminding us that human wisdom, knowledge, and technology will not somehow "save" us from the current ecological crisis. Wisdom Christology offers a healthy dose of humility to our anthropology.[44] In addition, it teaches us responsible love for the Creation, in keeping with the biblical wisdom tradition. The antithesis of wisdom is sloth—refusing to act as neighbor to all of Creation and remaining inactive when action is necessary. Ellen Davis calls sloth "a style of life and work that is pursued without regard for the enduring health of community and place."[45] Wisdom calls us toward action, emulating Jesus's care for the Earth by tending and keeping it, honoring limits, and restoring it to God's intention. When we do so, we bear witness to the One who was, is, and always will be the Wisdom of God.

Thirdly we must investigate some of the implications of the *incarnation*, the divine becoming human. Few doctrines are as significant for a Christ-centered ecotheology as the incarnation. On Christmas Day in 386, Eastern Orthodox preacher and theologian John Chrysostom proclaimed that for Christ it was "no lowering to put on what He Himself had made. Let that handiwork be forever glorified, which became the cloak of its own Creator."[46] Incarnation is primarily about embodiment, about bringing nature into God's embrace. Too often our tendency is to spiritualize salvation and to remove anything

---

42. Elizabeth A. Johnson, "Jesus, Wisdom and Our World," *Priests and People* 13, no. 7 (July 1999): 260.

43. James D. G. Dunn, *Christology in the Making* (Philadelphia: Westminster, 1980), 163–212.

44. Deane-Drummond, *Eco-Theology*, 111.

45. Ellen F. Davis, *Scripture, Culture, and Agriculture* (Cambridge: Cambridge University Press, 2009), 142.

46. John Chrysostom, "Christmas Morning," in *The Sunday Sermons of the Great Fathers*, vol. 1, ed. M. F. Toal (Chicago: Regnery, 1957), 112.

salvific from the material. But the incarnation undermines those gnosticizing tendencies and allows us to see the divine in created things, the sacramentality of all life. Writing in the ninth century, Theodore the Studite made this bold affirmation: "What place is there where divinity is not present, in beings with or without reason, with or without life?"[47]

Jesus's divinity has the power to form our Christian discipleship. Dorothy L. Sayers, in a 1940 radio broadcast on the BBC, made this insightful statement on the divinity of Christ: "If Jesus Christ is God of God, and made the world to His own pattern, then . . . by disregarding Christ we shall come into collision with the very nature of the universe."[48] The Creator has taken on createdness; as our lives by grace are aligned with the cosmic Christ, the wisdom of God, and the incarnate One, we step into synchronicity with the design and nature of the universe itself, with who and what we were created to be.

■ ■ ■

Jesus Christ and his salvific life, death, and resurrection are the center of an evangelical ecotheology and ecopractice. In our present crisis, understanding Jesus's purposes and teachings—his comprehensive vision of the common-wealth of God—becomes one of the central tasks of the church. For it is Jesus Christ through whom all was created, and it is through Jesus Christ that all things will be reconciled to God.

Pneumatology

Only the Spirit of creation is strong enough to be the Spirit of resurrection. . . . The whole creation is home to the Spirit's operations, and the cosmic fruits issue in new creation.

—Clark Pinnock[49]

In the fourth century, Gregory of Nazianzus referred to the Holy Spirit as the *theos agraptos*—the God about whom no one writes. Finnish theologian Veli-Matti Kärkkäinen calls the Spirit the "Cinderella" of both the Trinity and theology.[50] Our conviction, though, is that pneumatology—the theology of the Holy Spirit—has a critical and often overlooked role in a holistic investigation of God and ecology.

47. St. Theodore the Studite, *On the Holy Icons*, trans. Catharine P. Roth (Crestwood, NY: St. Vladimir's Seminary Press, 1981), I.12, p. 33.

48. Cited in Simmons, *Creed without Chaos*, 84.

49. Clark Pinnock, *Flame of Love* (Downers Grove, IL: InterVarsity Academic, 1996), 63.

50. Veli-Matti Kärkkäinen, *Pneumatology* (Grand Rapids: Baker Academic, 2002), 16.

The Complexity of Creation

Our perception of the universe is increasingly marked by complexity. Humankind's comprehension of the nature of the universe has evolved significantly over time, most particularly over the last five centuries. Through the insights and discoveries of Copernicus (1473–1543), Kepler (1571–1630), and Galileo (1564–1642), humans came to perceive the expansive grandeur of a galaxy of which planet earth and humanity were no longer the center. Isaac Newton (1643–1727) awakened us to gravity, and Charles Darwin (1809–1882) argued that earth's life span began billions of years ago, evolving into what we see today. All of these portrayed a Creation that is more mysterious and more complex than what was portrayed in earlier static models.

Recent discoveries have led to massive alterations in cosmological understanding, leapfrogging earlier views. Edwin Hubble's discovery in the 1920s of an apparently enlarging galactic system led to what has been called the "Big Bang" theory.[51] By the mid-1950s, a number of scientists and cosmologists were speaking of *nucleosynthesis*, proposing that all existing cosmic material essentially remains recycled matter from the "Big Bang" event.[52] The discovery in 1965 of expanding background radiation harmonized with Hubble's thesis. Albert Einstein's theory of relativity would continue to disrupt a once safe and static view of the universe.[53] In spite of the fact that many within the Christian tradition continued to have reservations about any (or all) of these theories, late modern human experience is re-situating itself in the wake of staggering revolutions not only in scientific and cosmological, but also in theological, paradigms.

A vital theological resource for conversing with an increasingly vibrant scientific understanding of Creation is pneumatology. However pneumatology until recently has remained generally disconnected from larger theological discussion, even though it has much to offer the ecological conversation.[54] To engage theological dialogue from the perspective of pneumatology and

---

51. Cosmologist and physicist Stephen Hawking, *A Brief History of Time* (New York: Bantam, 1988), 39, comments that the discovery of the expanding universe is "one of the great intellectual revolutions of the twentieth century." The "Big Bang" theory was first proposed in 1931 by the Belgian physicist and Roman Catholic priest Georges Lemaître, contending that if the universe was indeed expanding, there must have been a point at which it was all centralized in one place—the "primeval atom."

52. Denis Edwards, *Jesus and the Cosmos* (Mahwah, NJ: Paulist Press, 1991), 65–66.

53. On the significance of Einstein's theory of relativity for scientific and Western understandings of God, see Gregory Ganssle and David Woodruff, eds., *God and Time* (Oxford: Oxford University Press, 2002).

54. Kärkkäinen, *Pneumatology*, 19–20. This divide is undeniably part of the larger "atomization" of theology, the fruit of a categorization in the eighteenth century by which theology was splintered into specific parts (e.g., Christology, ecclesiology, pneumatology). It is illustrative that pneumatology as a formal "area" of theology did not even exist until the eighteenth century.

the ever-dynamic nature of God's Spirit is like "'beating the crust back into the batter,' . . . to go behind the later incrustations of doctrine to the living experience of faith with all of its ambiguities, temptations, and struggles," borrowing from Old Testament scholar Bernard Anderson.[55] Because of our emerging understanding of God's living Creation, we need the creative vitality of a pneumatology that engages all arenas of life, including ecology.

Spirit and Creation in Scripture

In the Old Testament we discover an oft-neglected connection between the Spirit and Creation. The Spirit (*rûach*) of God hovers over the chaos (*tohu vovahu*), bringing organization and completion (Gen. 1:1–2). Augustine describes the creativity of the Spirit of God "as exercising a skill in making and fashioning things, in the way that the intention of a craftsman is 'borne over' the wood."[56] But the Spirit's role in the Creation narrative is not the whole biblical testimony; the Spirit continues to give Creation its life (*creatio continua*). God's Spirit is the life-breath of all beings without which they would wither. The psalmist ponders, "When you take away their breath, they die / and return to their dust. / When you send forth your spirit [*rûach*], they are created; / and you renew the face of the ground" (Ps. 104:29b–30). Donald Gelpi refers to the Spirit as a "scrutinizing omniscience" who is everywhere and always searching out Creation—"Where can I go from your spirit?" (Ps. 139:7).[57] Bezalel is filled with the creativity of the "divine spirit [*rûach*]" to help construct the tabernacle (Exod. 31:2–5).[58]

The New Testament bears witness to a similar relationship between Spirit and Creation. For instance, the Gospels describe the presence of the Spirit as that of a created "dove" that descends at the baptism of Jesus (Matt. 3:16). St. Paul describes a person's newness in Christ as being a "new creation" like that of the Genesis account (2 Cor. 5:17). The eighth chapter of Romans is a treatise on the nature of the Spirit: "The law of the Spirit of life in Christ Jesus has set you free from the law of sin and of death" (v. 2). With intimations of the Trinity, Paul speaks of "the Spirit of him who raised Jesus from the dead" (v. 11). Joseph Sittler extols Paul's writing in Romans 8: "It is probably fair

55. Bernard W. Anderson, *Contours of Old Testament Theology* (Minneapolis: Augsburg Fortress, 1999), 3, suggests that the point of theology in general is to keep the doctrines we have created always informed by the relational thrust that created theology in the first place.
56. Augustine, "Unfinished Literal Commentary on Genesis," in *On Genesis*, trans. Edmund Hill, OP, ed. John E. Rotelle, OSA (Hyde Park, NY: New City, 2002), 16.
57. Donald L. Gelpi, *The Divine Mother* (Lanham, MD: University Press of America, 1984), 48.
58. Colin Gunton, "The Spirit Moved Over the Face of the Waters: The Holy Spirit and the Created Order," *International Journal of Systematic Theology* 4, no. 2 (2002): 201.

to say that never before or since in the history of literature has such a group of powerful, enormous notions and concepts been compacted into so small a space."[59] Embedded in Paul's theological masterpiece on life in the Spirit is his description of the waiting, futility, bondage, groaning, and hope of Creation (vv. 19–23). That very Spirit who dwells in us (v. 9), who bears witness with our identity (v. 16), and who intercedes when we do not know how to pray (v. 26), groans with the whole Creation as we await redemption and freedom (v. 23). Paul's vision of the work of the Holy Spirit is expansive and life giving, as seen in the words of the Nicene Creed: "We believe in the Holy Spirit, the Lord, the giver of life."

One connection between the Spirit and Creation, Ephesians 4:7–11, has solicited debate. The discussion of Christ's ascent to and descent from the heavenlies is considered by many to be a rabbinic conversation with Psalm 68, a traditional psalm of the Hebrew festival of Pentecost that celebrated the giving of the law on Mount Sinai fifty days following Passover. There have been numerous interpretations of the nature of "descent." Some have suggested that this descent was Christ's incarnation in the flesh, while others that it was his descent to hell after his death on the cross.[60] Yet some recent scholarship suggests that this descent was that of the Holy Spirit at Pentecost (Acts 2).[61] The argument, according to George Caird, is that a traditionally Jewish Pentecost psalm related to Moses is spun into a Christian Pentecost psalm, "celebrating the ascension of Christ and his subsequent descent at Pentecost to bestow spiritual gifts upon the Church."[62] In this interpretation, Ephesians 4:7–11 turns out to be a distinctively pneumatological text about Creation. The passage notes, in a classic Pauline parenthetical phrase, that in his final ascent to heaven Christ "fills [*pleroun*] the whole universe [*ta panta*—'all things']" (v. 10), a phrase often used to illustrate God's omnipotence and omnipresence.[63] Therefore the descent is the outpouring of the Spirit on the church *and* the whole universe, implying both an *ecclesiological* and *ecological* interpretation

59. Joseph Sittler, "Nature and Grace in Romans 8" (1975), in *Evocations of Grace*, ed. Steven Bouma-Prediger and Peter Bakken (Grand Rapids: Eerdmans, 2000), 209.

60. J. Clifford Hindley, "The Christ of Creation in New Testament Theology," *Indian Journal of Theology* 15, no. 3 (1966): 89–105.

61. W. Hall Harris III, *The Descent of Christ* (Grand Rapids: Baker, 1996).

62. George Caird, "The Descent of Christ in Ephesians 4:7–11," *Studia Evangelica*, vol. 2, ed. Frank L. Cross (Berlin: Akademie, 1964), 541. Others who take a similiar view include T. K. Abbott, *The Epistles to the Ephesians and the Colossians* (Edinburgh: T&T Clark, 1897), 115–16; H. von Soden, ed., *Hand-Kommentar Zum Zeuen Testament* (Freiburg: Mohr, 1893), iii.135–36. The argument was first proposed by von Soden, revived by Abbott, and reconstituted by Caird.

63. For exegetical options on the meaning of "filling the whole universe," see Rudolf Schnackenburg, *Ephesians: A Commentary* (Edinburgh: T&T Clark, 1991), 179.

Tension Point: Evolution

Evolution is a thorny issue for evangelicals. By itself, the issue has led to division among theologians and teachers, pastors and parents, from all walks of life and from all types of traditions. The vast majority of scientists, including evangelical scientists, accept evolution (and the basic realities of climate change).

While it may appear as though we have glossed over the issue, there are hours of dialogue not recorded in this book. In the end, we unanimously agreed that the Bible definitively narrates a story of God as Creator. Two of us accept the fundamental ideas of evolution: common ancestry and descent with modification. One of us continues to wrestle with these concepts. Many (if not most) evangelical scientists, historians, philosophers, and theologians hold the convictions of evolution.[a]

The primary conflict between the three of us was whether or not we should address evolution at all in this text. To be frank, the strong temptation is to avoid or stay on the fringes of this question because it is such a "make or break" issue for many evangelicals. The church needs theologians who are willing to do the hard work of engaging science when delineating a theology of human origins.

- Why do you think evolution is such a "make or break" issue for evangelicals? Is it one for you? Why or why not? Do you have trouble imagining how people who are persuaded differently can care for Creation with intellectual integrity?
- How can Christian communities and places of learning create hospitable space where people on both sides of this question can interact with each other with civility?
- What do you think or feel about the fact that as writers we have not tackled this issue more directly? What would have been the fallout, in your opinion, if we had landed on one side or the other?

a. See Calvin College, Office of the Provost, "Calvin College Seminar Series: Human Origins" (2010–2013), http://www.calvin.edu/admin/provost/seminars/human-origins.html, accessed January 14, 2014.

of Psalm 68. At Pentecost Christ fills the church with charismatic gifts; at the same time the Spirit "fills the universe" with Christ's presence and authority.[64]

In both the Old and New Testaments we encounter a Spirit involved in creating the universe, sustaining and continually creating life on this planet, and empowering the new Creation arising from the incarnation, life, death, and resurrection of Jesus Christ.

64. Although there are undoubtedly some exegetical issues with this interpretation, it still retains intriguing implications for a connection between pneumatology and a creation theology. For an illustrative examination of the textual and hermeneutical issues, see Harold Hoehner, *Ephesians* (Grand Rapids: Baker Academic, 2002), 532–33.

A Theology of the Spirit and Creation

To explore further the relationship between the Spirit and Creation, we turn to consider the Spirit's vocation. Mark Wallace proposes four traditional elements of the Holy Spirit—vivifying breath, living water, cleansing fire, and earth's fruit bearer/divine love.[65] Wallace demonstrates a comprehensive role for the Spirit that embraces Creation and moves beyond the historic tendency to limit the Spirit predominately, if not solely, within the context of the church. Kärkkäinen laments restricting the Spirit to the church where "it gives men and women the assurance of the eternal blessedness of their souls. This redemptive Spirit is cut off from both bodily life and life of nature. It makes people turn away from 'this world' and hope for a better world beyond."[66] A broader pneumatology seeks to reappropriate the Spirit in political, social, and ecological dimensions. In this way we are able to recognize that the Spirit gives divine life to and vivifies both the communion of saints (the church) and the community of Creation.[67]

A number of notable Spirit-sensitive ecotheologies have been constructed in recent decades.[68] Dennis Edwards proposes a pneumatology whereby the Spirit infuses life into Creation, giving it the fundamental ability freely to adapt and grow to its fulfillment. Edwards's construction makes room for evolution from a pneumatological perspective; the Spirit providentially creates the ability for Creation to change and evolve.[69] Not only is the Spirit involved in restoring human relationships, but also, on a broader level, the Spirit is the relational, dynamic presence between all creatures, human and other-than-human. That is to say, the divine Spirit is not simply a force or entity, but an active, inviting, reconciling presence within the whole created order, bringing all creatures together.[70] The same Holy Spirit who unites believers in worship beckons humans and the rest of the natural world into relationship. The Spirit is a flame of love, kindling our love for animals, plants, stars, and the Earth.

65. Mark I. Wallace, *Finding God in the Singing River* (Minneapolis: Fortress, 2005).

66. Veli-Matti Kärkkäinen, *An Introduction to Ecclesiology* (Downers Grove, IL: InterVarsity, 2002), 132.

67. Jürgen Moltmann, *The Spirit of Life*, trans. Margaret Kohl (Minneapolis: Augsburg Fortress, 1992).

68. For example, A. J. Swoboda, *Tongues and Trees: Towards a Pentecostal Ecological Theology* (Blandford Falls, UK: Deo, 2013).

69. Edwards, *Jesus and the Cosmos*. This view is similar to "evolutionary theodicy" or "cosmic theodicy." See Christopher Southgate, *The Groaning of Creation* (London: Westminster John Knox, 2008), 47–48.

70. John V. Taylor, *The Go-Between God* (Philadelphia: Fortress, 1973), 31.

The Healing Spirit

When Jesus arrived in Nazareth at the beginning of his public ministry, he opened the Isaiah scroll and read:

> The Spirit of the Lord is upon me,
> because he has anointed me
> to bring good news to the poor.
> He has sent me to proclaim release to the captives
> and recovery of sight to the blind,
> to let the oppressed go free,
> to proclaim the year of the Lord's favor. (Luke 4:18–19)

In this passage, Jesus presents himself as the messianic figure anticipated by the Jewish community, as a "Spirit-anointed" one. The Messiah was to proclaim the good news of freedom—from poverty, blindness, captivity, and hopelessness. The Creation is oppressed, hurt, broken, and imprisoned. Elizabeth Johnson speaks of the Creator Spirit as the emancipator of all Creation, as the One "who pervades the world in the dance of life."[71] One might emphatically suggest that the Spirit seeks to free the oppressed whoever, whatever, and wherever they may be.

Jesus the Messiah healed many people, often through personal touch (e.g., Matt. 8:1–4). Paul and the early church continued the practice of the "laying on of hands" (Acts 8:17; 13:3; 19:6). James specifically charged the Christian community to lay hands on the sick (James 5:14). In Pentecostal and charismatic communities today, the conviction continues that this practice has redemptive and healing power. Could we envision the Spirit's healing power in ecological terms, through a personal encounter by the Spirit with the marvel of Creation? For those who have lost "touch" with the reality of God's enlivening Creation, the greatest means of healing is a return to personal relationship and touch.

■ ■ ■

It is no coincidence that this chapter began with a story of physical action gone wrong (Moses striking the rock) and ends with the restorative power of touch. There is a visceral difference, beyond just cognitive dissonance, when one places side by side the image of Moses striking the rock with that of Jesus healing by the laying on of hands. Jesus—Afua Kuma's Liberator and ours—came to restore to health all forms of brokenness. This restoration, this healing, this salvation, as we will see in the next chapter, includes both

71. Elizabeth A. Johnson, *Women, Earth, and Creator Spirit* (Mahwah, NJ: Paulist Press, 1993), 2.

a sin-marred humanity and a wounded and oppressed Creation.[72] It is nothing less than miraculous that in working out our salvation Jesus invites us to partnership—to "become partners of Christ" (Heb. 3:14)—in the reconciliation of all things, to participate in healing that which we have spent most of human history harming.

72. See section "Redemption and Salvation" in chap. 6.

6

Restoring Eden

Ancient Theology in an Ecological Age

M y (Dan's) friend Tom Durant is a retired businessman and former
student of mine who now teaches global business management and
directs a ministry called EcoCafé Haiti, located in Ranquitte in the
steep foothills of north central Haiti, population 20,000.[1] The vision of the
ministry is to help restore economic self-sufficieny, heal the heavily deforested
environment, provide food for the poor, and restore broken relationships in
Christ. The story of EcoCafé Haiti revolves around coffee. French colonists
first brought the crop to the country, and by the late 1700s Haiti furnished
over 70 percent of the coffee consumed in Europe and the United States. After
Haiti's revolution in 1804 when the new nation abolished slavery (the first in
the Western Hemisphere to do so), tragically most countries, including the
United States, were unwilling to trade with Haiti out of fear that abolition
would spread like an infection. As a result of this boycott, Haiti's coffee enterprise collapsed. But the Arabica Typica coffee plants remained on the island,
and now EcoCafé Haiti is developing a sustainable coffee enterprise using
natural and sustainable cultivation practices. Slowly, the ecological, economic,

---

1. EcoCafé Haiti, "EcoCafé Haiti. Good Coffee. Good Cause," http://www.ecocafehaiti
.com, accessed October 31, 2012. For an interview with Tom Durant, see University of Oregon,
"UO: A couple minutes with . . . Tom Durant," December 28, 2011, https://www.youtube.com
/watch?v=xMRXd-P3OI8. On what follows, Tom Durant, "EcoCafé Haiti," presentation at
George Fox Evangelical Seminary, Portland, Oregon, February 4, 2011.

societal, and spiritual estrangement is being reversed. This is restoration; it is also redemption, shalom, and salvation.

This chapter examines the theological categories of creation, sin, redemption and salvation, and eschatology. The Western church has not kept these aspects of the story of God's saving work in equilibrium. By undervaluing the doctrine of Creation, we have diminished the breadth and inclusivity of the doctrine of redemption. A robust ecotheology enables us to restore all these theological components to a healthy balance and tension. Since we can speak of an "ecology"—an interrelatedness and interdependence—within the whole created order, then it is also important to see an interconnectedness in the brokenness and salvation of Creation, an "ecology of sin" and an "ecology of grace."[2]

Creation

> Sunrise—an event that calls forth solemn music in the very depths of one's being, as if one's whole being had to attune itself to the cosmos and praise God for a new day, praise Him in the name of all the beings that ever were or ever will be—as though now upon me falls the responsibility of seeing what all my ancestors have seen, and acknowledging it, and praising God, so that, whether or not they praised God back then, themselves, they can do so now in me.
>
> —Thomas Merton[3]

"We believe in one God, the Father, the Almighty, maker of heaven and earth, of all that is, seen and unseen." With these words, the Nicene Creed places the Creator and the Creation at the forefront of our confession as Christians. At this moment in history, it is more important than ever that theology arise out of our experience of Creation. With a solid foundation in Creation theology, we are better able to explore what has "fallen" and the breadth of what God has done to redeem and save.

The Goodness of Creation

Joseph Sittler wrote, "Reason says that destroying clean air is impractical. Faith ought to say it is blasphemous."[4] Destroying clean air should be con-

2. See Howard A. Snyder, *Salvation Means Creation Healed: The Ecology of Sin and Grace* (Eugene, OR: Cascade, 2011), 65–109.

3. Thomas Merton, *The Journals of Thomas Merton*, vol. 4, *Turning toward the World: The Pivotal Years, 1960–1963* (New York: HarperOne, 1997), 292.

4. Cited in John Bayard Anderson, *Between Two Worlds* (Grand Rapids: Zondervan, 1970), 139.

sidered blasphemous because it diminishes the self-revelation of the Creator whose "eternal power and divine nature, invisible though they are, have been understood and seen through the things he has made" (Rom. 1:20). All that God created is very good (Gen. 1:31; *tôb mĕ'ōd*). If everything and everyone that the sovereign God made is *tôb mĕ'ōd*, then to be what the Creator intended must also be very good—creatureliness is good. Curiously we have invested considerable theological and philosophical wrangling throughout the centuries attempting to unravel "the problem of evil." But, is not "the problem of good" equally bewildering? Does not Creation itself speak to grace? Sittler declares, "The fundamental meaning of grace is the goodness and lovingkindness of God and the activity of this goodness in and toward his creation."[5]

This created grace has an undeniable potency. In her iconic novel Virginia Woolf portrays the looming presence of the lighthouse: "Only the Lighthouse beam entered the rooms for a moment, sent its sudden stare over bed and wall in the darkness of winter, looked with equanimity at the thistle and the swallow, the rat and the straw."[6] My (Dan's) son gave me Woolf's novel to read because of my own love affair with one particular lighthouse. In the northwest corner of Washington state a spit of land stretches out five miles into the Straits of Juan de Fuca. At the end of that spit and wildlife refuge sits the New Dungeness Lighthouse, accessible only by foot or kayak. Every week of the year volunteers maintain the lighthouse as it sends its "sudden stare" over land and sea. On four separate occasions my wife and I and four friends spent a week at the end of the longest natural spit in North America, watching over that lighthouse and building relationships with each other and with God's Creation. There, hemmed in by variances of sea and storm and witness to bald eagles, elephant seals, gray whales, scores of migratory bird species, the Olympic Mountains, and stunning sunrises and sunsets, we were uniquely aware of a harmony, a goodness, a wonder in created wildness. The experience was undeniably compelling, and the most natural thing, perhaps the most essential calling in that moment, was to wonder.

The fact that the human creature can, in Thomas Merton's words, "attune itself to the cosmos" gives evidence that the Creator's goodness and grace make possible a relationship between humanity and the created order. Steven Bouma-Prediger insists, "An adequate Christian ecological theology must take more seriously the responsiveness of creation. That is to say, the common

5. Joseph Sittler, *Essays on Nature and Grace* (Philadelphia: Fortress, 1972), 24.
6. Virginia Woolf, *To the Lighthouse* (Orlando, FL: Harcourt Brace, 1927), 138.

view of the natural world as essentially autonomous and unresponsive—as 'nature'—must be replaced by a perspective in which the natural world is seen as grace-full and response-able. All creation is a place of grace."[7]

Genesis 1 and 2

The cosmogonies in Genesis 1 and 2 provide origin stories with distinct emphases. In Genesis 1:1–2:4a (hereafter, the Genesis 1 account) we are told of the goodness of Creation, including those created in the image of God; Genesis 2:4b–25 (hereafter, the Genesis 2 account) emphasizes that the human, like other-than-human Creation, is made of dust (Heb. *aphar*).[8] German social activist and mystic Dorothee Soelle finds a paradox in these two descriptions, differences she maintains must be held in tension with one another:

> Can I affirm myself as one who is made from dust? Can I say that my having been created is very good? . . . Is it possible for me to value my "creatureliness" in the knowledge that my existence was willed prior to my birth, that I am not here on this earth simply by chance, that I am needed, that I am not a disposable object, and that I am designed for freedom and equality?[9]

Recurrently, Christianity has been conspicuous both for its disregard of the goodness of Creation and for its denial of the "dust factor."

Throughout history, both Creation narratives have frequently been utilized as foundational texts to reinforce humanity's supposed license to disregard the goodness of Creation and to exploit the Earth and its resources. Readers of Genesis 1 have been prone to emphasize that humankind was identified with the Creator through the image of God; by contrast, nature was not identified with the divine in the same way, leading to the privileging of humankind over nature in the hierarchy of created order.[10] The Creation account in Genesis 2 portrays God as gardener and the first man as a caretaker placed in the garden to "till it and keep it" (Gen. 2:15). This account is more overtly agrarian; nevertheless traditional interpretations of Genesis 2 may still perpetuate themes

---

7. Steven Bouma-Prediger, *The Greening of Theology* (Atlanta: Scholars, 1995), 281.

8. The vast majority of biblical scholars assume that Genesis 1:1–2:4a and 2:4b–25 are separate accounts of Creation. See John Walton, *The Lost World of Genesis 1* (Downers Grove, IL: InterVarsity, 2009); Tremper Longman III, *How to Read Genesis* (Downers Grove, IL: InterVarsity, 2005); Peter Enns, *The Evolution of Adam* (Grand Rapids: Brazos, 2012).

9. Dorothee Soelle with Shirley A. Cloyes, *To Work and to Love* (Philadelphia: Fortress, 1984), 29.

10. Hava Tirosh-Samuelson, "Judaism," in *The Oxford Handbook of Religion and Ecology*, ed. Roger S. Gottlieb (Oxford: Oxford University Press, 2006), 34.

of dominion and hierarchy: the male demonstrates power over both woman and created nature by naming them. Genesis 2 has often served historically as a mandate to position certain humans above other humans, and humanity over other-than-human Creation.[11] Modern scholarship is demonstrating that these formative texts do *not* have to be read in ways that perpetuate systems of domination; nonetheless, they have regularly functioned in that way. To focus on differences and "power over" is Othering, something Larry Rasmussen refers to as an "apartheid mindset" through which we "identify all else by declaring what it is not. 'Nonhuman' is not us. 'Not us' is its significance, moral and otherwise."[12]

Theological Anthropology in the Creation Story

To speak of how we understand our relationships as humans with God, with other people, and with all Creation is to engage theological anthropology. What does it mean to be a human? Or, to be in relationship with others (both human and other-than-human)? I (Jen) like to think that I expect nothing from the three felines that live with me, that I am simply content to witness their cat*ness* and to wonder at their created grace. In actuality, I am obsessed with personifying the cats—creating them in my own image, saying they are happy or sad, depressed or lonely. I think they are pouting or punishing or comforting. Daniel Miller writes, "Bears do not actively pursue bearness; they simply are bears."[13] My compulsion to personify my cats is rooted, I suspect, in my own anthropocentrism. In truth, my cats live fully into their catness without my anthropomorphizing tendencies.

Could it be that humanity, by contrast, is the only part of Creation that can fail at being what we were created to be? If responsibility means we have the capacity to live into our human*ness*, it also means that we can become *other than* what we have been called to be.[14] In our brokenness, in our failure to live into our calling to responsibility, we think of the cat only in terms of its usefulness to us, its ability to keep us company or to make us laugh. We think about natural resources in the same way, what they can give us, how they can improve the quality of our lives. We stopped living into our calling when we trespassed the original boundary in the garden, consuming what was not ours to consume—valuing the tree for what it could do for us rather than for its tree*ness*.

11. Ibid. See also Rosemary Radford Ruether, *Womanguides* (Boston: Beacon, 1985), 62–63.
12. Larry L. Rasmussen, *Earth Community, Earth Ethics* (Maryknoll, NY: Orbis, 1997), 32.
13. Daniel K. Miller, *Animal Ethics and Theology* (New York: Routledge, 2011), 45.
14. Ibid.

Image of God

At the heart of theological anthropology is what it means to be created in the image of God, *imago Dei*. Historically, Christianity has tended to talk about *imago Dei* in three ways. The *substantialist* model is the oldest and, until recently, most prominent. It describes the unique capacity that humans possess—consciousness, will, reason, intellect, freedom, soul—that separates us from the rest of the created order. Because substantialism has affinities to dualism and can lead to an irresponsible anthropocentrism, many theologians are shifting away from this model.[15] Some scholars have tended to favor the second model, the *functional* or *representational* approach. In this paradigm the human person, made in the *imago Dei*, is given dominion over and functions as God's representative ruler within nature.[16] Functionalism, however, has a propensity toward hierarchy and a corresponding emphasis on the male sex as more representative of a male deity. More prevalent among contemporary theologians is the *relational* model propagated, among others, by Karl Barth, Jürgen Moltmann, and John Zizioulas. Relationalism argues that the *imago Dei* corresponds to social Trinitarianism and to the belief that relationality is the most fundamental attribute of God. But too often this perspective grants humans license to maintain a qualitative distinction between human and other-than-human life.

In all three models, Christianity has routinely managed to use the doctrine of *imago Dei* to sanction the godlike status of humanity *over* Creation, to value natural resources not for intrinsic value but for their utility, and even to elevate certain humans over others. If we are going to move toward a more holistic and ecologically mindful theological anthropology, it will mean re-imagining *imago Dei*. While *imago Dei* has long served as a way to talk about what makes humanity distinct from the rest of Creation, modern science is forcing us to talk about continuity between humans and the rest of the natural world. Humanity shares 96 percent of genetic material with our closet relatives, chimpanzees.[17] It turns out, as a species, we are not as "other-than-nature" as we might like to think. Genesis 2 is rooted in the primal element of dust as the common component of all created things. Wendell Berry calls

---

15. Anna Case-Winters, "Rethinking the Image of God," *Zygon* 39:4 (2004): 814; Claus Westermann, *Genesis 1–11: A Continental Commentary* (Minneapolis: Fortress, 1994), 153.

16. Nathan MacDonald, "The Imago Dei and Election: Reading Genesis 1:26–28 and Old Testament Scholarship with Karl Barth," *International Journal of Systematic Theology* 10, no. 3 (July 2008): 303–4; Marc Cortez, *Theological Anthropology* (New York: T&T Clark, 2010), 22; J. Richard Middleton, *The Liberating Image* (Grand Rapids: Brazos, 2005), 26–27.

17. Stefan Lovgren, "Chimps, Humans 96 Percent the Same, Gene Study Finds," *National Geographic News*, August 31, 2005, http://news.nationalgeographic.com/news/2005/08/0831_050831 _chimp_genes.html.

us to recover a theological memory of what it means to hold our createdness in common with every other being: "The breath of God is only one of the divine gifts that make us living souls; the other is dust. Most of our modern troubles come from our misunderstanding and misevaluation of this dust."[18] We are thoroughly earth-bound creatures and such a part of Earth's systems that "we are utterly dependent on their thriving."[19]

Christian theologians have tended to prioritize humanity to the detriment of the rest of Creation. Anne M. Clifford comments, "Theologians have directed their attention almost exclusively to human existence or human history . . . and have implicitly treated nature as a timeless and static backdrop."[20] An ecological hermeneutic enables us to understand *imago Dei* not as something that privileges humanity above Creation, but as that capacity for loving responsibility that starts with a recognition of our mutuality and relationship with all of Creation. Rasmussen suggests that to be created in the image of God "means that precisely *as* the creatures we are, situated in threefold relatedness to God, other human creatures, and otherkind, we would be turned toward God. . . . Imaging God is loving earth fiercely, as God does."[21]

The time to return our minds and hearts to the land, from and in which we exist, has come. It is our own Teacher who models for us an essential conversion to the Earth. Before Jesus announced his ministry of liberation for captives, healing for the blind, and freedom for the oppressed in Luke 4, he went into the wilderness "full of the Holy Spirit" (v. 1). In the wilderness, he did his work. He kept company with the Devil and the ancient stories of his people. He was tempted by economic privilege—"command this stone to become a loaf of bread" (v. 3)—and power—"To you I will give their glory and all this authority" (v. 6)—and rejected both. When he emerged, he knew his calling and mission. Our path must be the same. Modern humanity has become alienated and rootless. In our journey back to the Earth, we must acknowledge our sameness and solidarity with Creation. We must reject the temptation to accumulate resources and use privilege for our own purposes. And in our return to the land—coming home—we will see the work to which we have been called.

18. Wendell Berry, *Sex, Economy, Freedom, and Community* (New York: Pantheon, 1994), 107.

19. Kathleen Dean Moore and Michael P. Nelson, introduction to *Moral Ground* (San Antonio: Trinity University Press, 2012), xix.

20. Anne M. Clifford, "When Being Human Becomes Truly Earthly: An Ecofeminist Proposal for Solidarity," in *In the Embrace of God*, ed. Ann O'Hara Graff (Maryknoll, NY: Orbis, 1995), 177.

21. Rasmussen, *Earth Community, Earth Ethics*, 280.

An Expanded Vision: Holistic Relational Model

An earthbound theological anthropology must more critically explore the concept of connection rather than distinction, and consider what a relational understanding of *imago Dei* might look like not only for the God-human relationship, but also for the human-nature relationship. We must speak of our calling as humans in terms of our interconnectedness with God, other humans, and the fullness of the natural world. We propose a fourth perspective of theological anthropology building on the relational model: the *holistic relational* model.

Throughout Christian history, theology has been predisposed toward anthropocentrism, in which the Earth is created primarily for the benefit of humanity; but more and more theologians are questioning this assumption. David Fergusson suggests, "The life of the planet and its manifold species belong to God's good creation; these have a divinely appointed place not reducible to the service of human interests."[22] The divine image uniquely endows humans with responsibility rather than permission to dominate one another and Creation.[23] De-centering humanity from the apex and pinnacle of Creation reorients our single-minded focus from the human to all of the created order.

What might it look like to reinterpret theological anthropology as holistic relationality? To begin with, we must call attention to both the transcendence and the immanence of God. The Western church has consistently elevated transcendence over immanence. In doing so, God's transcendence has been transferred to humans—those "like-God"—making them transcendent to and essentially unlike everything else that is "not-God." It follows that in a theology focused on holistic relationality and the interconnectedness of all life with the Creator, God's transcendence must be counterbalanced by God's immanence. To hold transcendence and immanence alongside each other, in tension, enables us to see that what matters in the gospel is not that we are different from the Other, but that God is most closely encountered in the Other. In our current social and historical moment this would mean the marginalized person *and* the marginalized Earth. A radical conversion to the neglected and oppressed—both human and other-than-human—is necessary to rethink anthropology in a holistic and inclusive way.[24]

Moltmann stresses a broad construction of relationality and contends that the human person is "a being that can only exist in community with all other

22. David Fergusson, "Creation," in *The Oxford Handbook of Systematic Theology*, ed. John Webster, Kathryn Tanner, and Iain Torrance (Oxford: Oxford University Press, 2007), 73.
23. Kathryn Tanner, "The Difference Theological Anthropology Makes," *Theology Today* 50, no. 4 (January 1, 1994): 573.
24. Eleazar S. Fernandez, *Reimagining the Human* (St. Louis: Chalice, 2004), 31.

created beings and which can only understand itself in that community."[25] Humans are constituted by their relationships with the other-than-human world as much as by their relationships with other humans.[26] To define ourselves in relationship to others compels us to be responsible and accountable to the others with whom we are in relationship. Thinking about being human in a relational way provides a paradigm that focuses on persons in community, held responsible and accountable by other humans and by the Earth itself.

While it is unnecessary to avoid differentiating and categorizing entirely, this model of anthropology begins to deconstruct the dualism between humans and the Earth. A holistic relational theological anthropology rests on both the transcendence and immanence of God. Such a model provides a foundation for interrelated, communal relationships that affirm the solidarity of humans with God and all Creation. Theological anthropology must take a cue from God's own embodied solidarity in and through the life and teachings, death and resurrection of Jesus Christ.

Re-reading the Creation Narratives

It is possible to read the stories of Creation with new eyes and to find more hopeful and liberating strands that respond to our present time and place. It is imperative that we replace inadequate interpretations and implications of the Creation story with accounts that are life giving for all of Creation. We must do the very work commanded by God—"Choose life so that you and your descendants may live" (Deut. 30:19)—rather than choosing death for those whom the dominant interpretation has forgotten. Good theology, as discussed in chapter 2, is always resituating itself in response to the current situation of the planet and humanity.

The stories of our origins describe our condition and relationship with the Creator.[27] How we read the Creation accounts influences how we think about God. By removing the limited lens we have inherited, we uncover, recover, and discover elements in the text that reveal oft-hidden aspects of God, the human creature, and all Creation. Ellen Davis emphasizes, for example, that the poetry of the first Creation narrative is "confrontational"; it challenged the Canaanite fertility gods and defied the Mesopotamian ideology that humans were to supply food to the gods; instead, Genesis revealed a generous

---

25. Jürgen Moltmann, *God in Creation*, trans. Margaret Kohl (Minneapolis: Fortress, 1993), 186.
26. Bouma-Prediger, *Greening of Theology*, 270–71.
27. Michelle A. Gonzalez, *Created in God's Image* (Maryknoll, NY: Orbis, 2007), 13.

Creator "who provides food for every living creature."[28] Similarly, our orientation toward nature shifts if we remember that in Genesis 2 God sees neither humanity nor the garden in isolation but as created for one another—in a mutually dependent, symbiotic way: humankind needs the land, and the land needs humankind. Humanity tills and keeps the garden, in contrast to the idea that the Earth belongs *to* humanity. By re-reading the narrative in its social and historical context, we open up new insights into Creator and created.

We *can* interpret the Creation narratives in ways that transform a traditional paradigm that is no longer conversant with our social and historical context. An ecotheology that makes room for nature is nothing less than a return to our Hebrew and Christian roots.[29] These scriptural roots, notes Sallie McFague, "appear novel due to centuries of focus on human well-being alone."[30] When we speak of relationships characterized by mutuality and justice, we are rediscovering the roots of our own tradition and remembering the heritage of Emmanuel ("God with us"), the immanence of God in Creation, and the words spoken by God of the whole Creation: "it was very good" (Gen. 1:31). When we read our sacred Creation texts, we can discard harmful interpretations of domination with ones of mutuality and interdependence. This vision is realized by the image of God as gardener who sees all of Creation as worthy of care and benevolence, of Jesus the savior and liberator, and of the vivifying Spirit, who calls everyone and everything toward reconciliation and shalom.

Sin

> Under the present conditions of life, humanity and nature are caught in a web of mutual alienation and abuse. The separation of human beings from God insinuates itself into all other relationships, including that between humanity and nature.
>
> —Daniel Migliore[31]

Many years ago, the *London Times* asked a number of writers for essays on the topic: "What's wrong with the world?" G. K. Chesterton sent this reply:

---

28. Ellen F. Davis, *Scripture, Culture, and Agriculture* (Cambridge: Cambridge University Press, 2009), 51; see also Albert Baylis, *Creation to the Cross* (Grand Rapids: Zondervan, 1996).

29. Sallie McFague, *Life Abundant* (Minneapolis: Fortress, 2001), 34; see also Davis, *Scripture, Culture, and Agriculture*, "Reading the Bible through Agrarian Eyes," 21–41.

30. McFague, *Life Abundant*, 34.

31. Daniel L. Migliore, *Faith Seeking Understanding* (Grand Rapids: Eerdmans, 1991), 83.

Dear Sirs:
  I am.

             Sincerely yours,
             G.K. Chesterton

This much is clear: a comprehensive, biblical understanding of sin is essential for a healthy interpretation of salvation. Douglas John Hall notes, "Until the depths of the human predicament have been plumbed, in any age, there can be no response to that anxiety from the depths of the Christian gospel."[32]

Our theology of sin has much to do with how we understand our relationship to the Earth. In the Scriptures, for instance, the Earth suffers the reverberations of humanity's sin in the Creation story (Gen. 3:17–18). The prophet Hosea connects the sin of Israel with the degradation of Creation: because of Israel's sin "the land mourns, / and all who live in it languish; / together with the wild animals / and the birds of the air, / even the fish of the sea are perishing" (Hosea 4:3). The apostle Paul makes a similar correlation in his treatise to the Romans: "For the creation was subjected to futility, not of its own will but by the will of the one who subjected it, in hope that the creation itself will be set free from its bondage to decay and will obtain the freedom of the glory of the children of God" (Rom. 8:20–21). But where there is hope for the liberation of nature, there is also hope for humanity. Our purpose here is to examine why such hope is necessary, or in what ways human sin has contributed to Creation's "bondage to decay." Genesis 3 tells us that sin is rooted in the human desire to transcend our finiteness, to become like God.[33] Indeed Hall points out, "The desire *for* God is subtly interwoven with the desire to *be* God."[34] The root of sin is located in the craving to be what we are not, the results of which have profound ramifications for both humanity and ecosystems around the planet.

Personal Sin

In many churches Christians confess on a weekly basis that we have sinned against God "in thought, word, and deed, by what we have done, and by what we have left undone."[35] These sins are rooted in our individual actions, resulting

---

32. Douglas John Hall, *The Cross in Our Context* (Minneapolis: Fortress, 2003), 131.

33. Jeannine K. Brown, "Being and Becoming: The Scriptural Story of Formation," in *Becoming Whole and Holy*, by Jeannine Brown, Carla M. Dahl, and Wyndy Corbin Reuschling (Grand Rapids: Baker Academic, 2011), 67.

34. Hall, *Cross in Our Context*, 100.

35. For example, "A Penitential Order: Rite One," *The Book of Common Prayer*, http://www.bcponline.org/HE/penord1.html, accessed January 15, 2013.

in personal guilt. Consider David's anguished cry: "Against you, you alone, have I sinned, / and done what is evil in your sight, / so that you are justified in your sentence / and blameless when you pass judgment" (Ps. 51:4). Our culture experiences the enslaving power of sin through rampant addictions, dependencies, and attachments. This dominant Western view, in which "sin" is reduced to *personal moral sins*, is intertwined with the prevailing Western perspective of salvation as the forgiveness of the guilt of sin through the substitutionary death of Jesus.[36]

A second way to conceptualize personal sin is as *relational*. From this standpoint, sin is primarily understood as broken relationship, as estrangement or alienation. It is a view more attuned to Eastern Orthodoxy, in which salvation becomes the process of restoring broken relationships through the life, death, and resurrection of Jesus Christ. Bryant Myers delineates the extent of this relational estrangement, stating that people experience broken, unjust relationships "with ourselves, with our community, with those we call 'other,' with our environment, and with God."[37] Instead of a healthy sense of our self, our belovedness, and our vocation, our relationship with ourselves is marred by self-deprecation and a poverty of being. Instead of a reciprocated connectedness with our community, we exploit our neighbors and isolate ourselves. Instead of justice and shalom with "others," we dominate and oppress those not like us. Instead of being rooted in and caring for our created environment, we overuse the land and its resources. Instead of a dynamic spiritual relationship with God, we fall prey to the idolatry of consumerism and substitute gods.

To understand personal sin as relational is a critical enhancement to the prevailing Western view of sin as moral failure. Our hamartiology—our theology of sin—inescapably impacts our soteriology—our theology of salvation. The broader our understanding of sin, the more comprehensive will be our understanding of salvation.

Systemic Sin

Sin is not just personal. As creatures that exist in relationship with each other and the rest of the world, our individual broken relationships contribute to and are interwoven with a systemic brokenness. Wherever there is

---

36. The substitutionary theory of atonement was prominently purported by Anselm of Canterbury (1033–1109) and remains the most prevailing view of salvation in the Latin West. See Hall, *Cross in Our Context*, 129–30.

37. Bryant L. Myers, *Walking with the Poor*, rev. and expanded ed. (Maryknoll, NY: Orbis, 2011), 144. Myers builds on the works of Jayakumar Christian.

relationship—any relationship—we find both the invasiveness of sin and the possibility of restoration. Those distorted relationships are manifest among individuals, societies, and the natural world.

One way to see systemic sin is as the *disruption of shalom* in our world.[38] Walter Brueggemann describes shalom as a "central vision" in the Bible, whereby "all of creation is one, every creature in community with every other, living in harmony and security toward the joy and well-being of every other creature."[39] Similarly, Jim Wallis draws correlations between shalom, a relational worldview, justice, and Creation:

> The vision of shalom requires us to establish "right relationships." It is a call to justice in the whole community and for the entire habitat. Shalom is an inclusive notion of justice extending even to the rest of God's creatures and the whole of creation. . . . It pushes us to see ourselves as part of a community, even as members of an extended but deeply interconnected global family, and ultimately as strands in the web of life that we all share and depend upon.[40]

Sin is anything that disrupts the harmony of God's Creation. The classic pillars of oppression—classism, sexism, racism—are representative of the systemic disruption of shalom. In each of these interconnected systems, those "on top" maintain power and privilege—marginalizing and silencing those who are unlike them. Most importantly in terms of our discussion of sin, oppression becomes integrated *systemically* in society.

The inescapable reality is that those in positions of power have the freedom to ignore the connection between their choices and the welfare of others and of the planet. Ignorance and indifference (intentional or not) perpetuate systems of injustice and oppression that must be named for what they are—broken relationships and disruption of shalom. These sins are the kind of actions the apostle Paul spoke of in Romans 8 when he addressed the groaning of Creation under the exploits of humanity. Daniel Migliore writes,

> Under the present conditions of life, humanity and nature are caught in a web of mutual alienation and abuse. The separation of human beings from God insinuates itself into all other relationships, including that between humanity and nature. . . . According to the biblical witness, we human beings exist in a solidarity of life and death with the whole groaning and expectant creation.[41]

38. Ibid., 143.
39. Walter Brueggemann, *Peace* (St. Louis: Chalice, 2001), 13–14.
40. Jim Wallis, *The Soul of Politics* (Maryknoll, NY: Orbis, 1994), 73.
41. Migliore, *Faith Seeking Understanding*, 83.

If we insist on ignoring the reality of systemic sin, we have failed to un-derstand the ramifications of broken relationships. Similarly, if we ignore the interconnectedness of our relationships with one another we will miss the point that personal action and inaction contribute to the disruption of shalom and result in something more egregious than individual guilt.

Redemption and Salvation

> We know that Christ is raised and dies no more.
> Embraced by death he broke its fearful hold;
>   and our despair he turned to blazing joy. Alleluia!
> A new creation comes to life and grows
>   as Christ's new body takes on flesh and blood.
> The universe restored and whole will sing: Alleluia!
> —John Brownlow Geyer[42]

It is an 80-degree November day in Manalapan, Florida. I (Jen) woke up to the sound of the Atlantic and a gentle wind rustling through the palm trees. Today is my seventh wedding anniversary. It is also the day my grandfather will die.

My mother called me yesterday. "Sissy," she said, "I hate to give you bad news on your vacation, but Po is in the ER. We don't think he'll come home." I had received a similar phone call six months earlier. On that day, I packed a bag and drove the five hours across the Blue Mountains to Eastern Oregon, where my parents and grandparents live. When I walked through the front door of my parents' home, my dad (the original cowboy) felt fragile and shaky as he wrapped his arms around me. His eyes were glistening, and his voice faltered. That night, the whole family, including relatives from Arkansas and Kansas, gathered at my grandparents' home to do what families do when they are losing someone they love—we told stories and shared a meal. Uncle Ben, tall and lanky with a Virginia Slim hanging from the side of his mouth, told stories about when my grandpar-ents first moved West. In between the stories were long periods of silence, as we all stared into the rugged outline where the mountains that frame that part of the valley collide with the sky. Every so often someone would comment that Po was headed to a better place. To be honest, I have no idea what that means. As an ecotheologian, I am drawn to N. T. Wright's analysis of those Old and New Testament passages that undergird a theology of an integrated new heaven and new earth, the concept of heaven as the *present* reality of God's reign.[43]

---

42. John Brownlow Geyer, hymn 296, in *The Hymnal 1982: According to the Use of the Episcopal Church* (New York: The Church Pension Fund, 1985).
43. N. T. Wright, *New Heavens, New Earth* (Cambridge, UK: Grove Books, 1999).

That week in May was the last time I saw my grandfather. As I sat next to his bed, he slipped in and out of lucidity, in and out of being the grandfather I remembered. Sometimes he sang old gospel music. He recognized me only occasionally. "Is that Jenny?" he would ask with the sweet voice I remembered from my childhood, an occasional hint of a whistle in his words, an endearing sort of speech impediment. My niece was born that week. My younger sister and her family live in the same town as my parents and grandparents, and so my trip to say good-bye to him allowed me to welcome Aubrianna into the world.

On this day in Manalapan, I am celebrating the aliveness of my partnership as I sit on the very water my grandfather spent so much of his life as an officer in the Navy. Thousands of miles away, my father and grandmother are sitting by his bedside . . . holding a hand no longer alive, weeping over a body. Where is his spirit? Hovering over the Atlantic? Wrapped around my grandmother? What, exactly, is immortality?

Much of the language we use surrounding death approaches gnosticism. The truth of a Christian theology of eternity is broader than the story we tell about going to heaven when we die. As ecotheologians, we need a more holistic soteriology, a foundation that provides answers both for personal salvation—where do we go when we die?—and corporate salvation—what is our responsibility toward making the kingdom of heaven a present reality?

Soteriology

Soteriology—the study of salvation—has dominated Christian theology from the earliest centuries; Christ became incarnate, in the words of the Nicene Creed, "for us and for our salvation." Christ's salvific work on the cross and his resurrection from the grave have made a way for all of humanity, through faith in the power of the gospel, "to become children of God" (John 1:12). Thus God's grace is made available to the world through the loving incarnation of Jesus Christ who died for the sins of the whole world (1 John 2:2).

Yet never has it been more important to revisit this central doctrine and re-conceptualize it through an ecotheological lens. Biblically the doctrine of salvation is much broader than an explanation of life after death. Historically the prevailing focus of soteriology, especially in the American evangelical tradition, has been how individual sinners are redeemed spiritually for heaven. However to limit salvation to humans alone is to shortchange both Scripture and our theological traditions.

"Salvation" comes from the Latin word *salvare*, meaning to salve or heal. The New Testament uses the word "salvation" (Gr. *sōtēria*) in a variety of ways. *Sōtēria* can mean healing, rescue, peace, or, indeed, salvation. Furthermore, *sōzein*—the New Testament verb for "saving"—might mean to save, to keep safe, to rescue from danger, or to heal spiritual, emotional, or physical suffering. Paul often employs *sōzein* in a way more closely aligned with the traditional understanding with which many of us are most familiar, as a parallel term to being justified by Christ's blood (Rom. 5:9–10). However, *sōzein* is also used eighteen times to refer to physical or material healing, as it does in many of Jesus's miracles. The New Testament offers a comprehensive view of "salvation" that includes both the spiritual and the material as realms of God's salvific power. Given the present-day suffering of Creation, our theological imagination must grasp a more comprehensive soteriology, one that includes the "healing" of God's created order.[44]

Biblical evidence for this kind of sweeping view of salvation is ample; the visions of redemption within Scripture are, according to Migliore, "staggeringly inclusive."[45] Even as both humanity and other creatures are recipients of divine judgment in Genesis 3, so both are recipients of a divine covenantal promise in Genesis 9. The first story of Creation culminates with Sabbath rest for God, humans, *and* the created world.[46] In terms of *Heilsgeschichte*, or salvation history, Leonardo Boff suggests that we see the doctrine of salvation with "two eyes . . . one looks back toward the past, where salvation broke in; the other looks toward the present where salvation becomes reality here and now."[47] The biblical drama of redemption encompasses humans *and* other-than-humans, the spiritual *and* the material, space *and* time.

Salvation, Shalom, and Healing

A vital, comprehensive meaning of salvation, especially regarding ecotheology, is as reconciliation, the restoration of relationship, the healing of a broken people and a broken Creation with a holy God. The "central vision" of shalom described by Brueggemann connects the reconciliatory work of Christ to the five areas of unjust broken relationships: with ourselves, our community, those we call "other," our environment, and God. A holistic soteriology takes into account the healing of fragmented relationships between not only humans and God but also with the created order. We cannot remove any part of Creation from the realm of God's salvation. In one breath, we can speak

---

44. J. Schneider and C. Brown, "Soter," in *The New International Dictionary of New Testament Theology*, ed. Colin Brown (Grand Rapids: Zondervan, 1986), 219.

45. Migliore, *Faith Seeking Understanding*, 84, observes that Gen. 9; 1 Cor. 15; Rev. 21; and Isa. 11 all speak "of a time of universal shalom when all creatures will live together in harmonious and joyful community."

46. Moltmann, *God in Creation*, 287.

47. Leonardo Boff, *Way of the Cross—Way of Justice* (Maryknoll, NY: Orbis, 1980), viii.

of the salvation of souls and the salvation of soils. If sin is the distortion of right relationships manifesting in injustice, greed, selfishness, and alienation from God, among individuals, societies, and the natural world, then healing for humanity will likewise mean healing for all Creation. We cannot speak of hope for redeemed humanity without the hope of liberation for the cosmos. This holistic shalom will involve personal as well as corporate redemption.

For those steeped in the Western Protestant tradition of an otherworldly, individualistic salvation *from* this world of pain, an inclusive understanding of redemption may feel disconcerting. Again it is worth emphasizing that the biblical understanding of salvation is a comprehensive one. The Reformation narrowed its meaning predominately to the individual; the American evangelical and revivalist tradition continued in that paradigm. The history of Western Protestant salvation theology often falls short of communicating the breadth of Christian soteriology. Elizabeth Theokritoff writes:

> Salvation for [Eastern] Orthodoxy is not a discrete theme or sub-section of theology. It is very hard to find Orthodox writings focused specifically on salvation; rather, the saving work of Christ is the matrix within which we understand the meaning and purpose of all creation. . . . We are thus looking for a concept of salvation that connects us with the rest of creation. Such a concept sees salvation as involving the whole created world and our relationship with it, which in turn entails an eschatological vision of salvation with the world, not from it. Any narrowing of the idea of salvation to focus primarily on the redemption of humans from sin would seem profoundly unhelpful.[48]

Our time and our context require us to recover and restore the breadth of the fullness of the Christian tradition and the earliest biblical understanding.

The key to curtailing the Protestant predilection for an individualistic, otherworldly salvation is in reconceptualizing Creation *within* the realm of salvation. Creation history and salvation history are linked through the very nature of a loving Creator who is continuously seeking the healing and restoration of the whole Creation. Catherine LaCugna refers to God's resolute movement, through Jesus Christ and the Holy Spirit, toward shalom and salvation, "so that we may come into communion with God and with one another. . . . God and all of God's creatures dwell together in a common household."[49] Ultimately, this movement is consummated in the "eschatological . . . fulfillment of all in God."[50]

48. Elizabeth Theokritoff, "The Salvation of the World and Saving the Earth: An Orthodox Christian Approach," *Worldviews: Environment Culture Religion* 14, no. 2/3 (2010): 142.
49. Catherine Mowry LaCugna, "The Practical Trinity," in *Exploring Christian Spirituality*, ed. Kenneth J. Collins (Grand Rapids: Baker, 2000), 281.
50. Ibid., 275.

Ecological healing, the Christian notion of salvation, and the eschatological future should rightly be interconnected. We can combat the lingering effects of the compartmentalization within Christian theology by an approach that envisions Spirit and matter as intertwined entities.[51] Salvation as healing is a fundamental aspect of God's mission. Ecological degradation is a symptom of human sin in the same way as unjust patterns of broken human relationships. Redemption in all of these areas relies on liberation for all, a holistic view of God's salvation, and a healed humanity. Essential to this vision of redemption and liberation is human responsibility and accountability in transforming relationships of brokenness. As co-creators, humanity must work in partnership with God as we address both the consequences of sin and the roots of evil while working toward ultimate reconciliation.[52] Forgiveness of personal guilt through Christ has not yet been enough to make shalom a reality. John Wesley wrote, "By salvation I mean, not barely, according to the vulgar notion, deliverance from hell or going to heaven, but a present deliverance from sin; a restoration of the soul to its primitive health, its original purity; a recovery of the divine nature; the renewal of souls after the image of God."[53]

Eschatology

The reason that eschatology is such an indispensable element in theological thinking is that it responds to the question of the total meaningfulness of the present creation, a meaning that can only finally be found beyond science's extrapolation of contemporary history.

—John Polkinghorne[54]

A year into my (A. J.'s) first pastorate, the church where I served discovered major environmental dangers in its children's building. Erected in the 1970s, toxins from the building were leaking into the groundwater, air quality was unhealthy, and it was constantly at risk of being flooded in our rainy Oregon climate. The church rightfully decided to have it destroyed and rebuilt. The spring morning they tore it down was clear and warm. Standing with my pastor, we watched as they demolished the building. The material of the building was of such low quality that it stripped away like papier-mâché. Surprised, I

---

51. Snyder, *Salvation Means Creation Healed*, 3–27.
52. Ernst M. Conradie, "The Salvation of the Earth from Anthropogenic Destruction," *Worldviews: Global Religions, Culture & Ecology* 14, no. 2/3 (2010): 125.
53. John Wesley, *The Works of John Wesley*, ed. Frank Baker (Oxford: Clarendon, 1983), viii.47.
54. John Polkinghorne, *The God of Hope and the End of the World* (New Haven: Yale University Press, 2002), 140.

wondered out loud why it had been built so poorly; thirty-five years seemed, to me, a short time for a building's lifespan. The senior pastor looked at the building and pondered my question, "Well, they needed more space and didn't have much money." Then, over the sound of the bulldozer and only half-joking, he shouted, "And they thought Jesus would return in the next ten years." That day I learned a powerful lesson: our theological convictions—for better or worse—*will inevitably shape our ecological landscape*. Little did I recognize at the time, watching that building fall in one fell swoop, that I had gained a valuable lesson in Christian eschatology.

Eschatology and Millennialism

Eschatology is the theological discipline that has to do with last things, or end times, and specifically with death, judgment, heaven, and hell.[55] A vision of apocalypticism surrounding the abrupt end of history, the judgment of God, and the return of Christ has been found within Christianity from the beginning. The New Testament presents a community of faith hoping and waiting for the near return of Jesus in the midst of painful persecution. However certain apocalyptic beliefs, particularly dispensational millennialism ("dispensational" referring to different dispensations or periods in history; "millennialism" referring to the thousand-year reign of Christ on earth), have played a uniquely prevalent role in American evangelicalism. Millennialism broadly speaks to the vision set forth by John in Revelation 20:1–10 that has captured the thinking of generations of Christians. In many interpretations, this vision predicts a time in history during which unmatched *shalom*, peace, will reign. In sweeping terms, three dominant millennial views prevail: amillennialism, that the thousand-year reign of Christ is to be understood symbolically within present reality and the hearts of believers; premillennialism, that the second coming of Christ occurs at the end of the present age and *before* the thousand-year reign; postmillennialism, that Christ's return will occur *after* the millennium and that the church in the present age expands Christ's kingdom through the Spirit until then.[56] Stanley Grenz associates each position with a theological mood: amillennialism is realistic, premillennialism pessimistic, and postmillennialism optimistic. Most importantly, each eschatological attitude brings with it a particular set of assumptions regarding human responsibility and action.[57]

---

55. *OED*, s.v. "eschatology."

56. Premillennialism is further divided into historicist and futurist; futurist premillennialists are either pretribulationist, midtribulationist, or posttribulationist. Likewise, pretribulationism, midtribulationism, and posttribulationism are terms referring to *when* the rapture of the church will take place, whether it be before, during, or after the period of tribulation.

57. Stanley J. Grenz, *The Millennial Maze* (Downers Grove, IL: InterVarsity, 1992), 213–14.

Of particular interest for constructing an ecotheology is how evangelicalism throughout its history has fluctuated between pre- and postmillennialism.[58] The early Puritans were unquestionably premillennial, but during the time of Jonathan Edwards (1703–1758) and the first Great Awakening, the conviction arose that through the proclamation of the gospel God was establishing the millennial reign in America.[59] The second Great Awakening saw a further outpouring of postmillennial optimism that led to an emphasis on revival and social reform; evangelicals formed voluntary societies that advocated the abolition of slavery, worked with the poor, and promoted temperance, education, and world missions. During this time revivalists, such as Charles Finney, connected conversion to Christ with social duties, such as abolition. In fact, they believed that the purification of society from social sins actually *prepared* the way for Jesus's coming reign. Evangelicals in that historical moment believed they could actively participate with Christ in establishing God's kingdom on Earth. But, as the nineteenth century drew to a close, so did its optimism. Christians (and society in general) began to lose hope in societal transformation. Dispensational premillennialism came to the fore; instead of a culture constantly advancing, the world was hurtling toward God's judgment and the imminent return of Christ. Two world wars drove the final nail in the postmillennial coffin, while premillennialism flourished.

As a result of the shift from post- to premillennialism, the evangelical community on the whole withdrew from being active partners in ushering in God's reign and focused even more on the salvation of souls. Evangelical historian Timothy Weber writes:

> One must finally conclude that premillennialism generally broke the spirit of social concern which had played such a prominent role in earlier evangelicalism. Its hopeless view of the present order left little room for God or themselves to work in it. . . . Consequently, though there were significant exceptions, premillennialists turned their backs on the movements to change social institutions. In time, the social conscience of an important part of American evangelicalism atrophied and ceased to function. In that regard, at least, premillennialism broke faith with the evangelical spirit which it had fought so hard to preserve.[60]

This shift also led to a more pessimistic view of the Earth. Now hope was centered not on societal renewal as a preparation for Christ's return but on a

58. Randall Balmer, "Apocalypticism in American Culture," Divining America, Teacher Serve©, National Humanities Center, http://nationalhumanitiescenter.org/tserve/twenty/tkeyinfo/apocal.htm, accessed April 13, 2013.
59. Timothy P. Weber, *Living in the Shadow of the Second Coming* (Oxford: Oxford University Press, 1979), 13–14.
60. Ibid., 183.

Tension Point: Eschatology

Eschatology has received a great deal of attention in evangelical theology. Premil lennialism, especially the dispensational premillennialism found in popular evangelical end-time fiction, seems to *require* the destruction of the Earth for the salvation of the world. Thus the question was raised: can a premillennialist care for the Earth while remaining faithful to his or her eschatology?

We were divided over the issue, largely because we did not come to a united position on millennialism. We wondered whether premillennialism was actually a detriment to Creation care. Or does postmillennialism offer a more hopeful approach to earthkeeping?

We agreed that "blueprint" interpretations of the book of Revelation—that there exists a prescriptive divine timetable for the future—are not the only way to understand eschatology. Most importantly, we believe that hospitality is essential for engaging these complex and challenging conversations.

- Can a premillennialist care for the Earth while remaining faithful to his or her eschatology? If so, in what ways?
- Why do you think "blueprint" interpretations of Revelation have proven so popular in American evangelicalism?
- What do you believe has been the long-term impact of popular end-time fiction on the attitudes of Christians toward Creation?

hope in Christ's return that would usher in a new Earth. It is worth re-engaging Scripture in its historical context in order to discover an eschatological perspective that offers a transformative hope for humanity *and* the rest of Creation.

Reimagining the Apocalypse

It is difficult to deny that at least part of Christianity's ambiguous history with Creation lies in a traditional eschatological perspective in which the Earth is ultimately destroyed by fire and Jesus returns to create anew. Catherine Keller calls this perspective "unearthly," in that "the indifference toward nature implied in traditional eschatology becomes lethal. That is, its distraction from the earth complies with the destruction of the earth."[61] Because a theology of Creation is essential to our vision of redemption, our conviction is that a belief in the physical afterlife does not have to result in disregard and disdain for the present life.

61. Catherine Keller, "Eschatology, Ecology, and a Green Ecumenacy," *Ecotheology: Journal of Religion, Nature, and the Environment* 5, no. 2 (January 1997): 87.

Yet we acknowledge that there are a collection of ostensibly "destructive" texts in the New Testament. For instance, as the author of 2 Peter reflects on the coming eschaton, he appears to imagine a future destruction of the Earth:

> By the word of God heavens existed long ago and an earth was formed out of water and by means of water, through which the world of that time was deluged with water and perished. But by the same word the present heavens and earth have been reserved for fire, being kept until the day of judgment and destruction of the godless. . . . But the day of the Lord will come like a thief, and then the heavens will pass away with a loud noise, and the elements will be dissolved with fire, and the earth and everything that is done on it will be disclosed. (2 Pet. 3:5b–7, 10)

What do we do with texts like this? What does the transformation of the world (*transformatio mundi*) and "a new heaven and a new earth" (Rev. 21:1) look like? Or, to put it another way, will the Earth be *renovated* or *replaced*?

Evangelical biblical scholar Douglas Moo offers three rationales for why he surmises 2 Peter 3 should not be read apocalyptically, signaling the physical end of the planet. First, the text is problematic for translators—he points out that few agree on an acceptable rendering. Second, the Old Testament image of "fire" commonly refers to God's purifying judgment and not a literal destruction, even as Noah's flood was the judgment of God against humanity, but did not destroy the entire planet. The final judgment does not have to be different. Fire, writes Moo, "need not bring total destruction."[62] And third, Moo points out that the Greek word for "dissolve" (*lyō*, in vv. 10, 11, and 12) does not, in other biblical texts, convey entire destruction or annihilation, but rather "a dissolution or radical change in nature."[63] When *luō* is used elsewhere, it denotes a loss of fruitfulness, the wasteful use of ointment, the uselessness of wineskins when they have holes in them, or the loss of a coin. In not one of these cases does the object being referred to *cease to exist*. Nor should we expect it with Creation. While it is essential we do not undermine the pointedness and abruptness of texts such as 2 Peter 3, we also must not overemphasize them, building theologies of destruction on uncertain readings or difficult translations.

In our attempt to deal responsibly with the biblical texts, one approach to bringing heaven to Earth might begin with re-examining John's Apocalypse— the book of Revelation—and with releasing much of the baggage surrounding

---

62. Douglas Moo, "Nature in the New Creation: New Testament Eschatology and the Environment," *Journal of the Evangelical Theological Society* 49, no. 3 (September 2006): 468.
   63. Ibid.

Armageddon, the lake of fire, and a burning Earth. In many premillennial eschatologies, Revelation has become a kind of road map for the end of time with current events serving as signposts both to Christ's soon return and proof of the Bible's prophetic accuracy. However Eleazar Fernandez points out that an increasing number of scholars attest that Revelation "emerged out of the experience of the persecuted, the outcasts, and the powerless, . . . people who were living on the brink of despair; people who believed in the ultimate and sovereign power of an ultimately good God, but experienced in their daily lives the oppression of idolatrous power."[64] Barbara Rossing juxtaposes the New Jerusalem in Revelation 21 with the "ecological imperialism, violence, unfettered commerce, idolatry and injustice" of the Roman Empire.[65] Such (political) interpretations of the new heaven and the new Earth, claims Keller, argue that, "properly understood, the biblical apocalypse, whatever else it may be, is one long act of protest against the power of the state."[66]

The vision of heaven descending to Earth—of the experience of the presence and kingdom of God in our current home, of relationships transformed from suffering and estrangement into something new—spoke to the needs of a beleaguered community striving to find meaning in the midst of crisis and looking toward a future hope. John's vision keeps company with the prophet Isaiah—another promise of heaven descending to Earth—"I am about to do a new thing; / now it springs forth, do you not perceive it? / I will make a way in the wilderness / and rivers in the desert" (Isa. 43:19). The hope of heaven on Earth is not a hope of escape from our home planet. Read in its historical context, John's Apocalypse can best be understood as a text of hope *for* the marginalized and as a sign *against* the prevailing attitudes of the Roman powers. Woefully, what began as resistance literature symbolizing hope for an oppressed people was all too quickly diverted into a blueprint of the future more appealing to a powerful majority.

An Active Eschatological Hope

It is often said: Christians are so heavenly minded that they are no earthly good. Does our hope in the coming of Christ permit us to ignore the great global challenges of our time? Not in the mind of Moltmann: "Christian

64. Fernandez, *Reimagining the Human*, 213.
65. Barbara Rossing, "River of Life in God's New Jerusalem: An Eschatological Vision for Earth's Future," in *Christianity and Ecology*, ed. Dieter T. Hessel and Rosemary Radford Ruether (Cambridge, MA: Harvard University Press, 2000), 212; see also John E. Stanley, "The New Creation as a People and City in Revelation 21:1–22:5: An Alternative to Despair," *Asbury Theological Journal* 60, no. 2 (2005): 27.
66. Catherine Keller, "Why Apocalypse, Now," *Theology Today* 49, no. 2 (July 1, 1992): 187.

expectation of the future has nothing whatsoever to do with the end, whether it be the end of this life, the end of history, or the end of the world. Christian expectation is about the beginning: the beginning of true life, the beginning of God's kingdom, and the beginning of the new creation of all things into their enduring form."[67] Eschatology must be rooted not just in the future but also in the present, in the "not yet" and the "already." Its goal is the transformation of the present into a more hope-filled, liberating future. According to Gregory Brett, "Eschatology does not dissolve human responsibility but rather radicalizes it. Human beings have the capacity and the responsibility of enabling the world to be more open to its absolute future."[68]

In *Surprised by Hope*, N. T. Wright explores a new way of imagining what he calls "life *after* 'life after death.'" Wright argues that heaven and Earth are "two different dimensions of God's good creation."[69] However we should not envisage salvation as a skyrocket escape *from* this Creation but as resurrected bodies *within* this Creation. By examining key eschatological texts in the Old and New Testaments, as well as an extensive reading of early church doctrines, Wright argues that any Christian theology of the end must incorporate all of Earth in the new Creation. The physical universe becomes the cradle within which heaven comes to rest. Our Christian goal becomes not to escape into some postmortem destiny but to embrace God's kingdom in the present. This calls for a rekindling of belief in a physical resurrection that will restore the Earth to its garden shalom. Wright says, "Heaven, in the Bible, is not a future destiny but the other, hidden, dimension of our ordinary life—God's dimension, if you like. God made heaven and earth; at the last he will remake both and join them together."[70] Apocalypse, therefore, is not a future destructive judgment but a future creative judgment; God resurrects the world within which a new humanity will live.

In *our* historical moment, apocalyptic texts are best understood as a description of the work at hand for the people of God—the movement toward God's vision of shalom. Being attentive to our contemporary experience helps us place emphasis on how eschatology can provoke transformative hope. We *can* read the Apocalypse in a way that resists escapism, focusing instead on what it means to be earthbound, good-news-bearing Christians. It is a non-escapist

67. Jürgen Moltmann, *In the End—The Beginning*, trans. Margaret Kohl (London: SCM, 2004), ix–x.

68. Gregory Brett, CM, "A Timely Reminder: Humanity and Ecology in the Light of Christian Hope," in *Earth Revealing—Earth Healing*, ed. Denis Edwards (Collegeville, MN: Liturgical Press, 2001), 167.

69. N. T. Wright, *Surprised by Hope* (London: SPCK, 2007), 122.

70. Ibid., 26.

theology that "bases its post mortem hope on a reality inaccessible to scientific investigation, the faithfulness of a living God."[71] Reading Revelation as a promise of supernatural rescue from our own recklessness allows us to divorce humanity from the natural world and removes any responsibility we have toward the rest of Creation. Living on the edge of the chaos with faith in a different future anchors us, writes Keller, in "an ecosystemic rather than a merely systemic theology [which] neither repeats nor shuns but rather recycles, grounds, and deepens eschatology."[72] When our ecotheology deepens eschatology, it does so in order to create hope for a transformed present rooted in a new future. Eschatology means learning to live on Earth as it is in heaven. It does not promise that we will live to see this new future fulfilled, but it demands we participate in the work of creating that future in *this* moment.

■ ▓ ▪

This chapter has re-examined the broad theological categories of Creation, sin, redemption and salvation, and eschatology. In it we set forth an ecotheological perspective that is grounded in relationship and in the theological interconnection between the goodness of God's created world, *imago Dei*, personal and corporate sin, salvation and healing in this world, and an eschatological reconciliation in the world to come. Moving past broken relationships, through Jesus Christ, toward the experience of shalom in the commonwealth of God must begin with and will demand nothing less than repentance and conversion. Pietist and social activist Christoph Blumhardt spoke of two conversions—first from the world to God and then from God back to the world.[73] As converted humanity, we must become keenly aware that *our* experience of shalom is dependent on the possibility of shalom for all Creation. Until the time that humanity is moved toward justice for the entire Earth community, this planet will groan.

---

71. Polkinghorne, *God of Hope and the End of the World*, 10.

72. Catherine Keller, "No More Sea: The Lost Chaos of the Eschaton," in *Christianity and Ecology*, 192.

73. Quoted by Johannes Harder, introduction to Christoph Blumhardt, *Ansprachen, Predigten, Andachten, und Schriften*, vol. 1, ed. Johannes Harder (Neukirchen-Vluyn: Neukirchener, 1978), 12.

Part III

Doing Ecotheology

7

Breaking the Bonds

Do Justice, Love Mercy, Walk Lightly

Nathan, a former student at our seminary, was an essential collaborator in the creation of the Christian Earthkeeping concentration. He gave himself to a small group of people who spent hours together—reading, writing, dialoguing, arguing—compelled by a call to the Earth and to action. For two years he dedicated a significant part of his life to this project. His relationships bore the burden of his devotion. After graduation, instead of pursuing further academic studies, Nathan went to Mozambique with his wife and their youngest daughter. Maybe it was a strategy to rebuild the relationships that had suffered because of his steadfast devotion to our work. Or maybe he was consumed by a passion to transform what he had discovered in the classroom—a blueprint for living earthbound lives in relationships of shalom—into the real world.

Nathan works for a Christian NGO (non-governmental organization) in Mozambique. Every day Mozambicans die of starvation from ecologically related disasters, their deaths forgotten in reports of environmental degradation. Nathan drives through rural countrysides, doing his best to provide the suffering with basic necessities: food, water, medicine. Sometimes Nathan sends us messages that end with a tone of desperation: "I struggle for the poor and forgotten here in Mozambique. I have spent the last days with people dying from famine due to climate change. Some days I feel that I have chosen wrongly [by not going into academics]. I stand with the poor, but the world could care less. . . . We have no voice."[1] Life is hard; his heart is breaking. Theology has driven him to praxis, to bearing witness by opposing inaction and injustice toward the invisible.

We three authors teach in the Christian earthkeeping program that Nathan helped design. Each of us has witnessed—and participated in—many ecotheological conversations that revolve around ideology, ethics, and scriptural authority. Too few of those dialogues have converted into praxis. This pattern disturbs us as we seek to improve our pedagogy. It would be impossible to justify our theological wrangling to the suffering in Mozambique. A thoughtfully constructed Christian ecotheology *must* lead to a renovated spirituality and praxis. Our primary concern in these next chapters is to re-engage the Bible, theology, and history, seeking concepts most likely to inspire a shift in practice. By focusing on an engaged and praxis-oriented theology, we hope to move into a holistic transformation of both mind and lifestyle.

In many ways, we write these chapters as a confession, an effort to honor Nathan's story and an acknowledgment that too often we have failed to take action. Ours are sins of omission. We write aware of our own tendency toward complacency and of our comfortable, North American social location; yet we also write out of a sense of conviction and hope that it is possible (and necessary) for Christians to live an ecotheological ethic personally, communally, and globally. The previous chapters of this book have been guided by an ethos of truth telling—the truth of a planet in crisis, of a people who have too often rejected their vocation as caretakers, of the ambiguous relationship of Christianity with the Earth, and of a system diseased by its entrapment to commodification. In our journey toward truth and the wellness of Creation, we seek a holistic discipleship, rooted in concrete action and a vision for creating real change.

Developing an Ecotheological Mind-Set

> I would define asceticism as: traveling light . . . letting go . . . opening up . . . softening up . . . treading light . . . living simply . . . simply living.
>
> —John Chryssavigis[2]

Most people in congregational leadership are continuously dealing with change. In a shifting world, we suspect our old way of "being" the church no longer works as it once did—we need to move into a new paradigm, worldview,

1. Personal electronic communication, November 15, 2012. Used by permission.
2. John Chryssavigis, introduction to *Cosmic Grace, Humble Prayer*, by Patriarch Bartholomew I, ed. John Chryssavigis (Grand Rapids: Eerdmans, 2003), 31.

system. The problem is that shifting a system is disruptive—even when we know the old way of being can no longer support us. The ecocrisis is not dissimilar from the church's dilemma. We know that our current way of life no longer works, that the system is not sustainable. Yet it produces intense stress and anxiety to imagine how we might succeed in "being" any other way. Environmental systems analysts suggest that thinking about systems "can lead us to the edge of what analysis can do and then point beyond—to what can and must be done by the human spirit."[3] We might say something similar about ecotheology. It can take us to the edge of what human thinking can do, and point us beyond—to what can and must be done by the Spirit of God moving among the faithful.

This chapter suggests that a critical component of developing a new paradigm for the church in an age of ecological crisis is acquiring an ecotheological mind-set.

Defying "Spirit-Body" Dualism

One of the more fascinating (albeit unsettling) characters in Christian monastic history is Simeon Stylites (c. 390–459).[4] In his longing to live as a recluse, Simeon was drawn to extreme forms of monasticism, eventually retreating into the sky, onto the tops of pillars that became successively higher. Ultimately his "spirituality" led him to spend the last forty years of his life perched on a pillar about sixty feet in the air. His career as a holy man and pillar ascetic balanced on his small parcel of space between earth and heaven was spectacular. Emperors and peasants sought his counsel on everything from foreign policy to cucumber crops.

Simeon's extreme and radical lifestyle serves as a metaphor for the perception within the Western tradition that Christian spirituality is primarily about climbing toward perfect union with God, who is Spirit. Ascending spiritually has inevitably also meant rising above and escaping nature and the body. Even today Western Christianity struggles with ambiguity between spirituality and the body. The church has undeniably played a major part in perpetrating this dualism by prioritizing a spirituality of ascent and denigrating nature. Wendell Berry piercingly addresses this unbiblical dichotomy:

> For many of the churchly, the life of the spirit is reduced to a dull preoccupation with getting to Heaven. At best, the world is no more than an embarrassment

3. Donella Meadows, The Donella Meadows Institute (website), http://www.donellameadows.org/about-dmi/, accessed August 17, 2013.
4. S. Ashbrook Harvey, "The Sense of a Stylite: Perspectives on Simeon the Elder," *Vigiliae Christianae* 42 (1988): 376–94; David Frankfurter, "Stylites and Phallobates: Pillar Religions in Late Antique Syria," *Vigiliae Christianae* 44 (1990): 168–98.

and a trial to the spirit, which is otherwise radically separated from it. The true lover of God must not be burdened with any care or respect for His works. While the body goes about its business of destroying the earth, the soul is supposed to lie back and wait for Sunday, keeping itself free of earthly contaminants. . . . As far as this sort of "religion" is concerned, the body is no more than the lusterless container of the soul, a mere "package," that will nevertheless light up in eternity, forever cool and shiny as a neon cross. This separation of the soul from the body and from the world is no disease of the fringe, no aberration, but a fracture that runs through the mentality of institutional religion like a geologic fault.[5]

Berry's voice, though sharp, hardly seems overstated when one considers the ways in which much of Christianity is observed today and the ramifications of those practices for Creation. An embodied approach to discipleship must engage both the mystical and the earthly.

To counterbalance Western Christendom's overemphasis on a spirituality of ascent, we can draw attention to a God who is as present on Earth as in heaven. At the dedication of the first temple, Solomon prayed, "Can it be that God will actually move into our neighborhood? Why, the cosmos itself isn't large enough to give you breathing room, let alone this Temple I've built" (1 Kings 8:27, Message). The mystery of the incarnation is not simply that the Second Person of the Trinity came to *redeem* Creation through the cross but that God also came to *reveal* humanity. In Jesus we witness the original "goodness" of the human creature and come face-to-face with how God intended humanity to live from the genesis of the world.[6] In Christ "there is a new creation" (2 Cor. 5:17). "Spiritual" formation, then, involves discovering in Christ what it means to be human and who we were originally created to be.

Practically, this incarnational spirituality opens the door for a greater sense of "earthiness" and the "natural" in the Christian life. It is time to speak less often of denying our bodies and more often of embracing the body as a vehicle of wisdom and divine grace.[7] It is time to end the dichotomy between exercises that are "spiritual"—prayer, meditation, Scripture

5. Wendell Berry, "The Body and the Earth," in *The Art of the Commonplace*, ed. Norman Wirzba (Washington, DC: Shoemaker & Hoard, 2002), 103–4.

6. Douglas John Hall, *The Cross in Our Context* (Minneapolis: Fortress, 2003), 93; N. T. Wright, *Matthew for Everyone*, 2 vols., 2nd ed. (Louisville: Westminster John Knox, 2004), i.49.

7. Henri Nouwen, *The Inner Voice of Love* (New York: Doubleday, 1996), 32–33, talked about a "new spirituality" that is not "body denying or body indulging but truly incarnational"—a way to "bring your body home."

reading—and those that are "embodied"—taking walks, practicing Pilates, eating well. It is time to cease speaking of God's immanence in the created order as nature worship.

Stewardship

The English word "steward" was used as far back as the eleventh century.[8] Originally the word was *stigweard*; *stig* probably referred to house or dwelling—think pig*sty*—while *weard* meant "warden" or "keeper." A *stigweard*, then, was someone who kept or cared for the affairs of a household.[9] In his old age, when David was handing the realm over to Solomon, he gave a careful account of the people responsible for sustaining the realm: Levites, priests, temple musicians, gatekeepers, treasurers, judges, military leaders, tillers of the fields, vinedressers, managers of the orchards, and keepers of sheep, camels, and donkeys (1 Chron. 22–27). At the end of the list, we read: "All these were stewards of King David's property" (27:31). In the New Testament the primary Greek word translated as "steward" or "manager" is *oikonomos* (e.g., Luke 12:42; 1 Cor. 4:1; 1 Pet. 4:10). *Oikos* means "house" or "household," while *nomos* means "law" or "order," so that *oikonomos* means the person who "has responsibility for planning and administrating (putting into order, or *nomos*) the affairs of a household (*oikos*)."[10] Likewise, the Greek word *oikonomia* carries the idea of stewardship, although various words are used in translation: "management" (Luke 16:2); "commission" (Col. 1:25; 1 Cor. 9:17); "plan" (Eph. 1:10); "divine training" (1 Tim. 1:4). Significantly, the root *oikos* lies at the heart of "economics," "ecology," and "ecumenical."

Douglas John Hall, while acknowledging that the concept of stewardship has been truncated, argues that the steward is a biblical metaphor that has come of age. He asserts that authentic, responsible stewardship should form an essential aspect of the church's prophetic, countercultural witness and of a praxis-based Christian ecotheology. Hall cites a secular eco-philosopher: "The coming age is to be seen as the age of stewardship: we are here not to govern and exploit, but to maintain and creatively transform."[11] Berry insists that "stewardship is hopeless and meaningless unless it involves long-term courage, perseverance, devotion, and skill."[12]

---

8. *OED*, "steward, n."
9. Douglas John Hall, *The Steward*, rev. ed. (Grand Rapids: Eerdmans, 1990), 40–41.
10. Ibid., 41.
11. Henryk Skolimowski, *Eco-Philosophy* (London: Marion Boyers, 1981), 54.
12. Wendell Berry, "The Gift of Good Land," in *Art of the Commonplace*, 299.

Still, some are asking if the concept and language of "stewardship" ought to be replaced or avoided altogether.[13] In many North American churches the word means little more than an annual pledge drive to undergird the congregation's finances. And to be honest, any concept Christians might have had in the past of stewarding Creation has functionally *not* altered humanity's relationship to the land, resulting in our current condition—ecological degradation and planetary crisis. Indeed Paul Santmire suggests the problem is not with the word itself but with "what is happening 'on the ground.'"[14] If thinking of ourselves as stewards of Creation undergirds an ethos that fails to consider the ramifications of commodifying the land, that reinforces an attitude of human dominance and power-over, that thinks of Creation as valuable only in its usefulness to humanity, and that does not acknowledge God's immanence, then perhaps the whole notion of stewardship is not only outdated but detrimental to the welfare of God's Creation. One thing is clear: if stewardship is to have a transforming effect on how Christians relate to Creation, it will need to be reimagined, reframed, and re-articulated in convincing ways.

Genesis 2:15 reads, "The LORD God took the man and put him in the garden of Eden to till it and keep it."[15] Perhaps "keeping" can be reimagined and nuanced as a relationship of solidarity with Creation, anchored in partnership as well as caretaking. The experience of belonging to a community—including the whole community of life—involves both membership and functioning as a co-creator of the community.[16] When we define ourselves in relationship to others, we become accountable to the Other—whether the Other be people who think, believe, or act differently from us or, in this case, the Earth and its creatures. If we do not imagine ourselves as part of Creation, if we globalize the ecocrisis and deny its pertinence to our local communities, if we do not live in relationships of accountability, we might well remain unresponsive to the ecocrisis and fail to see the biblical mandate of "keeping" Creation as a call to solidarity and action on behalf of the garden.

Relationships of belonging, solidarity, and action, with and for the world, must be rooted in love. Berry commends the person "who has undertaken to

---

13. See Clare Palmer, "Stewardship: A Case Study in Environmental Ethics," in *Environmental Stewardship*, ed. R. J. Berry (New York: T & T Clark, 2006), 63–75; Christopher J. Vena, "Beyond Stewardship: Toward an *Agapeic* Environmental Ethic" (PhD diss., Marquette University, 2009), http://epublications.marquette.edu/dissertations_mu/16/.

14. H. Paul Santmire, "From Consumerism to Stewardship: The Troublesome Ambiguities of an Attractive Option," *Dialog: A Journal of Theology* 49, no. 4 (Winter 2010): 333.

15. Rabbi Lawrence Troster, presentation at Green Faith Retreat, Pine Bush, New York, May 23, 2012, asserts that the garden is anything but an "it" in the creation story, calling the earth a "live and ethical actor."

16. Peter Block, *Community* (San Francisco: Berrett-Koehler, 2008), xii.

cherish it [the world] and do it no damage, not because he is duty-bound, but because he loves the world and loves his children; whose work serves the earth he lives on and from and with."[17] Terry Tempest Williams writes, "Our lack of intimacy with each other is in direct proportion to our lack of intimacy with the land. We have taken our love inside and abandoned the wild."[18] Our alienation from each other and from God is coupled with our disaffection from the Earth. Earthkeeping and discipleship must consistently return to love. We cannot be in relationships of stewardship and solidarity with the unloved.

Perhaps we are afraid to turn our affections toward the wild because we know we will fall in love. And perhaps we are afraid to fall in love with the Earth because we fear our hearts will be broken. But that is the risk of a restored vision of stewardship. Faith in Jesus Christ compels us toward the Other, dissolving false dichotomies between nature and culture, human and other-than-human. Bearing witness to our faith opens our eyes to the communion of all life—in which there is particularity but not "otherness."

Sustainability and Resiliency

In the Mbanhela community of Mozambique, community members raise chickens to support orphans and vulnerable children.[19] The goal of community leaders and of the evangelical NGO that invested in their venture is *sustainability*, the community's ability to keep the project going on its own, without further outside financial or technical assistance. However in the first two years of operation, the president of the association died suddenly and two cycles of chickens were destroyed through abnormal heat and then flooding. The community needs more than sustainability; it requires *resiliency*, an ability to withstand unexpected disruptions, self-reorganize, cooperate with others, and thrive through failure.[20] Admittedly the quest for resilience is more difficult for majority-world communities like Mbanhela, yet the volatility of the world leaves it little choice.

Interest in the idea of "sustainability" began in the 1970s, and its meanings have evolved over time. Initially sustainability was grounded in economics and revolved around "sustainable development." Its most recognized definition

17. Wendell Berry, *The Unforeseen Wilderness* (Lexington: University Press of Kentucky, 1971), 33.

18. Terry Tempest Williams, "Winter Solstice at the Moab Slough," in *Simpler Living, Compassionate Life*, ed. Michael Schut (Harrisburg, PA: Morehouse, 2008 [1999]), 215.

19. See chap. 1.

20. See "A Shift to Humility: Andrew Zolli on Resilience and Expanding the Edge of Change," *On Being with Krista Tippett*, May 16, 2013, http://www.onbeing.org/program/a-shift-to-humility-andrew-zolli-on-resilience-and-expanding-the-edge-of-change/5501.

comes from the World Commission on Environment and Development, known as the Brundtland Report. First published it 1987, it states:

> Sustainable development is development that meets the needs of the present without compromising the ability of future generations to meet their own needs. It contains within it two key concepts:
> - the concept of needs, in particular the essential needs of the world's poor, to which overriding priority should be given; and
> - the idea of limitations imposed by the state of technology and social organization on the environment's ability to meet present and future needs.[21]

While the Brundtland Report was a sweeping challenge to business as usual, many experts are asking whether or not the expanded economic growth it advocates for is either realistic or would actually eliminate poverty.[22] Some, including Larry Rasmussen, are seeking to broaden the concept of sustainability so that it embraces both human and earth processes and "encompasses the requirements of sustainable environments, sustainable societies, and sustainable livelihoods, economies, and ways of life."[23] This is a "whole-systems approach" that does not separate the needs of humanity from the needs of the Earth. The well-being and future of every member of the household is interdependent.

The concept of interconnectedness is bringing some thinkers to emphasize resiliency as an important next step. The only thing we can predict is the Earth's unpredictability. We have no choice but to expect the unexpected because, in the words of Andrew Zolli, "the ecological system, the economic system, the geopolitical system, the climate system, the food security system are all connected to each other in ways that cause very complex, highly unpredictable nonlinear outcomes."[24] Sustainability seeks a balance in which human beings learn to live in stability with the rest of Creation, knowing that we will collapse if we do not. Resilience thinkers question whether such equilibrium is possible, given the flux of the planet's systems. They argue that what we need are systems that adapt and thrive through failure because failure is inevitable. Zolli and Healy frame resilience "as *the capacity of a system, enterprise, or a person to maintain its core purpose and integrity in the face of dramatically changed circumstances.*"[25]

---

21. World Commission on Environment and Development, *Our Common Future* (Oxford: Oxford University Press, 1987), 43.

22. David C. Korten, "Sustainable Development: A Review Essay," *World Policy Journal* (Winter 1991–92): 158–59.

23. Larry L. Rasmussen, *Earth Community, Earth Ethics* (Maryknoll, NY: Orbis, 1996), 173.

24. "A Shift to Humility: Andrew Zolli on Resilience," *On Being*, May 15, 2013.

25. Andrew Zolli & Ann Marie Healy, *Resilience* (New York: Free Press, 2012), 7.

Christianity has strong resonances with resilience. After all, the heart of the gospel is redemption of failure and brokenness. While we are called to struggle against principalities and powers, systemic sin and oppression, the pervasiveness of sin and evil should not surprise us as we strive to bring about the commonwealth of God. The sustainability *and* resilience of a broad array of systems on Earth seem profoundly compatible with seeking God's will "on earth as in heaven."

Globalization and Economics

Numerous lists of the top global problems exist, from the Millennium Development Goals to Rick Warren's "PEACE" plan to the fifteen global challenges of the United Nations University. One cadre of Christian scholars—Goudzwaard, Vander Vennen, and Van Heemst—has narrowed the list of the top global problems down to three: global poverty, environmental devastation, and the insecurity of widespread violence and terror.[26] Whatever the catalog of critical global issues, comprehensive solutions have not proven within easy reach. One means of addressing these dilemmas is globalization. The Northwest Earth Institute defines economic globalization as "the process and economic activity fueled by the capital markets of the world seeking the highest total return, and the economic, environmental, and social and cultural characteristics and consequences of that process and activity."[27] Globalization is deeply controversial. According to one analysis, some experts believe globalization is "the panacea for preventing war and alleviating poverty," whereas others scourge it as "a system that benefits transnational corporations while degrading the environment and fostering labor abuses."[28]

Goudzwaard, Vander Vennen, and Van Heemst state, "The arrival of a better society by means of ongoing economic and technological progress has not lived up to expectations."[29] Whatever one's conviction about globalization, at the very least it compels us to examine systems and the larger frameworks by which we live. In an email a friend recently commented, "Praxis that does not connect with macro and mega system-stories is doomed to remain as charity—mending the casualties without looking upstream for the causal center of all this death and destruction." Systems analysis and leverage points may be helpful conversation partners if we intend to take our friend's comment

---

26. Bob Goudzwaard, Mark Vander Vennen, and David Van Heemst, *Hope in Troubled Times* (Grand Rapids: Baker Academic, 2007), 16–23.

27. Northwest Earth Institute, *Globalization and Its Critics* (Portland, OR: NWEI, 2004), 1.

28. Chris Frost, "Framework for Globalization," in ibid., 1–3.

29. Goudzwaard, Vander Vennen, and Van Heemst, *Hope in Troubled Times*, 24.

seriously—praxis must be connected to the narrative of the system and be able to identify leverage points within that system if things are going to change.

Brian McLaren offers a helpful "lay" approach to recognizing systemic roots to our global challenges. He describes three interlocking systems in our society: the "prosperity system," by which we come to believe that consumption will fulfill our desire for happiness and thriving; the "security system," which consists of an increasing array of war and policing subsystems; and the "equity system," which undergirds justice and fairness through laws, taxes, the courts, and the press.[30] All of these systems are supported by the Earth's ecosystems. The problem, McLaren observes, is that the societal goldfish—the three interlocking systems—is getting too big for the ecosystemic goldfish bowl in which we live.[31] These systems are ideally designed to yield the exact results they are now generating. All three societal systems are broken in major ways: in our drive for prosperity, we are not respecting environmental limits and are hell-bent on pursuing economic growth; our equity system is not bringing about the "common good," but instead rationalizes the widening gap between the economically privileged and underprivileged; and the expensive security system has increasingly relied on the threat of violence and armaments for protection.[32] McLaren insists that we need a new "framing story" for how we see our world, one rooted in the vision of Jesus of Nazareth for the kingdom of God as expressed in the Sermon on the Mount, and specifically in Matthew 6:19–34. He concludes: "So Jesus counters the imperial framing story that isolates humanity from creation by placing us back with our fellow creatures in a story of creation, secure and beautiful under the care of God, not driven by anxiety to remove ourselves from that natural system of care. In God's global economy of love we find all the prosperity, equity, and security we need."[33]

According to systems analyst Donella Meadows, the kind of reframing McLaren suggests is actually a powerful leverage point. Shifting the paradigm out of which a single individual acts is relatively simple, notes Meadows, but changing the framework of whole societies is much more problematic. In fact, she reminds us "societal responses to paradigm challenge have included crucifixions, burnings at the stake, concentration camps, and nuclear arsenals."[34] Meadows, building off of Thomas Kuhn's insights, says that we reframe paradigms by pointing out the incongruities and shortcomings of the

---

30. Brian D. McLaren, *Everything Must Change* (Nashville: Thomas Nelson, 2007), 54–58.
31. Ibid., 63.
32. Ibid., 68–70.
33. Ibid., 138–39.
34. Donella Meadows, *Leverage Points* (Hartland, VT: Sustainability Institute, 1999), 18.

old worldview, by empowering those working within new paradigms, and by engaging open-minded change agents in the middle ground.[35] A countercultural Christian community can be a powerful agent for transformation as it seeks to live out a global economy of love, the commonwealth of God.

Agrarianism

The contemporary agrarian dream is a movement, both urban and rural, both American and international, that values well-tended land, good food, honest work, beauty, and neighborliness.[36] More than a nostalgic return to bygone days of farming and rural life, agrarianism lifts up the interdependence of human well-being with the well-being of the land. Ellen Davis observes that in the wilderness, Moses urges "the Israelites to reimagine their land as blessed precisely in the fragility that necessitates and therefore guarantees God's unwavering attention." Agrarianism calls all of us to this kind of imagination, rooted in land and place and mutuality and reliance on God. The Bible, much more than many in our generation realize, fosters this kind of foresight and resourcefulness, "for the simple reason that agrarianism is the mind-set native to many if not most of the biblical writers themselves."[37]

For this text, we think of agrarianism in two ways: (1) a critique of industrialism; and (2) a proactive vision of the health of both culture and land. The "modern industrial/technological/economic paradigm" presumes the value of growth and the ongoing availability of resources to undergird that growth. In counterpoint, writes Norman Wirzba, agrarianism represents a "sustained attempt to live faithfully and responsibly in a world of limits and possibilities."[38] Berry highlights the far-reaching implications of this clash: "I believe that this contest between industrialism and agrarianism now defines the most fundamental human difference, for it divides not just two nearly opposite concepts of agriculture and land use, but also two nearly opposite ways of understanding ourselves, our fellow creatures, and our world."[39]

35. Ibid., referring to Thomas Kuhn, *The Structure of Scientific Revolutions* (Chicago: University of Chicago Press, 1962).

36. Brian Donahue, "The Resettling of America," in *The Essential Agrarian Reader*, ed. Norman Wirzba (Lexington: University Press of Kentucky, 2003), 36–37.

37. Ellen F. Davis, *Scripture, Culture, and Agriculture* (Cambridge: Cambridge University Press, 2009), 27.

38. Norman Wirzba, "Introduction: Why Agrarianism Matters—Even to Urbanites," in *Essential Agrarian Reader*, 4.

39. Wendell Berry, "Watershed and Commonwealth," in *Citizenship Papers* (Washington, DC: Shoemaker & Hoard, 2003), 144.

Agrarianism's denunciation of industrialism, and the "Green Revolution" associated with it, is multidimensional and global. A few of its reproaches will serve in summary. First, industrialism continues "an economy of colonialism" that puts power in the hands of a few, prioritizes gross domestic product over local practices, reinforces inequality in the distribution of food, and displaces small farmers in favor of large-scale agribusiness. Indian environmentalist and antiglobalization activist Vandana Shiva insists: "Industrial agriculture is an efficient system for robbing farmers."[40] Secondly, industrialism trusts uncritically and blindly in technology's ability to solve the big problems. Maurice Tellen warns: "Beware of nature-free equations and computer models, especially in the hands of those who talk glibly about 'the creation of wealth' and endless growth."[41] Lastly and most tellingly, industrialism to date has not resulted in equality of life: hunger and malnutrition worldwide are on the rise.

Beyond critique, however, Wirzba points out that agrarianism also offers an alternative to industrialism, one that seeks "the health and vitality of a region's entire human and nonhuman neighborhood."[42] Such a vision includes both land and culture, and requires more comprehensive and multifaceted ways of determining the overall health of a region. It is more dependent on biodiversity and small farming methods, practices that are much more transferable and effective in the majority world where labor is not the issue it is in the West. Shiva describes the results of agrarian traditions in India: "Here knowledge is shared, other species and plants are viewed as kin rather than 'property,' and sustainability is based on the renewal and regeneration of biodiversity and species richness."[43]

Agrarianism is not without its critics.[44] Some insist that technology is still our best hope for ending hunger and that small farms cannot feed the world. Others note that rural life has been unrealistically romanticized and that farming is boring, hard, insecure, stolen from indigenous people, and dominated by men. And chillingly, there are the voices arguing that people living in the Western world will not and cannot live without luxury and convenience. We admire prophets and activists like Berry and Vandana Shiva, but we also have the "privilege" to ignore their message.

40. Vandana Shiva, "Globalization and the War against Farmers and the Land," in *Essential Agrarian Reader*, 125.
41. Maurice Tellen, "The Mindset of Agrarianism . . . New and Old," in *Essential Agrarian Reader*, 60.
42. Wirzba, "Introduction: Why Agrarianism Matters," 4.
43. Shiva, "Globalization and the War against Farmers," 122.
44. See a summary of critiques in David W. Orr, "The Uses of Prophecy," in *Essential Agrarian Reader*, 171–76.

Repentance and Conversion

During his 1978 commencement address at Harvard University, Nobel Prize–winning writer Alexander Solzhenitsyn told the graduating class that the day of "voluntary self-restraint" had died. He believed the human race had lost the ability to curb its own selfish desires and ambitions for the benefit of the common good. Only in this day of no self-restraint, Solzhenitsyn chided, could an oil company purchase "an invention of a new type of energy in order to prevent its use," or a food manufacturer "poison" its product to preserve it.[45] Given the current state of the planet, it certainly appears that the human race is more dependent on fossil fuel than on the Creator, and that economics has trumped morality, ethics, and virtue.

The lack of "self-restraint" in the United States lies, at least in part, in our "individualism," a word used in 1835 by French politicist Alexis de Tocqueville as he toured the fledgling democracy. This rugged individualism has given rise to such benefits as personal initiative and hard work, self-sufficiency, and equal rights for everyone.[46] But unbridled individualism breeds an egoism preoccupied with self-realization and achievement and begets competition and consumerism, each person fighting for his or her own market share of the good life.[47] Despite all the advantages of this system—health care, transportation, food production, and education—much of the West continues to drown in a torrent of consumerism and fast-paced living that is squelching the abundant life. This way of life is deeply affecting the integrity and welfare of the Earth community.[48]

William Dyrness writes: "If the problem . . . is in our abuse of the land and of our neighbors, then things will not change apart from a radical spiritual change in our hearts and our communities. The Bible describes the radical response that is appropriate in a single word: *repentance*."[49] The "radical spiritual change" of repentance is incumbent upon both individuals and communities. The Greek word for repentance, *metanoia*, literally means "to change one's mind." Humanity stands in desperate need of *metanoia*. The cries of the land and its inhabitants are deeply rooted in the brokenness of human hearts and human systems. As individuals *and* as communities, followers of

45. Alexander Solzhenitsyn, "A World Split Apart," address at Harvard Commencement, June 8, 1978, http://www.orthodoxytoday.org.

46. David G. Myers, *American Paradox* (New Haven: Yale University Press, 2000), 162–63; Robert Wuthnow, *Sharing the Journey* (New York: Free Press, 1994), ix.

47. See J. Matthew Sleeth, *Serve God, Save the Planet* (Grand Rapids: Zondervan, 2007), 21.

48. Andrew Shepherd, "Creation and Christology: The Ecological Crisis and Eschatological Ethics," *Stimulus: The New Zealand Journal of Christian Thought & Practice* 18, no. 4 (November 2010): 51–57.

49. William A. Dyrness, "Are We Our Planet's Keeper?," *Christianity Today* 35, no. 4 (April 8, 1991): 42.

Christ are called to repent, to change our minds about our dominant position in the web of Creation.

Repentance compels us to conversion. Although today repentance and conversion are often used almost interchangeably, there are differences worth noting in the New Testament. The Greek verb for repent is *metanoeō*, to change one's mind; the verb, *epistrephō*, is usually translated "turn," "turn to," or "turn back."[50] The distinction between repentance and conversion is perhaps best illustrated in Paul's testimony before King Agrippa when he describes his proclamation to Jew and Gentile, "that they should repent [verb, *metanoeō*] and turn to [verb, *epistrephō*] God and do deeds consistent with repentance [noun, *metanoia*]" (Acts 26:20; see also 3:19). In other words, to repent is to recognize the need for change in one's life; to be converted is to bear witness to one's change of heart and mind through action and the way one lives.

Throughout this text we make frequent reference to conversion. Our conviction is that conversion is both a transformational moment in time rooted in God's grace *and* a process that involves continual renewal and risk. Gustavo Gutiérrez talks about the beginning of the way of discipleship in language that attends to both repentance and conversion: "A conversion is the starting point of every spiritual journey." Conversion involves both "a break with the life lived up to that point"—Jesus's explicit call to repentance (Mark 1:15)—and above all, the decision "to set out on a new path"—Jesus's invitation to "come, follow me" (Mark 10:21). Conversion marks a clear transition from the past and sets a "fixed horizon" for discipleship that provides a vision for the journey.[51]

As important as a "moment in time" change can be, Macrina Wiederkehr states, "Even people who have had a dramatic encounter with the Divine, still must go through that daily purifying process of continued conversion. A deep and lasting conversion is a process, an unfolding, a slow turning and turning again."[52] Not only is conversion an ongoing aspect of our everyday discipleship, but it also can happen in multiple areas of our lives. It involves a "daily purifying process" of returning to God, to Jesus's vision of the kingdom, to the Earth community, and to our original vocation as keepers and tenders of Creation. Dietrich Bonhoeffer reminded us of the cost of discipleship: "Whenever Christ calls us, his call leads us to death."[53] Perhaps our daily reaffirmation of

50. The noun "conversion" (*epistrophe*) is only used once in the NRSV (Acts 15:3).

51. Gustavo Gutiérrez, *We Drink from Our Own Wells*, trans. Matthew J. O'Connell (Maryknoll, NY: Orbis, 2003 [1983]), 95.

52. Macrina Wiederkehr, *A Tree Full of Angels* (San Francisco: HarperSanFrancisco, 1990), 18.

53. Dietrich Bonhoeffer, *Discipleship*, ed. Geffrey B. Kelly and John D. Godsey, trans. Barbara Green and Reinhard Krauss (Minneapolis: Fortress, 2001 [1937]), 87. The earlier translation may be more familiar: "When Christ calls a man, he bids him come and die" (87n11).

discipleship ("dying to self") is but a prelude of our ultimate conversion—our return to the dust from which, and the God from Whom, we came.

The prophet Joel documents the response of the people of God to an ecological crisis, in which the land is laid waste by an invasive species of locusts and subsequent drought: "The fields are devastated, / the ground mourns" (Joel 1:10). He laments the muted indifference of the human community while seeds shrivel, cattle groan, oxen are bewildered, sheep suffer, and wild animals cry out (vv. 16–20). Laurie Braaten notices that the prophet commands the human community to identify with the Earth in an act of repentance and conversion: "Earth is suffering and mourns. In this she serves as a model for proper human mourning, for she calls for humans to identify with her in her suffering. Earth also condemns human sin; her suffering stands as a sign to humans that they have not repented of the damage they have done to her."[54] This text, when read in light of the current ecocrisis, implies that conversion to the Earth will mean remembering our place as interconnected partners in the whole Earth community. It also serves as a reminder that before reconciliation can take place, we must acknowledge humanity's culpability in the crisis, repent of our participation in perpetuating the crisis, and respond with acts of restoration and healing.

If we repent, Scripture assures us that God will forgive. Will the Earth also forgive? Susannah Heschel, reflecting on the Holocaust, writes that forgiveness requires both atonement and restitution. Even when we believe divine atonement has been given, restitution is a critical part of repentance and therefore of conversion.[55] Whenever Christians and Christian communities repent for our trespasses against the Earth, we ought also to be engaging in actions of restitution. From planting gardens to ride-share programs for worship gatherings, Christ-followers are finding creative ways to practice restitution. If dry earth, bellowing cattle, and withering vines are signs of humanity's sinfulness against the land, perhaps water conservation projects, content chickens in the coop, and flowering gardens are signs of repentance, restitution, and conversion.

Grace

At the end of this section, we turn to grace as the spring from which praxis flows. To begin, nature models grace. The whole Creation exists because of,

54. Laurie J. Braaten, "Earth Community in Joel 1–2: A Call to Identify with the Rest of Creation," *Horizons in Biblical Theology* 28, no. 2 (2006): 121–22.

55. Susannah Heschel, "Symposium: Susannah Heschel," in *The Sunflower*, by Simon Wiesenthal, expanded ed. (New York: Schocken, 1997), 172.

and depends on, the Creator's love. Such reliance is true poverty of spirit (Matt. 5:3). In the incarnation, by which came "grace and truth" (John 1:17), nature and grace were fused together. Through Christ grace pervades the whole of nature, and through grace, notes Joseph Sittler, God works to restore nature "to his love and to its intended destiny."[56] Thomas Merton observes, "A tree gives glory to God by being a tree."[57] If a tree gives glory to God by being a tree, grace allows us to love the tree. Grace is the freedom to be what one is, to love what another is, and all of Creation unveils that freedom. The human journey, then, is about turning away from (in an act of repentance) our false selves reflected in personal and systemic sin and toward (in conversion) our most natural, grace-dependent selves.

Grace unleashes love for the broken, forgotten pieces of this world. An ongoing awareness of our dependence on the grace of God transforms our vision and creates a love for what the Creator loves. Grace and ethical action go hand in hand. Without grace, our actions become exhausting and unfruitful; without action, cheap grace leads to passive support of global systems. Bonhoeffer, writing in the mid-1930s and staring into the realities of the ruthless Nazi machine, reminded his students: "Cheap grace is the mortal enemy of the church. Our struggle is for costly grace."[58] The realities of the ecocrisis are intimidating and disheartening. Our common journey for the healing and restoration of the Earth is daunting. In the end, Ched Myers insists, our hope rests in a grace-filled discipleship: "The impediments to faith in the Jesus who calls us to radical discipleship are truly staggering. . . . The world in which we struggle for reconstruction is the same world dominated by the systems of addiction from which we struggle to defect. This is precisely why discipleship is entirely a matter of grace."[59]

■ ■ ■

From our conviction that Christians are called to grace-filled discipleship resulting from an embodied spirituality and willingness to repent and be converted, this section has been an attempt to suggest a practical, ecotheological mind-set. We favor a paradigm of stewardship that affirms the human creature's place in relationships of accountability and partnership with Creation—dissolving rather than perpetuating harmful dichotomies. From this theoretical

---

56. Joseph Sittler, "Commencement Address" (1959), in *Evocations of Grace*, ed. Steven Bouma-Prediger and Peter Bakken (Grand Rapids: Eerdmans, 2000), 35.
57. Thomas Merton, *New Seeds of Contemplation* (New York: New Directions, 2007 [1961]), 29–30.
58. Bonhoeffer, *Discipleship*, 43.
59. Ched Myers, *Who Will Roll Away the Stone?* (Maryknoll, NY: Orbis, 1994), 412, 416.

orientation, Christians can engage the world through care-filled practices like sustainability, resiliency, and agrarianism in a way that is faithful to Scripture and our faith tradition.

Ethics and Action

> A thing is right when it tends to preserve the integrity, stability, and beauty of the biotic community. It is wrong when it tends otherwise.
>
> —Aldo Leopold[60]

Yellowstone, one of the world's first national parks, is home to Old Faithful Geyser, numerous endangered species, and a wide array of ecosystems. It also provides fascinating case studies in environmental ethics. When bighorn sheep in Yellowstone contracted pinkeye, ethicists decided not to treat the disease, allowing 300 of them (over half the herd) to starve to death; they determined that letting nature take its course would ultimately strengthen the herd as a whole in its adaptation to the ecosystem. However when a mother grizzly and her three cubs were trapped on an island two miles from shore, ethicists had the bears rescued and released, in order to protect an endangered species. Letting the created world run its ecosystemic course meant allowing raging forest fires to incinerate almost a million park acres in 1988. We ought not underestimate the importance of these moral decisions. Holmes Rolston III writes, "Some people approach environmental ethics with a smile—expecting chicken liberation and rights for rocks, misplaced concern for chipmunks and daisies. Elsewhere, they think, ethicists deal with sober concerns: . . . questions of life and death and of peace and war. But the questions here are no less serious: The degradation of the environment poses as great a threat to life as nuclear war, and a more probable tragedy."[61]

Kathleen Moore and Michael Nelson argue that the ecocrisis is a *moral* challenge, not simply an economic, technological, or scientific one: "What will move people to act to save their beloved worlds? Clearly, information is not enough. What is missing is the moral imperative, the conviction that assuring our own comfort at terrible cost to the future is not worthy of us as moral beings."[62] Indeed psychologists have shown that there is no direct relationship

60. Aldo Leopold, *A Sand County Almanac* (Oxford: Oxford University Press, 2001 [1949]), 189.

61. Holmes Rolston III, "Environmental Ethics: Values in and Duties to the Natural World," in *Environmental Ethics*, 3rd ed., ed. Susan J. Armstrong and Richard G. Botzler (Boston: McGraw-Hill, 2004), 74.

62. Kathleen Dean Moore and Michael P. Nelson, introduction to *Moral Ground* (San Antonio: Trinity University Press, 2010), xvi.

between having more information and being more ecologically conscious: "Most researchers agree that only a small fraction of pro-environmental behavior can be directly linked to environmental knowledge and environmental awareness."[63] Moral motivation is more than knowledge.

Questions of ethics, morality, and justice are often missing from the conversation. What is our human responsibility? What is our moral imperative on behalf of the planet? Of course, it is possible to answer these questions *without* religion. People can act in moral and ethical ways without rooting their actions in a particular faith tradition. But in this text we presume that ethical reasons grounded in the Christian tradition and the Bible are the primary impetus compelling people of faith to action.

Ecojustice

Maps of the world are curious things. In the sixteenth century, Gerardus Mercator developed the map many of us grew up with: the Mercator projection, which served originally as a navigation tool. While its parallel lines of latitude and longitude worked well for ships, its use had other unfortunate and unethical consequences. Maps represent the perspective of the mapmaker. Thus maps can manipulate reality.[64] The Mercator projection puts the central meridian through Europe (and Greenwich, England) and makes Europe and North America look larger than they actually are on the globe, reinforcing an already existing sense of colonial dominance. Yet this map became the model for walls, atlases, and books, forming the mental image of the globe for most Westerners. In fact, to see a map representing more accurate landmass scale can be disarming.[65] Many people in the Northern Hemisphere have little concept of the size of the global South, let alone its diversity of history, culture, religion, economy, or ecology. Most "developed" countries are in the North, while the preponderance of "developing" countries is found in the global South.

The vast discrepancy between North and South is just one example of inequity and power differentials—systemic sin—in our world. Ecojustice is rooted in the "intersectionality" of classism, sexism, racism, *and* ecological degradation.[66] It is a central theological ethic for the flourishing of all life.

63. Anja Kollmuss and Julian Agyman, "Mind the Gap: Why Do People Act Environmentally and What Are the Barriers to Pro-Environmental Behavior?," *Environmental Education Research* 8, no. 3 (2002): 250.

64. Mark S. Monmonier, *How to Lie with Maps* (Chicago: University of Chicago Press, 1991), 94–99.

65. Compare, for example, the Mercator projection with the Mollweide projection.

66. "Intersectionality" refers to the way multiple systemic sins build on and intensify oppression. For example, a black woman often experiences the intersection of sexism and racism,

Ecojustice as Environmental Ethic

Who counts? Who has standing in the moral community and who does not? These are questions of belonging, membership, and ultimately, justice. The Western world, at least in part informed by the doctrine of *imago Dei*, has lived as if only humanity counts. Yet science reveals we are utterly dependent on the thriving of all Earth's ecosystems. Larry Rasmussen writes that all things "socio-communal, the biophysical, the geoplanetary . . . belong to a single moral universe."[67] Theories of justice founded upon Kant, Descartes, and Locke—most modern theories of justice—do not embrace the whole "community of life" as members of the moral community. Immanuel Kant wrote, "So far as animals are concerned, we have no direct duties. Animals are not self-conscious and are there merely as a means to an end. That end is man."[68] It is imperative to reject a worldview that positions humanity *against* nature: "Moral exclusion and privilege—'we' vs. 'they' as either human/human or human/the rest of nature—should not be considered normal and normative but deviant. . . . In point of fact, 'they' don't live there anymore. It's only 'we,' the whole Community of Life, together."[69]

Ecojustice affirms the interdependence of the whole created world, including humanity, and the right of that world to be free from unjustifiable destruction. God created the world in holistic relationship, yet sin has disrupted and fragmented every relationship by perpetuating alienation and oppression. A justice-centered Christianity does not separate culture from Creation, humanity from the natural environment, or "social justice" from "ecological justice"—all are inextricably connected. If social justice and the elimination of classism, sexism, and racism are central to the Christian faith, so is ecological justice, and thus our call to act on behalf of the planet.

Justice that is engaged on behalf of only *certain* oppression is inadequate and an insufficient response to the call of holistic justice Christ calls us to. Simon Schama describes one of the most ecologically friendly movements of the twentieth century. It initiated some of the first recycling programs, taught people how to garden for themselves, and intentionally took youth into the wilderness to experience the power of Creation. That movement

---

and, if she is economically underprivileged, classism. The intersection of gender hierarchy, racism, and disadvantage in the labor market forms a powerful nexus of oppression. In our world, ecological degradation must be added to this intersection.

67. Larry L. Rasmussen, "Is Eco-Justice Central to Christian Faith?," *Union Seminary Quarterly Review* 54, no. 3–4 (2000): 110.

68. Immanuel Kant, "Duties Towards Animals and Spirits," in *Environmental Ethics*, ed. David R. Keller (Chichester, UK: Wiley-Blackwell, 2010), 82.

69. Rasmussen, "Is Eco-Justice Central to Christian Faith?," 110–11.

was the Third Reich. From 1933 to 1935 Hitler enacted the first significant environmental legislation in modern history. Schama writes, "It is of course painful to acknowledge how ecologically conscientious the most barbaric regime in modern history actually was. Exterminating millions of lives was not at all incompatible with passionate protection of millions of trees."[70] Ecology did not exclude genocide. One-sided justice that takes into account *only* care of the earth or *only* concern for people is inadequate. And potentially dangerous.

The mainstream environmental movement has long been critiqued as an affluent, white movement—caring only for the "wilderness" and certain endangered species.[71] The environmental justice movement began to take shape in the 1980s as a way to raise awareness around issues of class and race and to raise awareness to the fact that marginalized populations often suffer disproportionate environmental impacts. The Environmental Protection Agency (EPA) defines environmental justice as "the fair treatment and meaningful involvement of all people regardless of race, color, national origin, or income with respect to the development, implementation, and enforcement of environmental laws, regulations, and policies."[72] In this text, we use the term "ecojustice" rather than "environmental justice." Ecojustice is a term used more commonly by theologians, ethicists, and social justice advocates who are concerned with the intersectionality of justice issues. While our focus here is how humans experience the effects of systemic oppression, we are not suggesting that other-than-human life is outside of our moral scope. Our very use of the term "ecojustice" implies that our concern encompasses all forms of life.[73]

Understanding Ecojustice

Historian and researcher Peter Montague suggests that understanding ecojustice begins with acknowledging that we exist in at least three

70. Simon Schama, *Landscape and Memory* (New York: Knopf, 1996), 119; see also Luc Ferry, *The New Ecological Order*, trans. Carol Volk (Chicago: University of Chicago Press, 1995), 91–92.

71. See the (controversial) speech of Adam Werbach, former president of the Sierra Club, called, "The Death of Environmentalism and the Birth of the Commons Movement" (often referred to as, "Is Environmentalism Dead?"), presented at the Commonwealth Club of San Francisco, December 8, 2004, San Francisco, California; reprinted at http://grist.org/article /werbach-reprint/, accessed August 3, 2013.

72. Environmental Protection Agency, "Environmental Justice," http://www.epa.gov/envi ronmentaljustice/, accessed August 3, 2013.

73. On the welfare of other species and ecosystems specifically, see chap. 3.

environments.[74] The *natural* environment is the one we usually think of: air, water, soil, wildlife, trees, rivers—God's Creation. Next is the *built* environment, which includes everything that humans make—cities, suburbs, highways, houses, skyscrapers, dams, power plants, chemicals, incinerators, etc. Lastly, the *social* environment of humans is the space in which we encounter classism, sexism, racism, and their acute effects on human health. The interface of these three "environments" shapes the quality of life for humans, as well as for the other creatures and ecosystems with which we share the planet.

Ecological *in*justice for people of color and/or the economically oppressed stems from four things.[75] The first is their disproportionate exposure to environmental evils, such as polluted air, fast food, unsafe neighborhoods, prejudice, and joblessness. The second is the unjust denial of environmental goods, like parks, public transportation, nutritional information, grocery stores with organic or healthy food, and clean air. Thirdly, these populations are more vulnerable or have less resistance than the "average" population to certain environmental evils. For example, a child's level of "vulnerability" to toxic lead poisoning is often governed by a parent's knowledge of and ability to pay for fresh vegetables (because a nutritious diet can decrease susceptibility to lead poisoning). The last factor is white privilege—a more systemic, less overt form of racism, and one to which most white people are oblivious. Privilege exists when one group has something valuable that is refused to others, not because they are undeserving but because of the group to which they belong.[76] It is about how society undergirds unshared power arrangements and the lack of access to self-determining power. These four elements blend into a perilous matrix for people of color and/or the economically oppressed in all three of their environments.

The puzzle of ecojustice has one final important piece: cumulative impacts, something Montague calls "the *central problem of our time*."[77] When it comes to both ecojustice and the ecocrisis, injustices are usually the result of multiple

74. On what follows: Peter Montague, "Research for Environmental Justice" presentation to GreenFaith Fellows, Newark, New Jersey, October 28, 2009, http://www.precaution.org/lib/greenfaith.091028.pdf.

75. Ibid., slides 10–26.

76. Peggy McIntosh, "White Privilege and Male Privilege: A Personal Account of Coming to See Correspondences through Work in Women's Studies," Working Paper No. 189 (Wellesley, MA: Center for Research on Women, 1988), http://files.eric.ed.gov/fulltext/ED335262.pdf; Allan G. Johnson, *Privilege, Power, and Difference*, 2nd ed. (New York: McGraw Hill, 2006), 21–34.

77. Montague, "Research for Environmental Justice," slide 29. For a presentation on cumulative impacts, see Peter Montague, "The Central Problem of Our Time," http://www.precaution.org/lib/win.090517.pdf, accessed March 27, 2013.

factors, not one, and are created by the cumulative impacts of numerous small decisions. Montague says, "The destruction of the planet as a place suitable for humans is occurring because of the cumulative impacts of many small decisions—most of which may seem unimportant when considered in isolation."[78] Once again we are reminded of the interdependence of life on this planet. Ecojustice teaches us that by protecting and ensuring the quality of life for the most vulnerable and those on the margins, we protect all people, creatures, and ecosystems.

Ecojustice and Oppression

> If you have come here to help me, you are wasting our time. But if you have come because your liberation is bound up with mine, then let us work together.
>
> —Aboriginal Activists Group, Queensland[79]

Historically, systems that function to advocate the domination of one human over another are labeled "isms." Classism, sexism, and racism make up the classic oppressive trio. Ecological degradation (naturism) is inextricably connected with these issues of systemic oppression, which multiply in harmful effect because of their intersectionality. Because of classism, the ecocrisis excessively and disproportionately impacts those without wealth, power, or position around the world. James Cone portrays a connection with racism: "The logic that led to slavery and segregation in the Americas, colonization and apartheid in Africa, and the rule of white supremacy throughout the world is the same one that leads to the exploitation of animals and the ravaging of nature."[80] Sexism also has an ecological side. Carolyn Merchant has shown how Western science has historically, at least since Francis Bacon, commodified both women and nature.[81] Moeletsi Mbeki, political economist from South Africa, illustrates the intersectionality of classism, sexism, racism, and ecological degradation in sub-Saharan Africa, which suffers from "declining life expectancy, falling school enrolment, capital flight, the brain

78. Montague, "Research for Environmental Justice," slide 30.
79. Lilla Watson, to whom this quote is usually attributed, credits it to a collective process in the 1970s.
80. James H. Cone, "Whose Earth Is It, Anyway?," in *Risks of Faith* (Boston: Beacon, 1999), 138.
81. Carolyn Merchant, *The Death of Nature* (New York: Harper & Row, 1989 [1980]), esp. 164–91. Brian Vickers, "Francis Bacon, Feminist Historiography, and the Dominion of Nature," *Journal of the History of Ideas* 69, no. 1 (2008): 117–41, charges Merchant with an anachronistic interpretation of Bacon.

drain, deforestation, desertification, conflict, massive and growing inequality, endemic and growing poverty, manipulation by outside forces and a growing dependence on foreign patronage and on solutions initiated from outside the continent."[82]

The redemption of Creation depends on our ability to see our uniquely Christian responsibility of living in just ways and of applying relational models that support the flourishing of all within the web of life.

Classism

The movie *Erin Brockovich* (2000) tells the true story of an unrelenting environmental lawyer representing a poor town whose population is suffering excessively from cancer. In taking on a major corporation that is dumping hexavalent chromium (a toxic carcinogen that can greatly harm those exposed to it) into the groundwater supply, Brockovich uncovers one of the greatest environmental coverups in US history. This story illustrates the often-overlooked connection between ecology and sociocultural factors, such as class.

We encounter classism when individuals or segments of society are given "differential treatment" based on social rank related to wealth, education, status, and/or power. These differences are perpetuated in systems that benefit certain (privileged) people, resulting in conspicuous wealth disparity and sharp discrepancies in how basic human needs are met.[83] Classism and the endangerment of Creation are inseparably joined. The underprivileged around the globe are suffering *disproportionately* from the ecocrisis. The economically privileged—who are *disproportionately* responsible for the planet's plight in the first place—benefit *disproportionately* from resource inequalities and are *disproportionately* protected from ecological perils. Our current social structures and dependency on accumulation, insists Leonardo Boff, lead inexorably to the "plundering" of God's Creation and require "a Hiroshima and Nagasaki in human victims every two days."[84] In this system a minority of the human population continues to take advantage of the majority for its own welfare. This "differential treatment"—classism—reveals how alienated we have become from one another, how far we have strayed from existing in true community.

82. Moeletsi Mbeki, *Architects of Poverty* (Johannesburg: Pan Macmillan South Africa, 2009), Kindle locations 386–89.

83. See "Class Definitions," Class Action (website), http://www.classism.org/about-class /class-definitions, accessed April 8, 2013.

84. Leonardo Boff, *Cry of the Earth, Cry of the Poor*, trans. Phillip Berryman (Maryknoll, NY: Orbis, 1997), 110–11.

Comparisons of Selected National Data (2010–2012)

	Energy Use	CO$_2$ Emissions	Rural Water Access	Internet	Population (Age 0–14)	GNI
Bolivia	746	1.5	72%	34.2	35%	$2,220
China	2,029	6.2	85%	42.3	18%	$5,720
India	614	1.7	90%	12.6	29%	$1,580
Iraq	1,266	3.7	67%	7.1	41%	$5,870
Italy	2,757	6.7	100%	58.0	14%	$33,860
Mexico	1,560	3.8	89%	38.4	29%	$9,640
Mozambique	415	0.1	33%	4.8	45%	$510
New Zealand	4,124	7.2	100%	89.5	20%	$30,640
Nigeria	721	0.5	47%	32.9	44%	$1,440
United States	7,032	17.6	94%	81.0	20%	$52,340

Source: The World Bank[85]

The chart above gives evidence of the gap between the economically privileged and underprivileged in our world and the connection of that disparity to such ecological practicalities as fossil-fuel energy use, CO$_2$ emissions, and access to water. Note particularly that, with the exception of China, lower-income, developing countries have significantly higher percentages of their population that are children. Methodist Bishop Bernardino Mandlate of Mozambique once said, "African children die so that North American children may overeat."[86] Few of these statistics should surprise us. As the world becomes smaller and more connected it is difficult not to be aware of the widening gap between the haves and have nots. The sin of classism, however, is revealed in the truth that the privileged can ignore these realities. At its worst, classism blames the impoverished and even creates theologies that justify class distinction as God's blessing.

At Nazareth Jesus announced that he had come "to bring good news to the poor" (Luke 4:18). He penetratingly and consistently challenged the rich and

85. The World Bank, "Data: Indicators," http://data.worldbank.org/indicator. Explanation of categories: Energy Use = kg of oil equivalent per capita (2011); CO$_2$ Emissions = metric tons per capita (2010); Rural Water Access = % of rural population with access to improved water (2011); Internet = users per 100 people (2012); Population (Age 0–14) (2012); GNI = gross national income per capita, Atlas method (current US$) (2012).

86. Bernardino Mandlate, in a presentation to the United Nations PrepCom for the World Summit on Social Development Plus Ten, New York, February 1999, cited in Cynthia Moe-Lobeda, *Resisting Structural Evil* (Minneapolis: Fortress, 2013), 23.

his followers to surrender their belongings and to live in simple dependence and poverty (e.g., Luke 5:28; 10:4; 12:33; 14:33; 18:18–23). Throughout Luke's Gospel Jesus makes it clear that wealth is toxic to a life of discipleship (e.g., Luke 6:24; 12:13–21; 16:19–31). At the same time, Jesus affirms that possessions could be rightly used for the sake of the poor (e.g., Luke 6:30; 14:12–14; 19:1–10).[87] Jesus refused to idealize the poor or spiritualize the involuntary "asceticism" of the deprived; quite the opposite, he prioritized the underprivileged, identified with them, offered them hope, confronted the political and religious systems that imprisoned them, disavowed the belief that class stratification was divinely ordained, and, inescapably, called his followers to do the same.

Sexism

Official reports now acknowledge an undeniable truth: empowering women and girls, representing 70 percent of the earth's poor, is essential to the eradication of poverty. While advancing women's rights is widely recognized as fundamental to breaking the cycle of poverty and slowing population growth, it has also proven distressingly elusive. Women do 66 percent of the world's work and grow 50 percent of the world's food, yet they only take home 10 percent of the world's income and own 1 percent of the land. UN Secretary-General Kofi Annan states: "As more cash and assets get into the hands of women, more of these earnings get into the mouths, medicine, and schoolbooks of their children, while at the same time increasing women's bargaining position and power in the family and community; and their ability to act against violence in the home and in the world. Indeed, study after study has confirmed that there is no development strategy more beneficial to society as a whole—women and men alike—than one which involves women as central players."[88]

Sexism is the use of either gender or sexual identity to advocate male domination and female subordination. Patriarchy describes the institutionalization of male dominance over women. Using the term patriarchy does not necessarily imply that women have no power, or that all women are victims, or even that men are not negatively impacted by sexism and patriarchy. On the contrary, patriarchy oppresses both women and men, notes Phyllis Trible, "denying full humanity to women and distorting the humanity of men."[89] Sexism can be unintentional, impersonal, subtle, and even benevolent.

---

87. Walter E. Pilgrim, *Good News to the Poor* (Minneapolis: Augsburg, 1981), 86.

88. United Nations Secretary-General Kofi Annan, address to the 23rd General Assembly Special Session, "Women 2000: Gender Equality, Development and Peace for the Twenty-first Century," New York, June 5, 2000, http://www.trickleup.org/poverty/women.cfm.

89. Phyllis Trible, "Five Loaves and Two Fishes: Feminist Hermeneutics and Biblical Theology," *Theological Studies* 50, no. 2 (1989): 281.

Tension Point: Engaging Oppression

A recurring struggle for our writing team was whether or not we had the right to contribute content on systems of oppression. In a very real sense, we held reservations because, as white, privileged academics, we wondered if we could speak *on behalf of* oppressed peoples, not knowing the depth of their experiences.

We cannot imagine the experience of an economically underprivileged, invisible-to-the-West, illiterate, HIV-positive Mozambican woman (see chap. 10). After a period of concentrated reflection and debate, we decided that an important act of justice *is* to leverage our privilege on behalf of the Other (when appropriate) and to engage in advocacy. Doing so has helped make us aware of how complex an issue privilege is. There are times when using our privilege may actually perpetuate oppression. Nevertheless, we are committed to practicing advocacy and learning how to function as allies.

- What steps can we take to begin to recognize our own privilege?
- Whenever we find ourselves in "privileged" positions or relationships, what are some of the things we need to think about in order to be compassionate Christ-followers striving for justice?
- What are the ramifications of this tension point in terms of our relationship to the Earth?

Sex and gender are not interchangeable or synonymous. Sex refers to biology, but gender refers to the expectations and roles of both women and men in society. We are socialized into gender roles; those social constructions are not inherently bad, and they can and do change over time. The concept of privilege adds another layer to the conversation. Privilege occurs when society confers or withholds status to particular groups based on class, race, gender identity, sexual orientation, age, able-bodiedness, etc. Privilege is fluid: we might benefit from social status in one category but find ourselves lacking in another. Male privilege is privilege held by men as a class in relationship to women. Privilege among individual men varies, but all men benefit in a systemic way.

Throughout history, women's work and social place were predominately restricted to the home and private spheres of the world, while men functioned as culture makers and inhabited public spaces. Rosemary Radford Ruether writes, "The establishment of this relationship between male and female spheres depends not only on males as definers of culture but also on the burdening of women with most of the tedious, day-to-day tasks of economic production."[90] Men as definers and creators of culture make women

90. Rosemary Radford Ruether, *Sexism and God Talk* (Boston: Beacon, 1993 [1983]), 74.

the object, rather than the subject, of discourse, dismissing the experience and voices of women.

The inequitable distribution of power between men and women is a transcultural reality. Women across the globe experience oppression: genital mutilation; sexual and domestic violence; inequitable distributions of labor, wealth, and resources; harassment; etc. Women worldwide experience gender inequity in varying ways: the oppression of a middle-class white woman in the West is not identical to the oppression experienced by a poor black woman in Africa. And women worldwide exercise agency distinctively as well: the ways they attempt to circumvent patriarchy may not look the same. Women's experience cannot be collapsed into a monolithic whole; their experiences are diverse and culturally complex. Feminism opposes the paradigm of domination and subordination in all forms.

Nature has suffered the same inferior status as women. Sallie McFague observes that the created order is a lifelong partner to women, even as naturism, the domination of nature, is a lifelong partner to sexism:

> The feminization of nature and the naturalization of women have been crucial to the historically successful subordination of both. One common legacy of this old partnership is our scolding of Mother Nature's fury whenever earthquakes, torrential rains, or hurricanes occur. The angry, out-of-control feminized nature gets back at her human tormentors through unleashing some solid strikes now and then. It is, sadly, one of the few times in our culture that we address nature as subject.[91]

As culture and history have defined nature as something that must be controlled, tamed, and dominated, so has it defined women.[92] Elizabeth Johnson writes that "within a sexist system the true identity of both women and the earth are skewed. Both are commonly excluded from the sphere of the sacred; both are routinely taken for granted and ignored, used and discarded, even battered and 'raped.'"[93] While feminism objects most particularly to the paradigm of male over female, it also rejects master over slave and humankind over the Earth.

The liberation of one marginalized group is interrelated with the liberation of the other. Thus women must see that there can be no liberation for them and no solution to the ecological crisis within a society whose fundamental model of relationships continues to be one of domination.[94] Ecofeminism

---

91. Sallie McFague, *Super, Natural Christians* (Minneapolis: Fortress, 1997), 20.
92. Ruether, *Sexism and God Talk*, 72.
93. Elizabeth A. Johnson, *Women, Earth, and Creator Spirit* (New York: Paulist Press, 1993), 2.
94. Rosemary Radford Ruether, *New Woman, New Earth* (New York: Seabury, 1975).

expands the feminist conversation to include concern for the marginalization of other-than-human life as well as for human life. The term was first used in 1972 by Françoise d'Eaubonne who wrote, "The destruction of the planet is due to the profit motif inherent in male power."[95] Both liberation movements—feminism and ecofeminism—have overlapping and interactive language. They seek to dismantle both the concept of male as the normative representative of humankind and that of humanity as the center and apex of Creation. In an ecofeminist ethic, relationships of domination—whether between men and women or humans and other-than-human life—are replaced by a web of interdependent relationships. In this historical moment, our theology must recognize that the integration of feminist concerns with ecojustice is vital for the healing of the Earth and of women.

Racism

The Slave House on Gorée Island, just off the coast of the capital city of Senegal, was part of the notorious triangular trade system. Europeans exported manufactured merchandise from Europe to West Africa in exchange for slaves. The slaves were then shipped to the Americas to help produce cotton, sugar, and tobacco, which were subsequently sent back to Europe.[96] The ground floor of the Slave House housed African slaves, who had been captured by fellow Africans to be sold to ship owners headed to the Americas. The back door of the Slave House opened to waiting ships and was known as "the door of no return." Today hundreds of oil rigs set the night sky afire along the coastline of Guinea from Nigeria to Namibia, with natural gas flares. Relating this story, Moeltsi Mbeki concludes: "The rigs are not connected to the mainland; they pump crude oil from the bowels of the earth to waiting oil tankers—those ships again!—which carry the oil straight from the rigs to the great oil-refining industries in the United States, Asia and Europe; another commodity Africa is selling to the rest of the world. In the past it was its people; today it is its natural resources."[97]

In 1987 the United Church of Christ (UCC) issued a groundbreaking report that demonstrated the essential connection between racism and environmental degradation.[98] The study found common factors between *where* ecologically harmful materials were discarded and the demographic among whom they

95. Rosemary Radford Ruether, *Integrating Ecofeminism, Globalization, and World Religions* (Lanham, MD: Rowman & Littlefield, 2004), 91.
96. Mbeki, *Architects of Poverty*, Kindle locations 77–98.
97. Ibid., Kindle locations 96–98.
98. United Church of Christ Commission for Racial Justice, "Toxic Wastes and Race in the United States" (New York: 1987), http://www.ucc.org/about-us/archives/pdfs/toxwrace87.pdf.

were dumped. Its conclusions were devastating: race and socioeconomic status were undeniable factors in the placement of toxic substances. Waste is much more likely to be dumped in places where people of color reside. The study was part of the launching of the "environmental justice" movement—a sharp critique of the white, elite power structures of the mainstream environmental movement. It exposed environmental racism: the disproportionate impact felt by populations of color and the systematic exclusion of those voices from the ecological conversation. Sadly when the UCC commissioned an anniversary report in 2007, the findings revealed that conditions had hardly changed in twenty years.[99]

The same findings were published by the EPA in a report on the city of Chester in Delaware County, Pennsylvania. Chester is a low-income, predominately African American city in a mostly white county. Chester possesses a median income 45 percent lower than the rest of the county, a poverty rate of 25 percent, an unemployment rate of 30 percent, and the highest infant mortality rate in the state.[100] And it is where unequal quantities of the county's trash goes. Of all of the waste produced in Delaware county, 100 percent is burned at the incinerator in Chester, 90 percent of the sewage is treated in Chester, and close to 100 tons of hospital waste are brought in every day from nearby states to be destroyed in Chester. The head of the EPA in the region stated that the processing of such hazardous materials and the resulting pollution would not have happened in nearby affluent white suburbs.[101] Carolyn Merchant has called Chester and cities like it "local sacrifice zones," where the waste of the rich is dumped on the heads and laps of the poor.[102] These global zones are disproportionately in places where non-white people live. Sulaiman Mahdi makes this connection vividly: "The crack in the ozone layer is directly related to the crack on the streets. The fact that African Americans don't live as long as Whites in the US is not genetic but social and ecological. We have to help make those connections."[103]

We must recognize that we more readily trash places that are farther away from us and out of sight. The first world's greatest export—and the majority

99. United Church of Christ Commission for Racial Justice, "Toxic Wastes and Race at Twenty: 1987–2007" (Cleveland: 2007), http://www.ucc.org/justice/pdfs/toxic20.pdf.

100. On what follows: Mark I. Wallace, "The Green Face of God: Christianity in the Age of Ecocide," *CrossCurrents* 50, no. 3 (2000): 322–26.

101. Howard Goodman, "Politically Incorrect," *Philadelphia Inquirer Magazine*, February 11, 1996.

102. Carolyn Merchant, *Radical Ecology*, 2nd ed. (London: Routledge, 2005), 169.

103. Sulaiman Mahdi, cited in Jane Blewett, "Social Justice: Its Link to a Spirituality of the Earth," in *Greening Congregations Handbook*, ed. Tanya Marcovna Barnett (Seattle: Earth Ministry, 2002), 40.

world's chief import—is garbage. This "colonialism of waste" is globalization at its worst, because we are quarantined from the effects of our choices and selective about what disturbs us. We oppose ecological impingements in our hometowns—"not in my backyard" (NIMBY)—but, because our waste has found a home in the backyards of the non-white poor, we display little concern. Nationalism and racism are indicators that something has gone profoundly wrong.

The Gospel and Oppression

The good news of Jesus Christ, who was anointed by the Holy Spirit "to bring good news to the poor" (Luke 4:18), speaks precisely to the intersectionality of systemic oppression. Over and over again in the Gospels Jesus points us toward the core directive of the Christian life: love God, love others. Our discipleship in Christ must be (re)oriented toward the poor, the oppressed, and the disregarded. Not only is the Earth itself oppressed and vulnerable, but those most affected by its suffering are marginalized by the interconnected systemic sins of classism, sexism, and racism. To resist systems of oppression in any form is, as Ruether emphasizes, part of a call to conversion: "If dominating and destructive relations to the earth are interrelated with gender, class, and racial domination, then a healed relation to the earth cannot come about simply through technological 'fixes.' It demands a social reordering."[104] This reorientation and reordering are embedded in the cost of discipleship, or as Carlo Carretto calls it, "the privilege of the cross," one that substitutes "humility for pride, simplicity for complication, poverty for wealth, service for power."[105]

The Gospel of Mark sheds light on how Jesus responded to structural hierarchies of his day by the use of the word "crowd" (*ochlos*).[106] Most of its thirty-eight uses refer to anonymous masses from underprivileged classes. Ched Myers states that the social outcasts—the impoverished, unwell, uneducated, and alienated—form the "omnipresent background" to the ministry of Jesus: "The portrait now emerging is of a Jesus who is continually surrounded by the poor, who attends their importune cries for healing and wholeness, and who acts not just to bind up their wounds but to attack the structures that perpetuate their oppression."[107] Jesus inaugurated an inclusive community in

104. Rosemary Radford Ruether, *Gaia and God* (San Francisco: HarperSanFrancisco, 1994), 2.
105. Carlo Carretto, *Why, O Lord?*, trans. Robert R. Barr, 3rd rev. ed. (Maryknoll, NY: Orbis, 1986), 49.
106. Ahn Byung-mu, "Jesus and the Minjung in the Gospel of Mark," in *Minjung Theology*, ed. Kim Yong Bock (Maryknoll, NY: Orbis, 1981), 139.
107. Ched Myers, *Binding the Strong Man* (Maryknoll, NY: Orbis, 1988), 156.

which no preference or priority was given to Jew or Greek, slave or free, male or female (Gal. 3:28).

Jesus literally gave the "nobody" a voice: "He has done everything well; he even makes the deaf to hear and the mute to speak" (Mark 7:37). The theme of "giving voice" continues in the book of Acts. When the Spirit descended at Pentecost, Peter quoted from the prophet Joel and proclaimed that God will pour out the Spirit on "all flesh" and that sons, daughters, and male and female slaves "shall prophesy" (Acts 2:17–18). One key thing links the coming of the kingdom of God through Jesus Christ and the coming of the Spirit at Pentecost: the giving of "voice" through the stunning diversity of humanity in what theologian Andrea Hollingsworth calls "the polyvocality of Spirit."[108] To "give voice" is liberating. Throughout the book of Acts, the Spirit often breaks patterns of injustice and provides liberation. Giving "voice" provides a meaningful way of engaging systemic oppression. It is our responsibility to fight against the silencing of the oppressed and to join the struggle in the giving and claiming of voice—"Speak out for those who cannot speak, / for the rights of all the destitute" (Prov. 31:8). In the polyvocality of Spirit, to give voice to marginalized people and to an unheeded Creation is an act of justice.

A Christian ethic of ecojustice calls us to relate to the natural world as neighbor, refusing to pit ecological and social justice concerns against one another. To move among different life systems without losing regard for the whole is to embrace the wide relationality within a community. This kind of intersystemic engagement must act decisively from the social and ecological margins, demonstrating an ethic of care and bringing to the foreground those made vulnerable by unjust power relations. Ecojustice invites the deconstruction of such arrangements—and a flourishing reconstruction—among the social, economic, and ecological systems of the web of life.

■ ■ ■

Our chapter started in Mozambique with our friend Nathan, who was in the States recently. We had coffee together and talked about his work in urban farming, alongside mothers who lack access to prenatal care, and with infants who are dying of malnutrition. He is lonely. He misses sitting around a table, talking and dreaming and arguing about ecotheology. He wonders out loud if he would be making more of a difference as a professor or a published theologian. We shake our heads in disagreement. It seems clear to us that Nathan is living the kind of life from which we are able to insulate ourselves. Nathan's

---

108. Andrea Hollingsworth, "Spirit and Voice: Toward a Feminist Pentecostal Pneumatology," *Pneuma: The Journal of the Society for Pentecostal Studies* 29, no. 2 (Fall 2007): 208.

embodied stories challenge us to integrate our own thinking, reading, and writing with ecologically aware lifestyles, to make sure that ecotheological conversations in our classrooms inevitably call us to praxis. Concrete action must be more than a footnote to lectures or PowerPoint presentations.

While dialogue without action has little effect on the ecocrisis, we are reminded that Nathan's journey began in a classroom and in a small group consumed with a hunger to learn and to make a difference for the planet. David Orr affirms, "From a variety of sources, we know that the things most deeply embedded in us are formed by the combination of experience and doing with the practice of reflection and articulation."[109] Ecotheology must include the stuff of *both* theological conversation *and* practical action, whether it concerns stewardship, solidarity, agrarianism, repentance, or ecojustice. Exploring ecotheology *and* doing ecotheology must be two sides of the same coin, even as they have become for Nathan.

109. David W. Orr, "Recollection," in *Ecological Literacy*, ed. Michael K. Stone and Zenobia Barlow (San Francisco: Sierra Club, 2005), 98–99.

8

Heavenly Minded, Earthly Good

Embodying Down-to-Earth Living

I (Dan) was finishing my 2013 visit to Mozambique with Nathan and his family. Over two weeks I'd stayed in their Maputo home and traveled with Nathan observing his fieldwork. During our many miles on the road, we had enjoyed enriching theological, political, and personal discussions. It was clear that he loved his work alongside the poor and invisible and that he was good at it. A respected leader, he was making a difference in rural Mozambique, and many people had a sustainable, even resilient, future because of him. It was also apparent that the work was demanding in every way: physically, relationally, and spiritually.

At the end of my visit, Nathan arranged to take me on a two-day safari through Kruger National Park in South Africa. En route I asked what sustained him in his ministry—I was concerned about *his* sustainability and well-being. He told me he does not need much sleep, so he reads voraciously and is forever listening to podcasts. However, every morning, wherever he was, he would spend twenty to thirty minutes in centering prayer, a life-giving discipline he'd practiced since seminary days. And then there was Kruger. Nathan goes there two or three times a year for renewal. Beginning our drive through the park, Nathan piled four field guides and a journal onto my lap. I told him I wanted to *see* the animals not *read* about them. He smiled. I wrote down every new species of animal we saw, forty-six of them, including the "big five"—lion,

177

elephant, leopard, cape buffalo, and rhinoceros. More often than not, even though he was driving, Nathan saw an animal before I did. He knew a lot about them: he told me an elephant's trunk has eight major muscles on each side and 150,000 portions of muscles (the entire human body has only 639 muscles); people miss the leopard because they don't look in trees; the male vervet monkey has bright blue and red parts of his body; the hippopotamus marks its territory in unpleasant ways. There I was, looking up each new animal in one of the guides on my lap. And it struck me: Nathan had long ago ceased being a tourist. He'd trained himself to "see" the wildlife of Kruger. He *knew* them, cared for them, grieved the seemingly unstoppable poaching of them, and was renewed in their presence. I only knew *about* them.

Nathan was sustained in his demanding vocation by a number of disciplines and practices, such as practicing centering prayer and cultivating awareness. These are just two of the ten practices we will explore in this chapter, each of which is a way of *doing* ecotheology, of living "down-to-earth," via lifestyles that are both aware of and accountable to global ecological realities. We will discuss staying rooted, cultivating awareness, practicing centering prayer, keeping the Sabbath, living simply, resisting consumerism, eating justly, conserving water, reducing waste, and keeping a garden.

Staying Rooted

> For in the end, we will conserve only what we love.
> We will love only what we understand,
> and we will understand only what we are taught.
> —Baba Dioum, Senegalese ecologist[1]

Numerous ecological writers and theologians have used Dioum's triad (conserving, loving, understanding) to try to explain humanity's lack of motivation in addressing the destructive tide of ecological degradation. When I (Jen) first heard the axiom as a college student, I tried to think about pieces of Earth I loved, and not a single place came to mind. My family moved frequently when I was growing up. Could lack of roots have contributed to my sense of alienation? Discomfort with isolation became my catalyst. I realized the only antidote to my growing sense of *displacement* was *replacing* alienation with rootedness.[2]

1. Baba Dioum, Speech to International Union for Conservation of Nature, New Delhi, India, 1968, quoted in Malcolm L. Hunter Jr. and James P. Gibbs, *Fundamentals of Conservation Biology*, 3rd ed. (Malden, MA: Blackwell, 2007), 338.
2. Ched Myers, *Who Will Roll Away the Stone?* (Maryknoll, NY: Orbis, 1994), 341–46.

The prophet Isaiah writes, "The surviving remnant of the house of Judah shall again take root downward, and bear fruit upward" (Isa. 37:31). So I began to burrow downward: into my blue-collar, solidly middle-class, white roots, into my evangelical Baptist heritage, into the lakes and mountains of northern Idaho and the farmland of eastern Washington. I sat first with things that once embarrassed me and then with the shame of believing I was better than those people and places I came from. On my journey upward, I remember what I love: the way my father always smells like a tire shop, how my mother has endured my arrogance, the stories my grandmothers tell of frying squirrel for supper and keeping financially afloat in the prairies during the Great Depression. And I recall the places that formed me: rivers and lakes, croplands and mountains, cherry orchards and gardens. The words of David Orr ring true: "I doubt that we can ever come to love the planet as some claim to do, but I know that we can learn to love particular places."[3] Dioum's ecological triad has been my North Star as I've embarked on this journey of replacement.

These days, it is common to read about being rooted, buying local, using public transportation, and becoming neighborly. Simone Weil, twentieth-century Christian mystic and social activist, once wrote, "To be rooted is perhaps the most important but least understood need of the human soul."[4] While such rootedness may stir up sentimental images of yesteryear, in reality American culture is rooted in root*less*ness. At the heart of this rootlessness lays American individualism, the freedom and means for self-improvement, the historic availability and abundance of land—all undergirded by a prevailing sense of mobility to go where and when we please.[5] Wendell Berry poignantly connects the ecological fallout to our obsession with improvement, technological supremacy, and personal success:

> The members of this prestigious class of rampaging professionals are the purest sort of careerists—"upwardly mobile" transients who will permit no stay or place to interrupt their personal advance. They must have no local allegiances; they must not have a local point of view. In order to be able to desecrate, endanger, or destroy a *place*, after all, one must be able to leave it and forget it. One must never think of any place as one's home; one must never think of any place as anyone else's home.[6]

3. David W. Orr, "Recollection," in *Ecological Literacy*, ed. Michael K. Stone and Zenobia Barlow (San Francisco: Sierra Club, 2005), 103.
4. Simone Weil, *The Need for Roots*, trans. A. F. Wills (New York: Routledge, 1995 [1949]), 41.
5. Wallace Earle Stegner, *The American West as Living Space* (Ann Arbor: University of Michigan Press, 1987), 22.
6. Wendell Berry, "Higher Education and Home Defense," in *Home Economics* (New York: North Point, 1987), 50–51.

Your Ecological Footprint

An activity to help raise your awareness about your impact on God's creation, especially in relation to others around the world, is calculating your ecological footprint. A number of quizzes or calculators are available online to do this (see below). In them you will find questions like:

- What kind of home do you live in? How big is it?
- How many people live in your household?
- What is your annual household income?
- Was any portion of your home built with green design features?
- What kind of practices do you use at home and work to be energy efficient?
- Which water saving features and habits do you have in your home?
- What kind of car do you drive?
- How do you get to work? How often do you fly?
- What best describes your normal diet?
- How often do you eat animal-based products?
- Where is your food grown, processed, and packaged?
- Do you have a garden to grow your own food?
- What choices do you make for maintaining your yard?
- How often do you select cleaning products that are biodegradable or nontoxic?
- What are some of your practices when you shop (e.g., bring your own bags)?
- How many standard size garbage bins does your household fill each week?
- What proportion of your waste do you recycle?[a]

a. Online resources: Center for Sustainable Economy, http://myfootprint.org; Conservation International, http://www.conservation.org/act/live_green/pages/ecofootprint.aspx; Earth Day Network, http://www.earthday.org.

A proactive vision reinforces an alternative lifestyle for Christians, one that prioritizes *rootedness*. Ched Myers writes that our challenge "is not so much one of cosmology, as of geography. We need a theology of *re-place-ment*."[7] Unfortunately much Christian theology has undervalued the importance of "place" by emphasizing heaven over earth, the spiritual over the physical. Rootedness helps counteract a kind of practical gnosticism that separates spirituality from earth and body. As Eugene Peterson observes: "Geography and theology are biblical bedfellows. . . . I find that cultivating a sense of place

7. Myers, *Who Will Roll Away the Stone?*, 345.

as the exclusive and irreplaceable setting for following Jesus is even more difficult than persuading men and women of the truth of the message of Jesus."[8]

The monastic fathers and mothers placed a high value on rootedness, refusing to evade their internal demons through escapism. Amma Syncletia, a desert mother, writes, "If you happen to live in a community, do not move to another place, for it will harm you greatly. If a bird leaves her eggs, they never hatch. So also the monk and the nun grow cold and dead in faith by going from place to place."[9] A significant value within new monasticism today is the discipline of staying put—pursuing the wisdom of stability and acknowledging our connection to the land.[10]

I (Dan) recently made a practical change in my life to move closer to an ethos of rootedness (I recognize, however, not everyone can or will choose this way of life). For twenty years my wife and I raised our two children in a suburb of Portland, Oregon. Everything we needed was there—church, schools, shopping malls, grocery stores, movie theaters, gym, coffee shops, restaurants, credit union, gas stations—all accessible in one of our two cars. In 2010, a year after my wife's death, I moved into an intentional community, Urban Abbey, in a north Portland neighborhood. I co-own a home with a young family that lives in the remodeled basement apartment. Students and other young people rent out rooms. Other Urban Abbeyites live next door or within easy walking distance. We share common meals twice a week, while we strive to live sustainably and to be involved in our neighborhood.[11]

Within months of moving into the neighborhood, I knew my new neighbors more than in twenty years of suburban living. I walk and bike more often and know neighborhood shop owners by name. My granddaughters and I frequent the community library. The change has inspired new feelings of *rootedness* and of being *placed*. I find myself resonating with Terry Tempest Williams: "It just may be that the most radical act we can commit is to stay home."[12]

8. Eugene H. Peterson, foreword to *Sidewalks in the Kingdom*, by Eric O. Jacobsen (Grand Rapids: Brazos, 2003), 9.

9. Hannah Ward and Jennifer Wild, eds., *The Monastic Way* (Grand Rapids: Eerdmans, 2007), 56.

10. Jonathan Wilson-Hartgrove, "The Spiritual Discipline of Staying Put," *Christianity Today* (February 9, 2012), http://www.christianitytoday.com/thisisourcity/7thcity/placeless culture.html, accessed July 25, 2012; cf. idem, *The Wisdom of Stability* (Brewster, MA: Paraclete, 2010); Scott R. Sanders, *Staying Put* (Boston, MA: Beacon, 1993).

11. Urban Abbey strives to live by these values: communal formation, relational integrity, grateful celebration, sustainable living, neighborhood involvement, and intentional inclusivity.

12. Terry Tempest Williams, *A Voice in the Wilderness*, ed. Michael Austin (Logan: Utah State University Press, 2006), 46.

Cultivating Awareness

> We almost never pay absolute attention. The minute we do, something happens. We see whatever we're looking at with such attention, and something else is given—a sort of revelation.
>
> —May Sarton[13]

In 1918, German youth came face-to-face with a disturbing reality: not only had their nation lost a war, but they were staring into a vast unknown regarding their culture and civilization. Some youth turned to nihilism, some to radical politics. Others, however, took a different course: they went walking. Searching for new answers, this groundswell of activism came to be known simply as "the Youth Movement." They embraced a newfound joy outdoors in the natural world—walking, camping, dancing, and singing—and strove to rise above class distinctions through simple living, deep friendship, and mutual respect.[14] In the midst of this revolution, a young Christian leader, Eberhard Arnold, wrote in 1919: "Our task is to live in active protest against everything that opposes God in this world. So poorly have we Christians filled this role that the question must be asked: Are we Christians at all?"[15] Awareness of God's Creation, peaceful protest, and radical living united many at a key moment in history.[16]

The practice of awareness is a way of embodying spirituality, of "seeing," of nurturing a deeper mindfulness of God's presence in the world and in our everyday, mundane lives. Henry David Thoreau said, "It's not what you look at that matters, it's what you see."[17] Early desert Christians were known as the "niptic" fathers and mothers, after the Greek word *nipsis*, which means mindfulness or attentiveness.[18] By "seeing" God's natural world, they fostered and heightened a sense of awe and wonder, as attested to in the Psalms: "Let all the earth fear the LORD; / let all the inhabitants of the world stand in awe of him" (Ps. 33:8). And seeing leads to praise: "O LORD, how manifold are

---

13. May Sarton, *Endgame: A Journal of the Seventy-Ninth Year* (New York: W. W. Norton, 1992), 337.

14. John Howard Yoder, introduction to *God's Revolution: Justice, Community, and the Coming Kingdom*, by Eberhard Arnold, 2nd ed., ed. the Bruderhof and J. H. Yoder (Farmington, PA: Plough, 1997), xxvi–xxvii.

15. Arnold, *God's Revolution*, 5.

16. Importantly, the movement of Eberhard Arnold and the Bruderhof was rooted in peaceful living and radical discipleship, which stood it in sharp contrast to the idealism, camping, singing, and love of nature in the Hitler Youth Movement. See Arnold, *God's Revolution*, 150–52.

17. Henry David Thoreau, *Journals*, August 5, 1851, The Walden Woods Project (website), http://www.walden.org/Library/Quotations/Observation, accessed January 18, 2013.

18. Steven Chase, *Nature as Spiritual Practice* (Grand Rapids: Eerdmans, 2011), 23–24.

your works! / In wisdom you have made them all; / the earth is full of your creatures" (Ps. 104:24). This tradition is exemplified in the writings of Annie Dillard, whom one biographer has called "a pilgrim on a mission to retrieve a sense of ecstatic wonder before the natural world."[19] Dillard writes, "We are here to witness. . . . That is why I take walks: to keep an eye on things."[20] To witness, to keep an eye on things, such are the foundations of awareness.

But becoming aware is difficult because of the "hurry sickness" in Western society. One writer emphasizes that "we must ruthlessly eliminate hurry from our lives." To do so, he recommends the practice of "slowing."[21] By slowing down and allowing nature to ground us in visceral reality, we see what is, and what *is* is enough. Macrina Wiederkehr writes, "When the simple gifts at our fingertips cease to nourish us, we have a tendency to crave the sensational."[22] How often do we overlook "the sacrament of the present moment" (Jean-Pierre de Caussade) simply because we are not aware? Through our hurriedness we miss those common elements that reveal the presence of God. Slightly changing Dioum's triad: we will not care for what we do not love; we will not love what we do not know; we will not know what we do not *see*. As we daily repeat the movements of cultivating awareness, our affections will be turned toward the wild, the commonplace, the tiny, and the overlooked. And we may just begin to experience, and be moved toward, love of Creation. In Simone Weil's words, "The kind of attention which is nothing else but attention is prayer."[23]

Many resources exist to help us with the practice of cultivating awareness. Here are just a few:

- Join nature in praise—Read Psalm 98, 104, or 148, taking note of how the psalmists describe nature praising its Creator. Then, go for a slow walk in the natural world and witness how Creation gives glory to God simply by being what it was created to be.[24]
- Take ten—During the Lenten season commit yourself to spending ten minutes every day outside, keeping an eye on the natural world and praying. I (Dan) practiced this during Lent 2013 when I was in freezing

19. Philip Lopate, "Annie Dillard," in *The Art of the Personal Essay* (New York: Anchor, 1994), 692.
20. Annie Dillard, "Teaching a Stone to Talk" (1982), in *This Sacred Earth*, ed. Roger S. Gottlieb (New York: Routledge, 1996), 34–35.
21. John Ortberg, *The Life You've Always Wanted* (Grand Rapids: Zondervan, 1997), 84.
22. Macrina Wiederkehr, *A Tree Full of Angels* (San Francisco: HarperSanFrancisco, 1990), xi.
23. Simone Weil, *The Notebooks of Simone Weil*, trans. Arthur Wills (New York: Routledge, 2004 [1956]), 527.
24. Adapted from Steven Chase, *A Field Guide to Nature as Spiritual Practice* (Grand Rapids: Eerdmans, 2011), 34.

Minnesota instead of rainy Oregon. Those ten minutes were an unexpected and surprising source of wonder and beauty.

- Learn from Creation—Biomimicry is a term that means imitating nature in order to solve complex problems.[25] Certainly we can learn about the Creator from Creation, but we can also learn many other things, including the interdependence of the web of life. Take time to "study" nature and reflect on what we can learn about life from it.

- Write a haiku—Go outside to reflect on, in, and with Creation. Be aware of any contrasts or tensions you see there. Write a haiku, consisting of seventeen syllables in three lines (five, seven, five). A haiku should describe the paradox or contrast you observe. Here's one written by a student in a recent class:

> Tall, majestic trees
> Rooted firmly in the ground
> Grasp earth and touch sky

Practicing Centering Prayer

Our outer environment can only begin to be healed by our inner, and I'm not sure we can ever truly tend to our polluted waters, our shrinking forests, the madness we've loosed on the air until we begin to try to clean up the inner waters, and attend to the embattled wild spaces within us. Action without reflection is what got us into this mess in the first place, and the only answer is not action, but, first, clearer reflection.

—Pico Iyer[26]

Another spiritual practice related to the natural world is centering prayer. Too often prayer is narrowly envisaged as a means of making requests and petitions *to* God. But centering, or contemplative, prayer emphasizes relying on God's grace, surrendering our agendas and wills, and aligning our whole selves *with* God. Dorothy Bass describes this transformation in how we understand prayer: "What I yearn for . . . is not simply to pray. What I yearn for is to view the world differently because I have viewed it in relation to God."[27] Thus, centering prayer seeks to see and love the world the way God sees and

25. Janine Benyus, "Biomimicry's Surprising Lessons from Nature's Engineers," TED Talk, May 27, 2009, http://www.ted.com/talks/janine_benyus_shares_nature_s_designs.

26. Pico Iyer, "The Inner Climate," *Orion Magazine* (September/October 2008), http://www.orionmagazine.org/index.php/articles/article/3259/.

27. Dorothy C. Bass, *Receiving the Day* (San Francisco: Jossey-Bass, 2001), 24.

Tension Point: Interventionism

How God intervenes in history is a difficult conversation—our team was split on the issue. Does God intervene and act to save humanity from its sin and disintegration? Or does God leave us to our own devices? Or something else? Where are we left if we visualize God as more than a cosmic clock maker who established the created order and then let it run on its own, if we somehow hold to a God who is both Creator and providential sustainer?

Interventionism—any theology that leans heavily on God's ability and willing-ness to break into time and space in order to *intervene* on the world's behalf—may easily lead to a lax attitude toward Earthcare. In other words, statements like, "God will ultimately save us," can easily lead to otherworldliness and to sidestepping the ecological work placed on us as human stewards. On the other hand, if we hold to a non-interventionist theology, the hope of the world rests on us, and in that case, our track record as a people has been far from exemplary, riddled by sin and selfishness as we are.

Certainly God out of love has intervened in the world through the incarnation of Jesus Christ to save and redeem the world in its brokenness. However, how far are we willing to expand our convictions about God's intervention, especially as they relate to the ecocrisis? We wrestled a great deal with this topic and have by no means reached consensus. Here are some questions to consider:

- In practical, ecological terms, what are some of the potential dangers and hopes if we believe in an interventionist God?
- What are the corresponding dangers and hopes if we trust in a God who will not intervene miraculously to save us?
- How might we speak to our Christian communities about a providential, sustaining Creator and our human responsibilities to be caretakers?

---

loves the world, which, in turn, enters us into the heartbeat of God and into the realities of the created world—"because as he is, so are we in this world" (1 John 4:17).

Christian mystics have often modeled this sort of prayer. Among the mystics we see the domain of what is encompassed by God's love unrelentingly expand, until ultimately it includes the created universe—"so that God may be all in all" (1 Cor. 15:28). Although mystics are often dismissed in our day as "New Age," at their most profound they give evidence of hearts, minds, and lives transformed by centering prayer. Trappist monk and priest Basil Pennington expressed well the growth that happens through this kind of deep prayer: "By the intuition of the Spirit we come to know our solidarity with all being. This cannot but lead to compassion—compassion for our fellow

humans who are one with us in our Source, in our call, and in our fate. . . .
Moreover, we will know that oneness and compassion with the rest of creation that is the source of good stewardship and a true ecology."[28] To care
well for nature, we must have the patience to sit in silence and learn to align
our hearts and lives with God.

Centering prayer can be a powerful exercise in the Christian life; its benefits
reach into the depths of our being, as well as the breadth of Creation. Centering prayer requires intentionality and a regular investment of time. Here we
offer one framework for centering prayer:[29]

- Establish a consistent time and place to open yourself regularly to God's
  presence. It could be morning, noon, or evening. The place might be a
  room in your home, or outdoors in mint fields, or on creek banks.

- Get comfortable, simply inviting your body and mind to rest. Take
  long, deep breaths, receiving each as a gift from your Creator. It takes
  time to detox from our anxious thoughts and to-do lists and for our
  minds to become aware of God's presence. When your mind wanders,
  just notice it without judgment and focus on breathing. After several
  minutes of deep breathing and settling in, you will begin to feel calm
  and centered.

- If words or images help you be present with God, choose one or two. You
  might use "Yahweh," which sounds like breath when vocalized: inhale
  on "Yah"; exhale on "weh." Other words could include "mercy," "let
  go," "Jesus," "Spirit," "Creator," etc. Or, you could choose a symbol
  like water, fire, earth, dove, etc. Some use the framework of the Lord's
  Prayer: "feed us" (Matt. 6:11), "forgive us" (Matt. 6:12), "be present
  to us" (Matt. 6:13). If helpful, consider opening up the Scriptures and
  meditating on a single phrase.

- After several minutes of practicing presence through breathing and
  centering, you are ready to listen. Not so much for the audible voice of
  God but for where God might be showing up in the world. Once when
  I (Jen) was engaged in this practice outdoors, I had been vaguely aware
  of a bird chirping insistently in the distance. Just as I transitioned from
  breathing to listening, to discerning where God might be showing up in
  the world, the chirping bird flew inches from my face to a low hanging
  branch of the oak tree next to me. It sat there, head cocked, suddenly

28. M. Basil Pennington, OCSO, "*Lectio Divina*: Receiving the Revelation," in *Living With
Apocalypse*, ed. Tilden H. Edwards (San Francisco: Harper & Row, 1984), 71. Thomas Keating,
Open Heart, Open Mind (New York: Continuum, 2006 [1986]), 43, maintains that in centering
prayer one is "embracing the whole of creation."

29. For another framework, see Keating, *Open Heart, Open Mind*, 177–81.

silent, gazing at me. Sometimes, as it turns out, we are very close to where God is showing up in the world.

• At the end of your time in centering prayer, spend a few minutes setting an "intention"—being willing to go where God is showing up in the world and committing yourself to living as a vessel of healing and reconciliation in the world.

• This prayer practice is most helpful when we attend to it every day. Practice builds muscle memory, imprinting this way of being into the very fabric of our lives.

Keeping the Sabbath

> This ordinary time is
> gifted with days,
> weeks of mundane grace
> routinely following the liturgy
> of hours anticipating creation
> tuning its prayer and praise to the
> rhythms of incarnate love.
> —Enuma Okoro[30]

My family and I (Dan) lived in England for three years in the 1980s. After breakfast, an average weekday began with a bike ride into town. The Bodleian Library at Oxford opened at nine o'clock in the morning, and I liked to start working right away. After two hours of study, we'd break for coffee, known affectionately as "elevensies." At one o'clock I'd meet my friends in the Balliol College dining hall for lunch, and afterward we would have coffee together in the common room. At four o'clock the library emptied, and people would head to the history common room for afternoon tea and biscuits. After twenty to thirty minutes we'd head back to the library. I would retire home for dinner around six or seven o'clock with the family. The day had an enticing rhythm to it, built around work, food, and relationships.

Our weeks had a rhythm as well. The library closed at one o'clock on Saturday afternoon, not opening again until Monday morning. Most stores were closed on Sunday, providing everyone a day of Sabbath rest. After worship, we would enjoy leisurely Sunday dinners and then, if the weather allowed, go for long walks. Britain was not nearly as driven as the fast-paced American

---

30. Enuma Okoro, "Passing Ordinary Time," in *At the Still Point: A Literary Guide to Prayer in Ordinary Time*, ed. Sarah Arthur (Brewster, MA: Paraclete, 2011), 24. Reprinted by permission of the poet.

lifestyle we'd known. It was quaint, charming, and perhaps unrealistic. But my soul still longs for a rhythm of life that prioritizes relationship, rejuvenation, and slow living alongside healthy work.

Recently there has been a revitalized interest in the importance of Sabbathkeeping as a personal discipline for finding rest, renewal, and freedom in our demanding and cluttered lives.[31] But what does Sabbathkeeping have to do with Creation or ecology?

Sabbath Rest

Sabbath revolves around rest: "And on the seventh day God finished the work that he had done, and he rested on the seventh day from all the work that he had done" (Gen. 2:2). God deemed this day *kadosh*, "holy"; time is holy. We might have expected the text to pronounce that God finished creating on the *sixth* day. But God was not finished—on the seventh day God created *menuha*, "rest."[32] Thus the crowning climax of the first creation account is not the creation of humankind on the sixth day but the creation of Sabbath rest on the seventh. The chief purpose of this account, therefore, is to highlight the centrality of God's rest in and for the created order rather than the cosmological significance of humanity.[33]

This intimate connection between Creation and Sabbath is also highlighted in the Ten Commandments. In the two Decalogue accounts—Exodus 20 and Deuteronomy 5—there is more variation between the Sabbath commandments (including two different rationales for keeping the Sabbath) than between any other pairs of commandments.[34] The justification for Sabbathkeeping in Exodus is God's *creative* work; however, in Deuteronomy the motivation for observing the Sabbath is God's *redemptive* work.

Sabbath and Creation

Exodus 20 reads, "For in six days the LORD made heaven and earth, the sea, and all that is in them, but rested the seventh day; therefore the LORD blessed the sabbath day and consecrated it" (v. 11). To speak of the creative

---

31. See Marva Dawn, *Keeping the Sabbath Wholly* (Grand Rapids: Eerdmans, 1989); Keri Wyatt Kent, *Rest: Living in Sabbath Simplicity* (Grand Rapids: Zondervan, 2008); Wayne Muller, *Sabbath* (New York: Bantam, 2000); Matthew Sleeth, *24/6* (Carol Stream, IL: Tyndale, 2012); Norman Wirzba, *Living the Sabbath* (Grand Rapids: Brazos, 2006).

32. Abraham Joshua Heschel, *The Sabbath* (New York: Noonday Press, 1951), 22.

33. Jürgen Moltmann, *God in Creation*, trans. Margaret Kohl (Minneapolis: Fortress, 1993), 277; Larry L. Rasmussen, *Earth Community, Earth Ethics* (Maryknoll, NY: Orbis, 1996), 232.

34. Patrick D. Miller, *The Ten Commandments* (Louisville: Westminster John Knox, 2009), 117.

action of God is to ground Sabbath rest in the makeup of the universe, a kind of cosmological natural law that applies to more than just the Hebrew people, indeed to more than just people.[35] Sabbathkeeping, in the words of Jon Levenson, is to relive "the primal structuring of time" and to bring life "into harmony with the intrinsic rhythm of the cosmos, instituted by divine fiat and observed by God."[36] There is something particular about Sabbath that is interwoven into the structure of the cosmos. Likewise humans are to lead Sabbath lives, as we have been created to do.

If Sabbath is cosmological, the implications are far-reaching, especially for Americans ensnared in an "unintentional wasteland of hyperactivity."[37] First, both work and rest are gifts of grace. God worked and rested—so do we. Sabbath puts work into its proper context as a response to rest, not as a preparation for it. Jewish theologian Abraham Joshua Heschel writes, "The Sabbath is not for the sake of the weekdays; the weekdays are for the sake of Sabbath. It is not an interlude but the climax of living."[38] God's affirmation, love, and acceptance set human action in the right framework. Secondly, Sabbath has power to instill within us neglected values. While the good life certainly entails vocation and work, life is also more than work. Work is vital for building a just and good economy, but, observes Wayne Muller, "during Sabbath, we specifically honor those precious things—courage, creativity, wisdom, peace, kindness, and delight—that grow only in the soil of time."[39] Sabbathkeeping is a revolutionary action against commodification and economic hoarding.

Sabbath and Redemption

Deuteronomy 5 reveals a second rationale for Sabbathkeeping: "Remember that you were a slave in the land of Egypt, and the LORD your God brought you out from there with a mighty hand and an outstretched arm; therefore the LORD your God commanded you to keep the sabbath day" (v. 15). Sabbath is rooted in the redemption of the Exodus event. Throughout the Old Testament the *sabbatical principle* consistently lifts up God's justice and mercy for humanity and the Earth.[40] This principle is directed toward male and female slaves, livestock, and outsiders living in their community (Exod. 20:10); it

35. Ibid., 126–27.
36. Jon D. Levenson, "The Theologies of Commandment in Biblical Israel," *Harvard Theological Review* 73, no. 1–2 (January–April 1980): 32.
37. Muller, *Sabbath*, 160.
38. Heschel, *The Sabbath*, 14.
39. Muller, *Sabbath*, 116.
40. Miller, *The Ten Commandments*, 134.

includes the land itself (Exod. 23:10–11); it involves the provision of release from economic oppression, including indebtedness and slavery (Deut. 15:1–18); and ultimately it is reflected in Jubilee (Lev. 25).[41] The sabbatical principle—providing rest even for animals—seeks to free the most vulnerable, the least, and the defenseless from unjust burdens.

We are invited, through God's redemption, into this kind of faithful living. "Those who live by these commandments," writes Patrick Miller, "do so as a freed people, always being set free. The Sabbath is both a remembrance of that being freed and its constant enactment."[42] Jubilee and the sabbatical principle insist that our work and rest engage economic fairness, ecological restoration, and social justice. As people liberated by the gospel, the way we exist in the world should proclaim Sabbath freedom for all those vulnerable to oppression—both human and other-than-human Creation.

Keeping Sabbath has many dimensions to its practice, a few of which we want to highlight.

- Sanctify a day—Traditionally the Jewish Sabbath is celebrated from Friday sundown to Saturday sundown. The Sabbath is "holy" (*kadosh*), set aside for a holy purpose from the rest of the week. However Saturday is not always the best day for modern people to keep Sabbath. The first step toward Sabbathkeeping is identifying one particular day in which one can cease the patterns of busy life.

- Ask two questions—As you think through Sabbathkeeping, begin with two questions: (1) What will I cease doing on the Sabbath? (2) What do I want to do on the Sabbath?

- Begin with Jesus—My (A. J.'s) family starts off each Sabbath (for us, Tuesday) by partaking together in the Eucharist on the oak dining room table in our home. We have found that this thoughtful practice not only sets the stage for Sabbath but also serves as a weekly reminder of where we find our real rest, the redemptive love and grace of Christ.

- Refuse consumerism—During the day, fast from the frenetic pace of consumerism. In other words, don't do anything that requires a transaction. Fasting from buying will be hard; don't expect to accomplish this every week.

- Light candles—In the evening, turn off electric devices and light candles. This is quite the exercise for modern people addicted to electricity.

41. Ibid., 133–49, provides an extensive and engaging overview of how the sabbatical principle was essential to the overall well-being of the Hebrew people.
42. Ibid., 149.

- Disconnect from the news—Undertaking a regular but intentional break from the media cycle allows one to be present to the moment, to relish loving relationships, and simply to rest in the love of God.
- Build in preparation time—Sabbathkeeping requires thoughtfulness, preparation, and work. Both ancient and contemporary Jewish communities observe "the Day of Preparation" beforehand, during which any necessary work is finished to enter Sabbath rest. Such a day includes planning meals, buying food, answering emails, etc.

Living Simply

> The trouble with simple living is that, though it can be joyful, rich, and creative, it isn't simple.
>
> —Doris Janzen Longacre[43]

It is embarrassing to admit that most of what we think we know about Amish people comes from movies like *Witness* and *The Devil's Playground*.[44] Of late, though, a number of authors have stirred up interest in and an appreciation for the simplicity, husbandry, and long-term sustainability of Amish farming.[45] Although Amish farms are small (their average size is 80 acres), as a whole, Amish farmers are more prosperous than other farmers—investing in community over equipment and utilizing centuries-old practices, like crop rotation and diversification. But here we are drawn to the Amish because of their commitment to simplicity in their lives, homes, and work. We have no desire to romanticize the Amish; in truth, many of their practices are simply not practical to the typical North American. Nevertheless our cluttered and marginless lives prove we have much to learn. Nancy Sleeth, for one, found much to admire in her exploration of Amish principles and practices: "The Amish are islands of sanity in a whirlpool of change."[46]

Simplicity is a consistent theme throughout the New Testament. The Gospels maintain that when Jesus beckoned disciples to "come and follow," it

43. Doris Janzen Longacre, *Living More with Less*, 30th anniv. ed., rev. and ed. by Valerie Weaver-Zercher (Scottdale, PA: Herald Press, 2010), 30.

44. The barn-raising scene in *Witness* (1985) is enlightening in its depiction of both the power of community and the lingering consequences of strict gender roles. The documentary *The Devil's Playground* (2002), though sensationalized, raises important dialogue around community and conversion.

45. See Wendell Berry, *Remembering* (San Francisco: North Point, 1988), 71–92; Wendell Berry, "Seven Amish Farms (1981)," in *Bringing It to the Table* (Berkeley: Counterpoint, 2009), 105–18; Wes Jackson, "Falsehoods of Farming," in *Nature as Measure* (Berkeley: Counterpoint, 2011), 155–64.

46. Nancy Sleeth, *Almost Amish* (Carol Stream, IL: Tyndale, 2012), xx.

inevitably involved leaving something behind. In response to that call, the disciples left behind tax booths, fishing nets and boats, and homes in order to journey with Christ toward the cross. This theme is also found in the story of the rich young ruler. Jesus challenged him to face the "one thing" that was holding him back from discipleship: "There is still one thing lacking. Sell all that you own and distribute the money to the poor, and you will have treasure in heaven; then come, follow me" (Luke 18:22). Unlike Zacchaeus, who made restitution and gave freely to the poor—and in so doing received the gift of "salvation" (Luke 19:8–9)—the rich young ruler rejected the call (Luke 18:23). On one hand, we acknowledge that the "giving up" motif of Jesus's teaching must be qualified—those *without* cannot "give up" what they have not. Furthermore these teachings can, and have, been used historically by the powerful to subjugate those without. On the other hand, there is a strong element of truth for first-world, Western peoples: following Christ means "giving up" outward securities and learning to trust in a God who provides for the birds of the air and the lilies of the field (Matt. 6:25–30).

Reflecting on Amish simplicity, Sleeth comments that there are two kinds of stuff or clutter: "the kind that fills our houses and the kind that fills our calendars."[47] Not only did those called to follow Jesus leave behind the material clutter of their lives, but they also gave up the stuff of their daily occupations, in order to entrust themselves to a new vocation of love, servanthood, and taking up the cross of Jesus. That kind of letting go, trust, and simplicity demanded—and demands of us today—nothing less than conversion. Simplifying and decluttering our lives starts with Jesus's call to discipleship.

An essential aspect of the practice of simplicity is contentment. In Philippians, Paul writes that he had learned "to be content with whatever I have" (Phil. 4:11). The word Paul used for being "content" implies an ability to rest in the sufficiency of Christ—"I can do all things through him who strengthens me" (Phil. 4:13). Similarly, in 1 Timothy we see the meeting of contentment and simplicity: "For we brought nothing into the world, so that we can take nothing out of it; but if we have food and clothing, we will be content with these" (6:7–8). The rich were called to good works and generosity, "so that they may take hold of the life that really is life" (v. 19).

The pages of Christian history are riddled with simplicity.[48] As the church became wealthier in the third and fourth centuries, many Christians protested by fleeing to the desert. Belden Lane's description of this early wilderness

---

47. Ibid., 94.
48. For more on simplicity among the saints, see Richard J. Foster, *Freedom of Simplicity* (San Francisco: Harper & Row, 1981), 52–73.

Christianity has much to say to us today as we seek to relate to the dominant culture:

> The desert Christians understood the church as an alien community no longer caught up in the anxious, self-interested preservation of the world-as-it-is. Their practice of indifference to the dominant social values of their age, exercised from the desert's edge, stood in stark contrast to the accommodating spirit of post-Constantinian, urban Christianity. Indeed, they understood their oddness to be an essential part of their faithfulness to Christ and the new community being formed in their midst.[49]

St. Francis of Assisi practiced radical simplicity by selling all his earthly possessions in order to preach Christ in his hometown.[50] William Stafford describes Francis as the standard of "downward mobility," emphasizing that he "was enamored with the poverty modeled by Christ and the disciples, and he insisted his followers live in radical poverty."[51] The Franciscans in the twelfth century were the first religious order formally to adopt the three "evangelical counsels" of chastity, poverty, and obedience.

Such simple existence has proven elusive in modern life.[52] Writing in 1936, Quaker reformer Richard Gregg remarked, "Simplicity seems to be a foible of saints and occasional geniuses, but not something for the rest of us."[53] David Shi states that since the seventeenth century, "again and again, Americans have espoused the merits of simple living, only to become enmeshed in its opposite. People have found it devilishly hard to limit their desires to their needs."[54] It is devilishly hard, indeed, as we come face-to-face with our drivenness. Technology, fast-paced workplaces, rootless living, financial indebtedness, and a drive-through culture all make simple living not only challenging but barely attainable. Yet something deep within us knows, with biting clarity, that this frenetic lifestyle is idolatrous, unsustainable, and deadly. And our souls are hurting.

As difficult as the practice of simple living is in the face of modernity, at its heart is centering our beings solely in God's love.[55] To simplify one's

---

49. Belden Lane, *The Solace of Fierce Landscapes* (New York: Oxford University Press, 1998), 192; see also Stanley Hauerwas and William H. Willimon, *Resident Aliens* (Nashville: Abingdon, 1998).

50. John Michael Talbot with Steve Rabey, *The Lessons of Saint Francis* (New York: Dutton, 1997), 17–35.

51. William S. Stafford, "The Case for Downward Mobility," *Christian History* 13 (1994): 30.

52. Duane Elgin, *Voluntary Simplicity*, 2nd ed. (New York: Harper, 2010); Warren Johnson, *Muddling Toward Frugality* (San Francisco: Sierra Club, 1978).

53. Richard B. Gregg, *The Value of Voluntary Simplicity* (Wallingford, PA: Pendle Hill, 1936), 1.

54. David E. Shi, *The Simple Life* (New York: Oxford University Press, 1985), 277.

55. Foster, *Freedom of Simplicity*, 80.

life must be *chosen* out of freedom and mutuality, out of an authentic love of God and neighbor. Forced simplicity, or poverty, is not the kind of simplicity we need. Christian simplicity is a choice—an emptying (*kenōsis*, see Phil. 2:7) of our own power and desire on behalf of the other. And is not this emptying, this love, what was modeled for us in the incarnation? Sleeth writes, "This is what simple living is all about: God made flesh—cooking, shopping, eating, walking, talking, working, and fellowshipping on this earth."[56]

In keeping with our commitment to do ecotheology, we want to suggest a few basic principles and practices for living simply.

- Make small decisions consciously—Simple living is ultimately about a myriad of everyday small decisions.[57] Each small decision ought to be made with a consciousness of Christ-centered values and convictions.

- Nurture relationships—If there is one thing I (Dan) have pondered since my wife's death it is that I have not regretted, for one moment, the time I spent nurturing that relationship. My previous workweeks of sixty to seventy hours become more incomprehensible (and inexcusable) as time passes. Staying home, working less, and playing more allow us time to nurture relationships.

- Take a virtual break—Take a weekly "Sabbath" from technology, including television, cell phones, email, computers, social media, video games—anything with a screen.

- Question technology—True, not all labor-saving gadgets are bad, but neither is labor itself bad. Those devices often distance us from other people and from the Earth, and reinforce our—and society's—misguided belief that technology will save us from the ecocrisis.

- De-clutter—Remember that less is more. De-clutter your homes and make an effort to invest in quality when purchasing new items.

- Go local—Support local businesses, schools, and houses of worship as much as possible. Make it your goal to know the name of your butcher, baker, and candlestick maker.

- Downshift—Downshifters are people who make living simply a governing priority in their lives. They figure out how to work fewer hours and are willing to live off of less money, in order to make space for what they value most. Downshifters take responsibility for their circumstances and confront head-on the chaos and clutter of their lives.[58]

56. Sleeth, *Almost Amish*, 94.
57. Janzen Longacre, *Living More with Less*, 30.
58. See John D. Drake, *Downshifting* (San Francisco: Berrett-Koehler, 2000).

Resisting Consumerism

> I was part of that strange race of people aptly described as spending their lives doing things they detest, to make money they don't want, to buy things they don't need, to impress people they don't like.
>
> —Emile Henry Gauvreau[59]

In the HBO documentary, *About Face: Supermodels Now and Then*, some of the best-known fashion models of the twentieth century are interviewed. Most of them admit that, whether they were fully aware of it or not, they were participating in actively recruiting to the cult of beauty normal women (read: not insanely gorgeous). Many of us in the West worship at that cult's altar. From the time we are young, we are inundated with messages about beauty. Yet on our own, none of us is ever quite beautiful or young enough to matter, so a multibillion dollar industry functions for that express purpose. The machine of consumption entraps us. So we, the enslaved, consume the industry's promises that we might be of worth if we were more attractive, thinner, drove a nicer car, or looked a little younger. By responding to that propaganda, we ourselves become commodities—pawns in a system that will never give us the power or the belonging we seek.

The documentary *About Face* may have targeted the commodification of women, but the process is not so different for men. Consumerism dehumanizes everybody. We are addicted to it, and it is sapping the human soul and ruining God's Creation.[60] Our addiction to consumption is not accidental. In 1955 economist and retail analyst Victor Lebow published a now infamous article on consumers and consumption:

> Our enormously productive economy demands that we make consumption our way of life, that we convert the buying and use of goods into rituals, that we seek our spiritual satisfactions, our ego satisfactions, in consumption. The measure of social status, of social acceptance, of prestige, is now to be found in our consumptive patterns. The very meaning and significance of our lives today is expressed in consumptive terms. . . .
>
> We need things consumed, burned up, worn out, replaced, and discarded at an ever increasing pace. We need to have people eat, drink, dress, ride, live, with ever more complicated and, therefore, constantly more expensive consumption. . . .
>
> What becomes clear is that from the larger viewpoint of our economy, the total effect of all the advertising and promotion and selling is to create and

---

59. Cited in Lauren Tyler Wright, *Giving—The Sacred Art* (Woodstock, VT: SkyLight Path, 2008), 87.
60. Albert J. LaChance, *Cultural Addiction* (Berkeley: North Atlantic Books, 2006 [1991]), 2.

maintain the multiplicity and intensity of wants that are the spur to the standard of living in the United States. . . .

As we examine the concept of consumer loyalty, we see that the whole problem of molding the American mind is involved here.[61]

We have been betrayed, and we are our own Judas. It should make us cringe to read phrases like "rituals," "spiritual satisfactions," "the very meaning and significance of our lives," or "molding the American mind."

But it is not just Westerners that suffer under the regime of consumer culture; our capacity to consume has global ramifications. Since 1950, a minority (20–25 percent) of the world's population, those in developed sectors of society, controls 80 percent of the world's production. The issue of overconsumption and its effect on others is not a new one. The psalmist writes, "Have they no knowledge, all the evildoers / who eat up my people as they eat bread, / and do not call upon the LORD?" (Ps. 14:4). Not only is the West addicted to overconsumption, but we are also actively propagating consumerism's false promises of self-fulfillment, to the detriment of cultures and Creation. In 2005 the CEO of Walmart Asia addressed the exploding market in China:

We started out with four feet of skin care; today it's twenty feet. Today we don't have deodorants, but someday down the road we will have deodorants in China. Five years ago perfumes were not a big business here. But if you look today it's the emerging market. . . . They drink more milk; they eat more bread and snack crackers and they eat more meat in their diet; there's a lot less bicycles, so that takes away from the exercise side of it, so the size of people are getting larger, so what's that tell you? Exercise equipment's getting good, exercise wear, jogging outfits and at some point, we'll have Slimfast and all those types of products.[62]

Today for the first time in human history, our unbridled use of the Earth's *people* and *resources* threatens us with a self-created apocalypse.

As Christ-followers, our faith drives us away from systems of power that are based on an ability to consume. Faith in Jesus moves us toward the kingdom of God—the kind of life Leonardo Boff depicts as "a non-consumeristic type of cultural practice that is respectful of ecosystems, ushers in an economy of what is sufficient for all, and fosters the common good not only in humans but also of the other beings in creation."[63] Boff's description of what is needed sounds

61. Victor Lebow, "Price Competition in 1955," *Journal of Retailing* 31 (Spring 1955): 7–8.
62. Joe Hatfield, interview with Paul Solman, "China's Vast Consumer Class" (transcript), PBS Newshour, October 5, 2005, http://www.pbs.org/newshour/bb/asia-july-dec05-consumers_10-05/.
63. Leonardo Boff, *Cry of the Earth, Cry of the Poor*, trans. Phillip Berryman (Maryknoll, NY: Orbis, 1997), 113.

suspiciously like the abundant life Jesus talks about in the Gospels, a world in which there is enough for all, especially the "least of these" (Matt. 25:40).

The early Christian community caught this vision of abundant life and the commonwealth of God. Early in the second century, Aristides of Athens wrote to Emperor Hadrian about what he saw in the early Christian community: "And from the widows they do not turn away their countenance: and they rescue the orphan from him who does him violence: and he who has gives to him who has not, and without grudging. . . . And if there is among them a man that is poor and needy, and they have not an abundance of necessaries, they fast two or three days that they may supply the needy with their necessary food."[64] In doing so, Christianity followed the apostle Paul, who spoke urgently to the Corinthians about "a fair balance between your present abundance and their need" (2 Cor. 8:13–14). Underscoring his plea, Paul cites a passage from the Exodus story of the provision of manna: "The one who had much did not have too much, and the one who had little did not have too little" (2 Cor. 8:15; see also Exod. 16:18). Daniel Erlander writes, "The way God gave the manna, and the way the people gathered it and shared it, taught the people how to live as a special people on this earth."[65] There is compelling evidence that the New Testament church and the early Christian communities strove to create a manna society that maintained a "fair balance" between abundance and need.

In our current system of commodification and consumption we have by and large failed to remember our connection with all created beings. As long as consumption continues without restraint or thought toward those it impacts, we will legitimize "the routine sacrifice of whole landscapes and species to the idols of technological hegemony and economic growth in a continuing holocaust of extraction and extinction. Mountain tops are blown off for coal and prairies poisoned for tar sand oil."[66] Too often our solutions have been to discover more carbon-based fuels or to develop new technologies; it is striking how seldom we think of consuming less. Ultimately in God's economy, our actions will not be inconsequential. The prophet Jeremiah warns, "Like the partridge hatching what it did not lay, / so are all who amass wealth unjustly; / in mid-life it will leave them, / and at their end they will prove to be fools" (Jer. 17:11).

Real power and true belonging come through a countercultural movement of community, a place where abundance is present through the actions of creating

64. *The Apology of Aristides on Behalf of the Christians*, 2nd ed., trans. and ed., J. Rendel Harris (Cambridge: Cambridge University Press, 1893), 49.
65. Daniel Erlander, *Manna and Mercy* (Mercer Island, WA: Order of Saints Martin and Teresa, 1992), 7.
66. Ched Myers, "Pay Attention to the Birds," *Sojourners* 38, no. 11 (December 2009): 33.

enough for all. Before suggesting a few practices to resist consumerism, we share just a few statistics reminding us of painful realities in the world today.

- In 2010 about 48.5 percent of the people in sub-Saharan Africa struggled in genuine poverty, on less than $1.25 a day; 69.9 percent survived on less than $2 a day.[67]
- With 4.5 percent of the world's population, the United States releases 16 percent of global greenhouse gas emissions.[68]
- In America there is over 19 square feet of retail space for every man, woman, and child.[69]
- The United States and Canada, with 5.2 percent of the global population, use 31.5 percent of the total amount spent worldwide on goods and services; sub-Saharan Africa, with 10.9 percent of the population, uses 1.2 percent of the total amount spent.[70]

These statistics are sobering. They can also be debilitating because, despite our power and privilege, we often feel powerless to deal with the all-pervading, systemic nature of transnational consumerism. Nonetheless we believe that there are some simple actions we can take to engage this devastating issue.

- Buy judiciously—Before buying new, consider the following questions: Can you afford it? Can you borrow it? Can you buy it secondhand? Can you live without it? Is it renewable and recyclable? Have you discussed major purchases with someone you trust?
- Avoid advertisements—Madison Avenue spent $285.2 billion in 1998 (more than the aggregate gross domestic product of sub-Saharan Africa). These days, with every click of the mouse, marketers are narrowing in on us. And that says nothing of the orchestrated bombardment on television—the average American sits through over 15 *days* of advertisements every year. To avoid advertisements, get off of junk mail and telemarketers' lists, and turn off the television.[71]

67. World Bank, "Poverty," http://data.worldbank.org/topic/poverty?display=map, accessed January 5, 2014.
68. World Resources Institute, "Country GHG Emissions," http://cait2.wri.org/wri/Country%20GHG%20Emissions?indicator[]=Total%20GHG%20Emissions%20Excluding%20LUCF&indicator[]=Total%20GHG%20Emissions%20Including%20LUCF&year[]=2010&chartType=geo, accessed July 15, 2013.
69. Dolores Hayden, *Building Suburbia* (New York: Vintage, 2004), 171.
70. WorldWatch Institute, "State of the World 2004: Consumption By the Numbers," http://worldwatch.org/node/1783, accessed Feb. 9, 2013.
71. The Center for a New American Dream, "Beyond Consumerism: Avoiding Advertising," http://www.newdream.org/programs/beyond-consumerism/avoiding-advertising, accessed February 9, 2013.

- Dress timelessly—Juliet Schor describes a "new clothing ethic," which is really an old ethic of frugality. In yesteryear, clothes lasted longer (in part because they were not washed as often), cost more (quality construction), and served multiple purposes (only the rich could afford multiple outfits). Her refashioned ethic values "quality over quantity, longevity over novelty, and versatility over specialization."[72] You might also consider shopping in vintage, consignment, and resale shops.

- Think globally—The economic world is getting smaller. It is important to investigate the "history" of products we purchase, including the kinds of raw materials used, whether or not workers were paid a fair wage, and transportation costs.

- Act communally—Because consumerism is so ubiquitous, staying aware of it is much like a fish trying to stay aware of the sea, and it is hard to battle alone. We are convinced that real countercultural Christianity is only possible in community, where people attempt to live more simply, hold up mirrors for each other, and share with neighbors. Make a covenant with a few friends to stand against the rat race of consumerism. For example, together spend a whole year resisting buying new products (except food, medicine, and hygiene products).

Eating Justly

Increasingly, obesity and hunger are two points on a continuum of poverty.

—Raj Patel[73]

Eating is one of the many God-given pleasures available to earthly life. Likewise feasting is a provocative image of the kingdom of heaven (Matt. 22:2). Eating connects heaven and earth. Food and drink are at the heart of the whole biblical tapestry. In Scripture's first chapter, God provides food to eat—for both human and other-than-human creatures—from the plants and trees in the garden (Gen. 1:29–30). The Bible's final chapter ends with an open invitation to drink from the wellspring of eternal life (Rev. 22:17).

Jesus was known for eating and drinking: "For John the Baptist has come eating no bread and drinking no wine, and you say, 'He has a demon'; the Son of Man has come eating and drinking, and you say, 'Look, a glutton and a drunkard, a friend of tax collectors and sinners!'" (Luke 7:33–34). Through his "table fellowship" with sinners and the outcasts, Jesus confronted the

72. Juliet Schor, "Cleaning the Closet: Toward a New Fashion Ethic," in *Voluntary Simplicity*, by Northwest Earth Institute (Portland, OR: NWEI, 2008), 37.
73. Raj Patel, *Stuffed and Starved*, 2nd ed. (Brooklyn, NY: Melville, 2012), 9.

Hungry for Change

Below we list some data related to food around the world. Facts and figures like these can help increase our awareness and choices surrounding food.

- Every day there are 219,000 added newcomers at the global dinner table.
- Americans spend 5–10 percent of their income on food. The earth's 2 billion poorest spend 50–70 percent. From 2007–2011 world grain prices doubled.
- For every 1 degree Celsius rise in temperature, farmers can expect a 10 percent decrease in grain yields.
- The last 50 years have seen a 90 percent reduction in the population of large commercial fish.
- Three companies—Archer Daniels Midland, Cargil, and Bunge—control 90 percent of the world's grain trade.
- Numerous chemicals and processes are banned in Europe but not in the United States—stevia, most genetically modified foods, bleached flour, and partially hydrogenated oil, to name a few.
- Twenty-three percent of energy used in the US food system goes to processing and packaging.
- Per capita, CO_2 emissions should not exceed more than 2 tons per year in order to avoid perilous climate change (according to the Potsdam Institute for Climate Impact Research).
  - In China the average per capita emission is 4–5 tons/year.
  - CO_2 emissions from Germany average 11 tons per person per year.
  - The United States averages over 20 tons per person per year.

Statistics come from Northwest Earth Institute, *Hungry for Change*
(Portland, OR: NWEI, 2011), 34, 41, 48, 61, 103, 108.

pharisaic holiness code and the principal expression of social interaction in his day.[74] Joachim Jeremias has commented that informed observers of Jesus's actions, including the Pharisees, "would immediately understand the acceptance of the outcasts into table fellowship with Jesus as an offer of salvation to guilty sinners and as the assurance of forgiveness."[75] The early Christian community welcomed Jesus's vision of inclusive table fellowship through the eucharistic bread and wine.

The modern experience of food has restricted what is on the table to a *product* rather than to an invitation to *participation*. All too often food and eating have become abstract concepts—not something experienced—which

74. Ched Myers, *Binding the Strong Man* (Maryknoll, NY: Orbis, 1988), 158–59.
75. Joachim Jeremias, *The Eucharistic Words of Jesus* (London: SCM, 1966), 204.

are largely commodified. But eating can and should be about participation, pleasure, and community.[76]

The apostle Paul once wrote, "In any and all circumstances I have learned the secret of being well-fed and of going hungry, of having plenty and of being in need" (Phil. 4:12). How are we to understand plenty and hunger in our world today? Moses told the people in the wilderness not to keep leftover manna for the next day, except before Sabbath, so that they might learn to trust God (Exod. 16:19–20). Yet in the miraculous story of the multiplication of the fish and loaves, there were plenty of leftovers. Proverbs states, "Those who till their land will have plenty of food, / but those who follow worthless pursuits have no sense" (Prov. 12:11). Again how are we to understand the reality that many in the majority world today who till their land do not have plenty? Is the abundance of the West the result of its righteousness?

"Food security" remains a conspicuous problem in the world today. People are "food secure" when they consistently have access to sufficient food and understand basic nutrition and sanitation.[77] It is estimated that 870 million people from 2010–2012 were not food secure and were suffering from chronic undernourishment.[78] The primary victims are children; malnutrition is a significant factor in more than a third of child deaths in developing countries. According to UNICEF, malnutrition "blunts the intellect, saps the productivity of everyone it touches and perpetuates poverty."[79]

Poignantly on the flip side of the food issue, numerous researchers are stating that obesity is now a bigger health crisis than hunger.[80] If almost one billion people worldwide are hungry and malnourished, it is estimated that over 1.5 billion are overweight. With the exception of countries in sub-Saharan Africa, obesity around the globe has increased 82 percent over the last two decades. For the first time in recent history, diseases like strokes, diabetes, and heart disease top the list of reasons people spend years sick or disabled. Sadly, for each person who is hungry, two people overeat. Raj Patel writes, "Global hunger and obesity

76. Wendell Berry, "The Pleasures of Eating" (1989), in *The Art of the Commonplace*, ed. Norman Wirzba (Washington, DC: Shoemaker & Hoard, 2002), 321–27.

77. World Health Organization, "Food Security," http://www.who.int/trade/glossary /story028/en/, accessed August 13, 2013.

78. World Hunger Education Service, "2013 World Hunger and Poverty Facts and Statistics," http://worldhunger.org/articles/Learn/world%20hunger%20facts%202002.htm, accessed January 5, 2014. The primary factors in the proliferation of hunger are poverty, harmful economic systems, conflict, hunger itself, and climate change.

79. UNICEF, "Nutrition: Introduction," http://www.unicef.org/nutrition/, accessed January 17, 2013.

80. Institute of Food Technologists, "Obesity tops hunger as global health crisis," December 19, 2012, http://www.ift.org/food-technology/daily-news/2012/december/19/obesity-tops-hunger -as-global-health-crisis.aspx.

are symptoms of the same problem and, what's more, the route to eradicating world hunger is also the way to prevent global epidemics of diabetes and heart disease, and to address a host of environmental and social ills."[81] Both undernutrition and overnutrition are facets of malnutrition, and both are issues of justice and human rights. As activist Frances Lappé has asked, "How do we build communities in tune with nature's wisdom in which no one, anywhere, has to worry about putting food—safe, healthy food—on the table?"[82]

What might eating responsibly mean in our context today? Here are some helpful practices:[83]

- Eat locally—Get close to the food you eat; know your farmers, their stories, and where your food comes from.
- Eat healthily—Eat food that is in season and fresh. Seek out nutritious food, especially produce.[84] Read labels. Avoid preservatives and foods that are highly processed. One of the major causes of both hunger and obesity is the difficulty in accessing genuinely nutritious foods because of the explosion in processed foods over the last thirty years.[85]
- Eat what *you* cook—As Michael Pollan reflected on how everyday individuals might change the American food system, live more healthily and sustainably, and gain a deeper awareness of their peculiar role in the natural world, he increasingly returned to an unexpected answer: cook. In his kitchen he learned to remove the raw stuff of nature from its abstraction and to transform it into nutrition. The art of cooking connects us with "a whole web of social and ecological relationships."[86]
- Eat less—Jesus's overall ethic hung on the notion of doing "to others as you would have them do to you" (Matt. 7:12). Stay aware of how your eating habits impact others both locally and globally. Doris Janzen Longacre cuts to the bottom line: "Intricate reasoning on the causes and solutions of world hunger has its place. But there are times when the only answer is, 'Because they have little, I try to take less.'"[87]

81. Patel, *Stuffed and Starved*, 9.
82. Frances Moore Lappé, "The Biotech Distraction," in *Engineering the Farm*, ed. Marc Lappé and Britt Bailey (Washington, DC: Island, 2002), 158.
83. For other helpful suggestions, see Luke Gascho, *Creation Care: Keepers of the Earth* (Harrisonburg, VA: Herald, 2008), 105–6, 109–10.
84. According to the World Health Organization, vegetable deficiency in people's diets globally causes 14 percent of gastrointestinal cancer deaths, 11 percent of heart disease deaths, and about 9 percent of stroke deaths. In developing countries, growing vegetables can be one of the most inexpensive and sustainable ways to provide essential micronutrients.
85. Ellen Gustafson, "Obesity + Hunger = 1 global food issue," TED Talk, May 2010, http://www.ted.com/talks/ellen_gustafson_obesity_hunger_1_global_food_issue.
86. Michael Pollan, *Cooked* (London: Allen Lane, 2013), 18.
87. Janzen Longacre, *Living More with Less*, 42.

- Eat together—In many homes the dining table has been replaced by the television. Eating together regularly has become disturbingly infrequent. Yet, coming together once or twice a week with family and/or neighbors around nutritious, local food is a wonderful way to celebrate life and build community.
- Eat slowly—Around the globe more and more people are protesting fast food and committing themselves to community and the environment by participating in the slow food movement, the goal of which is to "link the pleasures of the table with a commitment to protect the community, culture, knowledge and environment that make this pleasure possible."[88]
- Don't eat—If you are able, fast for a meal and give the money saved to local food pantries, food banks, or international relief agencies.

Conserving Water

Water is grossly undervalued. In the developed world, a cubic metre of high-quality drinking water is often worth no more than the price of a cigarette.

—Technical Centre for Agricultural and Rural Cooperation[89]

In most global societies, women and girls bear the major responsibility for collecting water, cooking, cleaning, hygiene, and growing food.[90] In rural settings women may spend four to five hours daily getting water, work that takes great physical toll on their bodies. In urban environments women may wait hours in a queue for water from unreliable hand pumps. This "time poverty" from fetching water constrains opportunities such as education, microenterprise, political decision making, and rest and leisure. Women also bear the burden of unsafe water and sanitation in their homes and communities. Toilets for women and girls are frequently unavailable in urban settings and remote in rural ones. Women are particularly vulnerable to, and their livelihoods threatened by, the ecological catastrophe upsetting the world's water supply.

Water is a consistent image in Scripture; the biblical narrative begins (Gen. 1:2) and ends (Rev. 22:1, 17) in the waters of life.[91] It is easy to forget that much

88. Slow Food USA, "About Us," http://www.slowfoodusa.org/about-us, accessed January 9, 2014.

89. Technical Centre for Agricultural and Rural Cooperation (CTA) (ACP-EU), "The water we eat—tackling scarcity in ACP [African, Caribbean, and Pacific] countries," *CTA Policy Brief*, no. 2 (June 2011), 2, http://publications.cta.int/media/publications/downloads/PB002E_PDF.pdf.

90. Prabha Khosla and Rebecca Pearl, *Untapped Connections: Gender, Water, and Poverty* (New York: Women's Environment & Development Organization, 2003), 2–5.

91. Ched Myers, "Everything Will Live Where the River Goes," *Sojourners*, April 2012, http://sojo.net/magazine/2012/04/everything-will-live-where-river-goes.

of the Bible was composed in the arid environs of Palestine. Desertification and scarcity symbolized alienation from the fertility of Eden and the destructive power of systemic sin. The prophets often present watery images of salvation and restoration: "For waters shall break forth in the wilderness, / and streams in the desert" (Isa. 35:6). Water symbolized justice for the marginalized: "When the poor and needy seek water, / and there is none, / and their tongue is parched with thirst, / I the LORD will answer them, / I the God of Israel will not forsake them" (Isa. 41:17; see also Amos 5:24). Jeremiah lamented that the people abandoned their God, "the fountain of living water" (Jer. 2:13). Importantly, then, Jesus cries out during the Festival of Tabernacles: "Let anyone who is thirsty come to me, and let the one who believes in me drink" (John 7:37–38). Finally, in the letter to Titus we read that God saved us "through the water of rebirth and renewal by the Holy Spirit" (Titus 3:5; see also Rom. 6:3–4). Spiritually and literally, water is essential to life. Water embodies restoration and brings salvation. Nigerian American poet Enuma Okoro expresses beautifully the intersection of these themes:

> This ordinary time is
> gifted in its quiet, marked passing
> Christ slips about
> calling and baptizing,
> sending and affirming,
> pouring his Spirit like water
> into broken cisterns,
> sealing cracks and filtering our senses,
> that we may savor the foolish
> simplicity of his grace.[92]

Water Security

Water security means having sufficient quality water available for the health and welfare of people, ecosystems, and economies, while controlling water-related risks.[93] The United Nations has determined that a human requires at least ten gallons of water daily. In many countries, the ability to meet this minimum mark is impaired by climate change, population growth, urbanization, pollution, escalating consumption of animal products, and the disproportionate availability of water resources. Over the last century water consumption per person has soared

92. Okoro, "Passing Ordinary Time," 25. Reprinted by permission of the poet.
93. David Grey and Claudia W. Sadoff, "Sink or Swim? Water Security for Growth and Development," *Water Policy* 9, no. 6 (2007): 545–71, http://www.iwaponline.com/wp/00906/wp009060545.htm, accessed July 20, 2013.

in developed countries, and reserves of freshwater are threatened.[94] Almost 23 percent of the world's population—1.6 billion people—lives where water security is endangered or unsustainable, either for ecological or economic reasons.[95]

Food security and water security are interdependent: "The world is thirsty because it is hungry."[96] This means that the majority of water is used for the food we eat (plants, livestock), and there is not enough water to produce the needed food. At current rates of population growth and food consumption, agricultural production and water use will need to double by mid-century, unless, of course, we alter those established patterns.[97] Globally 40 percent of our food comes from irrigated land. In India, for example, 50 percent of cultivated land is irrigated; however, only 4 percent of cultivated land in sub-Saharan Africa is under irrigation. A report from the African, Caribbean, and Pacific (ACP) countries emphasizes targeting low-yield farmers in rain-fed agriculture. We could meet 75 percent of the extra food needed over the next decades by improving the production of these farmers through small-scale, low-cost water management. In many places, that will mean focusing on women; in the words of one NGO director: "Women are the main subsistence farmers in sub-Saharan Africa, and general food security depends on their production." The scarcity of water is a global issue, but solutions must be local, with policies that prioritize women and that the farmers themselves influence.[98]

Virtual Water

The concept of "virtual water" is increasingly being raised in water security conversations.[99] Also known as "water footprint," it refers to the amount of freshwater used to produce food, commodities, and services—the water that is "virtually embedded" in the things we consume every day.[100] As vital as it is to reduce our carbon footprint, we cannot lose sight of our water footprint. Few understand that only about 4 percent of our water footprint arises from

94. Water Civilization International Centre, "Good Water, Water to 'Eat': What Is Virtual Water?" http://www.unesco.org/new/fileadmin/MULTIMEDIA/FIELD/Venice/pdf/special_events/bozza_scheda_DOW04_1.0.pdf, accessed July 20, 2013.

95. Technical Centre for Agricultural, "The water we eat," 1.

96. Slogan created by the Food and Agriculture Organization of the UN for World Water Day 2012.

97. Vaclav Smil, "Harvesting the Biosphere: The Human Impact," *Population and Development Review* 37, no. 4 (2011): 613–36.

98. Technical Centre for Agricultural, "The water we eat," 2–3.

99. Tony Allen, *Virtual Water* (London: I. B. Taurus, 2011), 1–20.

100. Arjen Y. Hoekstra, "The Water Footprint: The Relation Between Human Consumption and Water Use" (abstract), in *The Water We Eat*, trans. Michelle Nebiolo, ed. Marta Antonelli and Francesca Greco (Milan: Edizioni Ambiente, 2013), 25.

Fig. 8.1

THE FOOD AND ENVIRONMENTAL
DOUBLE PYRAMID

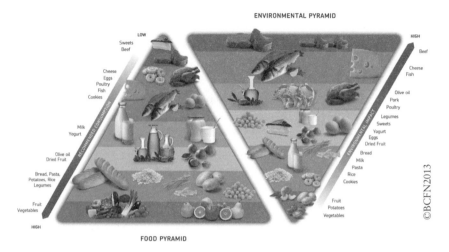

water use in our kitchens, bathrooms, and gardens (which is not to say that water conservation at home is unimportant). The vast majority of water used is in the food we eat—hence the phrase "the water we eat"—and in the goods and services we consume.[101] For example, to produce 1 pound of boneless beef requires 6.5 pounds of grain (oats, etc.) and 36 pounds of roughages (hay, grass, etc.) to feed the animal, which require about 1,830 gallons of water to produce. When you add more water for drinking and cleaning, it takes 1,845 gallons of water to produce one pound of beef.[102] Figure 8.1, The Food and Environmental Double Pyramid,[103] provides a unique perspective on the traditional food pyramid. The left side of the double pyramid addresses what foods are the healthiest to eat; the right side speaks to the environmental impact of the food we eat.

Up to 60 percent of the adult human body is made up of water. We are what we eat, and water is embedded in what we eat. The concept of virtual water is inspiring many people to reconsider their eating habits. It also unveils how

101. For an introductory video, see Barilla Center for Food and Nutrition, "The Water We Eat," April 2, 2013, https://www.youtube.com/watch?v=nQayvClunkM.

102. M. M. Mekonnen and A. Y. Hoekstra, *The Green, Gray and Blue Water Footprint of Farm Animals and Animal Products* (Delft, Netherlands: UNESCO-IHE Institute for Water Education, 2010), i.28, http://www.waterfootprint.org/Reports/Report-48-WaterFootprint -AnimalProducts-Vol1.pdf.

103. Barilla Center for Food and Nutrition. Used by permission.

much food we waste. Although the idea of "virtual water" is not without its critics, it is more easily graspable by the average person and has therefore stirred up considerable conversation and debate: "Virtual water has contributed to make water a public matter again."[104] And, hopefully, the more aware we are, the more we will change.

Here are a few things we can do to conserve water:

- Eat less water—A diet that is lower on the food chain and more plant-based uses much less water to produce. Take virtual water into consideration when making purchases.[105]

- "Zero mile food"—The food on the average North American dinner table travels 1,300 miles—it is (geographically) marinated in crude oil.[106] Food bought locally reduces water usage and helps the neighborhood economy. Make it a goal to eat food that is grown or produced no more than fifty miles away.

- Get a stainless steel thermos—Bottled water is not good value for the money, produces needless plastic waste, does not support local sources, and is no healthier than tap water.[107] If the taste of your local tap water is not agreeable, get a simple carbon filter.

- Use water sparingly in your yard and garden—Drip irrigation and rain barrels or cisterns can help in stewarding water. Consider using drought resistant native plants and getting rid of your lawn (or at least not watering it during the summer).

Reducing Waste

In the middle of the Pacific Ocean lies a floating garbage patch twice the size of Britain. A place where the water is filled with six times as much plastic as plankton. This plastic-plankton soup is entering the food chain and heading for your dinner table.

—Amanda Woods[108]

104. Mauro Van Aken, "Virtual Water, H$_2$O and the De-socialization of Water" (abstract), in *The Water We Eat*, 39.

105. Some people are willing to consume a little in order (ultimately) to consume a lot less, so one might consider purchasing a Virtual Water app for the smartphone, which calculates the amount of water consumed in the production of certain amounts of food items.

106. Gauscho, *Creation Care*, 104.

107. Chris Baskind, "Five Reasons Not to Drink Bottled Water," in *Choices for Sustainable Living*, 69; see the animated video, "The Story of Bottled Water" (2010), https://www.youtube.com/watch?feature=endscreen&NR=1&v=Se12y9hSOM0.

108. Amanda Woods, "The Plastic Killing Fields," *Sydney Morning Herald*, December 29, 2007, reprinted in Northwest Earth Institute, *A World of Health* (Portland, OR: NWEI, 2010), 71.

Virtual Water

Below are the gallons of water needed to produce some of our favorite foods and commodities.

- 7 gallons / 1 potato
- 18 gallons / 1 apple
- 32 gallons / 1 glass of wine
- 37 gallons / 1 cup of coffee
- 42 gallons / 1 cup of orange juice
- 45 gallons / 1 pint of beer
- 49 gallons / 1 bag of potato chips
- 62 gallons / 1 cup of milk
- 100 gallons / 1 slice of cheese
- 180 gallons / 1 loaf of bread
- 444 gallons / 1 pound chicken
- 576 gallons / 1 pound pork
- 713 gallons / 1 cotton T-shirt
- 1,845 gallons / 1 pound beef
- 2,166 gallons / 1 pair of jeans

Statistics come from Water Civilization International Centre, "Good water, water to 'eat,'" in *Hungry for Change*, ed. Northwest Earth Institute (Portland, OR: NWEI, 2011), 97.

In the visually stunning documentary *Manufacturing Landscapes*, renowned artist Edward Burtynsky takes viewers to the shores of Bangladesh, where oil tankers go to die. His film and artistry are a nonjudgmental meditation on the global effects of industrialization and the discarding of waste. The images are riveting: the iron walls of ships thundering to the ground, the cacophony of acetylene torches, winches, and sledgehammers, and the young Bangladeshis, scrambling over wreckage or wading through thigh-deep sludge to haul waste oil away bucket by bucket. In our consumption of oil we know little of oil tankers—except in cases like the *Exxon Valdez*—and even less of their dumping grounds. Photographing the demolition, Burtynsky comments: "Looking at these ships in Bangladesh the connection was clear. At some point I probably filled a tank of gas from the oil that was delivered by one of these tankers."[109] As children are learning in school these days: there is no "away" in "throw

109. Edward Burtynsky, *Manufactured Landscapes*, DVD, directed by Jennifer Baichwal (New York: Zeitgeist Films, 2006).

away." It is a reality most of us ignore: "Humans have the funny idea that when you get rid of something, it's gone."[110]

For our moment in time, the strongest biblical declaration against wastefulness is found in the core of Jesus's own ethic: "In everything do to others as you would have them do to you" (Matt. 7:12), and "You shall love your neighbor as yourself" (Matt. 22:39). The "transfrontier shipment" of waste involves transporting garbage, even hazardous waste, to another country with less restrictive environmental laws, avoiding penalties and costs in the country of origin. The intentionality behind this practice is sobering; the Montreal *Gazette* quoted the former chief economist for the World Bank: "The economic logic behind dumping a load of toxic waste in the lowest-wage country is impeccable, and we should face up to that. . . . I've always thought that under-populated countries in Africa are vastly under polluted."[111] In a well-known case of "ocean dumping," seventeen people in the Ivory Coast were killed in 2006 when the Netherlands-based tanker, the *Probo Koala*, dumped 500 tons of chemical waste around the port city of Abidjan.[112] Biblically, Jesus's call to love our neighbors impresses on us the need to become aware of the impact our trash has on others and on the earth.

Plastic Waste

An excellent learning experience for any group is a "garbage audit," whereby a garbage can is sorted to see how much is recyclable. One of the students in our first Christian earthkeeping class, Leslie, conducted such an experiment as a class project. For eight weeks she kept all of her garbage in the garage, just to get a picture of how much trash she accumulated. Mind you, Leslie is an avid recycler. What struck her most about her pile was "how much our society lives on plastic. From plastic-wrapped mailings, to plastic-covered food, to bubble wrap, to fast food-containers, plastic is the 'go to' for just about everything."

In the North Pacific Subtropical Gyre (a major ocean system of rotating currents), a thousand miles off the coast of California, there is a churning mass of garbage, including furniture, refrigerators, light bulbs, fishing nets, and televisions. But it is mostly plastic, and about 80 percent of that plastic

110. Elizabeth Grossman, cited in "E-Waste: Where Does It Go?" in *World of Health*, 75.

111. Lawrence Summers, quoted in the Montreal *Gazette*, March 28, 1992, cited in Stephen Bede Scharper and Hilary Cunningham, *The Green Bible* (New York: Lantern, 2002), 52.

112. "Two jailed for dumping toxic waste in Ivory Coast," nrc.nl (website), October 23, 2008, http://vorige.nrc.nl/international/article2035105.ece/Two_jailed_for_dumping_toxic_waste_in_Ivory_Coast.

washes out from the land. Fifty or sixty years ago there was no plastic there.[113] The scale of pollution of the marine environment by plastic debris is immense.[114] At least 267 different species of marine animals and birds have suffered from eating or getting entangled in debris. More than a million seabirds and 100,000 marine animals die every year from plastic.[115] It is estimated that there are over 13,000 pieces of plastic litter for every square mile of ocean surface.

Most plastic, when discarded, spends centuries along our byways or in our oceans or landfills. Most plastic does not disintegrate, although in the oceans it will break up into smaller pieces, making it that much more dangerous to marine life. Applying the three Rs—reduce, reuse, and recycle—to plastics would certainly make a significant difference; however the recycling of plastic is lagging considerably behind paper and cardboard, mainly because we are confused about how to recycle plastics. It takes intentional effort to learn which plastics can be recycled and where.

Food Waste

Another student in that first earthkeeping class, Jonathan, would regale us with stories of "dumpster diving." One summer he and his wife decided to save money for a trip by eating food redeemed from the trash. What began as an experiment in frugality took them to the bottom of every dumpster in their area and represented a turning point in their Christian journey. Their first dumpster—that of an organic food grocer—was surrounded by a twelve-foot, barbed wire fence. "They must have some great trash," Jonathan thought. Luckily the door to the trash paddock was open; they dove in, outfitted in raingear and headlamps. That summer they had more food than they could eat. Some nights the bags of bread were so heavy they struggled hauling them to their car. Other nights it was fifty pounds of slightly dented fruit. Jonathan reflected on how much energy, water, soil, resources, and sweat are required to transport and refrigerate food, and the requisite energy required of the Earth to reabsorb it as trash in landfills. He wrote, "I believe that my mission is to partner with Christ's efforts to redeem the whole world.

113. Woods, "The Plastic Killing Fields," 72; Katharine Mieszkowski, "Plastic Bags Are Killing Us," *Salon.com*, August 10, 2007, reprinted in Northwest Earth Institute, *Choices for Sustainable Living* (Portland, OR: NWEI, 2009), 49.

114. Michelle Allsopp et al., *Plastic Debris in the World's Oceans*, UN Environment Programme, http://www.unep.org/regionalseas/marinelitter/publications/docs/plastic_ocean_report.pdf, accessed March 2, 2013.

115. For a sobering video from the North Pacific Gyre on the effects of plastic on wildlife, see photographer Chris Johnson's "Midway: Message from the Gyre," http://vimeo.com/25563376, accessed January 5, 2014.

By rescuing, redeeming, and giving this food a second chance I believe I am doing just that."

Around the world, 30–40 percent of all food produced is either lost or wasted between production and consumption.[116] European and North American consumers waste 200–250 pounds of food per person every year, while in sub-Saharan Africa and Southeast Asia the waste is only 13–24 pounds per capita per year.[117] Billions and billions of pounds of food can be "lost" to waste, whether at farms, in processing, during marketing, or off of our plates. In 1995, for example, 26 percent of the edible food that could have been consumed was lost through the food service industry and from our own tables. Experts recommend food recovery programs, like gleaning, recycling food wastes, and education.[118] On the down side, however, is the policy among (too) many supermarkets *not* to donate outdated or bruised food to community food banks or food recovery organizations for fear of litigation.[119] Landfills are full; the poor are not.

E-waste

As painful as it is to read about the detrimental effects of plastic and food waste, a number of writers argue that the most worrisome and dangerous waste problem we face is one we seldom notice: toxic waste.[120] The production, processing, and disposal of chemicals are rapidly increasing, especially in the developing world. Take e-waste, for example.[121] Electronic equipment (such as computers and cell phones), which contains numerous hazardous substances (lead, nickel, mercury, cadmium, and brominated flame retardants), is often made in developing countries, sold in developed countries, and then recycled or disposed of in unprotected conditions back in developing countries.[122] In many countries the type of waste that is accumulating the fastest is electronics, in

116. Laura Reynolds and Sophie Wenzlau, Food and Agriculture Program, Worldwatch Institute, "Newsletter," February 12, 2013.

117. UN Regional Information Centre for Western Europe, "Food Waste," http://unric.org /en/food-waste, accessed January 9, 2014.

118. Linda Scott Cantor et al., "Estimating and Addressing American's Food Losses," *Food Review* (1997): 1–12.

119. For a personal reflection on this phenomenon, see Amy Johnson Frykholm, "Gone to Waste: Why Is Safeway Throwing out Good Produce?" *Christian Century* 128, no. 17 (August 23, 2011): 30–32.

120. Paul Hawken, *The Ecology of Commerce* (New York: Harper Business, 1993), 40.

121. For a "Story of Electronics" video by the Story of Stuff Project, see http://storyofstuff .org/movies/story-of-electronics/, accessed March 4, 2013.

122. UN Environmental Programme, *Global Chemicals Outlook: Towards Sound Management of Chemicals*, September 5, 2012, http://www.unep.org/pdf/GCO_Synthesis%20Report_CBDTIE_UNEP_September5_2012.pdf.

large part due to its high rates of obsolescence. Of the 304 million electronic products removed from US homes in 2005, *two-thirds were still in working order*.[123] About 80 percent of e-waste is not recycled.

Too often we are simply oblivious of our trash, let alone where it goes. Even though curbside collection has made recycling and even composting easier in many cities, the unfortunate fact is that nearly 60–70 percent of trash found in the average US garbage bin can be recycled or reused, and up to 50 percent can be composted.[124] Jesus's ethic of love, equity, and neighborliness calls us to take the time both to become aware of the effects of our waste on the Earth and on the poor, and to reduce, reuse, and recycle even when it might be less convenient to do so.

The reality of waste:

- In the US 1,609 pounds of trash is produced per person, per year. In Oregon, for example, 92 percent of that waste winds up in landfills.[125]
- Of the solid waste in US landfills, food waste is the overall number one material; landfills give off 34 percent of national methane emissions.[126]
- Only 1 percent of plastic bags worldwide are recycled—about 2 percent in the United States.[127]
- Global food production causes 80 percent of deforestation and 30 percent of all greenhouse gas emissions, and is the largest instigator of biodiversity loss.[128]
- Close to 300 million computers and 1 billion cell phones are produced every year. Global e-waste is estimated at 40 million tons per year.[129]

What we can do:

- Precycle—For thirty years Jeanne Roy has made reducing waste a priority in her household. In one year her family now accumulates just one trash can of waste! She emphasizes remaining aware of what happens before

123. According to the Consumer Electronics Association, cited in "E-Waste: Where Does It Go?," 75.
124. "Recycling Statistics and Facts," All-recycling-facts.com (website), http://www.all -recycling-facts.com/recycling-statistics.html, accessed March 1, 2013.
125. All-recycling-facts.com, "Recycling Statistics and Facts"; Oregon.gov, Department of Environmental Quality, "Rethinking Recycling: An Oregon Waste Reduction Curriculum," http:// www.deq.state.or.us/lq/pubs/docs/sw/curriculum/RRPart0304.pdf, accessed March 1, 2013.
126. Reynolds and Wenzlau, "Newsletter."
127. Mieszkowski, "Plastic Bags Are Killing Us," 49.
128. Nierenberg, FoodTank, email, June 6, 2013.
129. "E-Waste: Where Does It Go?," 75; UN Environmental Programme, *Global Chemicals Outlook*, 15.

and after you purchase a product. Her key is "precycling"—eliminating future waste by not buying it in the first place.[130]

- Reduce and reuse[131]—Buy less, especially new things. Buy used, at reuse centers or consignment shops. Make the amount of packaging an important consideration. Avoid as many disposable items as possible. Take your own tableware and cup to school or work. Borrow, rent, or share items that you don't use often.

- Recycle—Most people want to recycle; it's just too easy not to. Often all that is needed—in our homes, schools, workplaces, and churches—is someone to take ownership, to organize efforts, to generate interest, and to make the complicated less complicated. Does your local university, community college, or chamber of commerce offer recycling education?[132]

- Repair and reconsider—Ask if you must have the latest electronic gadget. Take a few minutes to find out if your electronic item or appliance can be repaired before you toss it. If it cannot be repaired, find an electronics recycler in your area.[133] Encourage manufacturers to implement "take-back" programs.

- Compost—A compost pile or a worm bin helps eliminate waste and provides beneficial mulch for your garden.

- Carry a trash bag—A number of our friends carry trash bags with them on their regular walks. It is a simple investment in their neighborhoods and in Earthcare.

- Bring bags to shop—To dodge completely the paper versus plastic debate, invest in reusable bags that you take with you to the market.

Keeping a Garden

The garden is a personal place of retreat and delight and labor for many people. Gardening helps them collect themselves, much like the activity of praying. For rich and poor—it does not make a difference—a garden is a place where body and soul are in harmony.

—Vigen Guroian[134]

130. Anna White, "What Does Not Buying Really Look Like?," *In Balance* 38 (Winter 2006/2007), reprinted in *Choices for Sustainable Living*, 52.
131. For more on the three Rs, see the US Environmental Protection Agency, "Reduce, Reuse, Recycle," http://www.epa.gov/recycle, accessed March 4, 2013.
132. Oregon State University offers a master recycling program (similar to a master gardening class) that trains citizens in all aspects of waste reduction.
133. Many reputable electronics recyclers can be found at e-Stewards, www.e-stewards.org.
134. Vigen Guroian, *Inheriting Paradise* (Grand Rapids: Eerdmans, 1999), xiii.

During my (Dan's) family's time in England, I developed such a fondness for the sprawling English garden that I planted one in my backyard when we returned home. Now in my current urban environment, my love for gardening has moved into new arenas. In our front and back yards, we have constructed eleven raised-bed planter boxes of various sizes, in which we grow zucchini, potatoes, pumpkins, kale, strawberries, herbs, tomatoes, green beans, peas, bok choy, carrots, onions, lettuce, and more. Added to the raised beds are a few dwarf fruit trees, a row of raspberries, and seven blueberry bushes. Needless to say, we have little grass to mow. Since she was a toddler, my granddaughter has loved the garden. It does not seem to matter to her that there might still be some dirt left on the carrots as she munches them to the nubs. I take authentic pleasure in a vine-ripened Sun Gold tomato or an organic French fingerling potato braised in butter or pancakes made with fresh pumpkin.

The kitchen garden—a potager garden in France or a kailyard in Scotland— is often planted in close proximity to the kitchen. It was common in Europe for people to keep their food close. Most of the Bible's characters—farmers, fishermen, vinedressers, gardeners, housekeepers, servants—were physically in touch with their food and its production. The earliest human communities knew the connection between land and food. It is estimated that in ancient civilizations 98 percent of the population worked the earth. Today, less than 1 percent of the US population makes their living off the land.[135] Because of this, we have lost our personal touch with the land. Leonardo da Vinci once wrote: "We know more about the movement of celestial bodies than about the soil underfoot."[136]

God created a garden, and then God created gardeners. In the first chapters of Genesis we note that God, the Earth, humanity, food, and work are all inextricably connected. "Earth" in Hebrew is *adamah*, and the one created out of earth is *adam*. In that first garden humans are depicted primarily as gardeners—to "till" and to "keep" (Gen. 2:15)—and not as landowners. The Jubilee celebration in Leviticus 25 allows the Israelites to return to their property and to their families (v. 10), all the while remembering that God is the true owner: "The land shall not be sold in perpetuity, for the land is mine; with me you are but aliens and tenants" (v. 23). Indeed, when it comes to the land, we are but aliens, tenants, and gardeners of what belongs ulti-mately to God. Gardening, tilling, and keeping are part of our holy calling to serve and to steward God's Creation; they can also, miraculously, take us back to Eden.

135. David R. Montgomery, *Dirt* (Berkeley: University of California Press, 2007), 2.
136. Quoted in ibid., 9.

A dirty theology, so to speak, is a theological call back to that from which we have come. Many are discovering that there is a unique spirituality to gardening. To get one's knees and hands dirty, to amend the soil with decomposed kitchen scraps, to feed and prune and divide and transplant and graft and cultivate and weed, to freeze and can and "put up" the produce of one's garden, and to enjoy God's bounty at harvest time and throughout the year—gardening and food preservation can be "spiritual" disciplines that bring healing and restoration in *both* the Christian life *and* the land.

Here are a few ideas to ponder in considering the "spiritual" practice of gardening:

- Start small . . . but start—In hindsight I (Dan) would say that eleven planter boxes were too ambitious, especially for my housemates (okay, for me as well). Even a small plot can produce healthy amounts of food, particularly if you coach your vines to grow vertically. More importantly, it gets you in touch with the earth.

- Urbanization is no excuse not to get dirty—Explore container gardens, sky-rise farming, community gardens, and even city co-ops, any of which can help restore a relationship to the food we are ingesting. Join a CSA (community-supported agriculture), if one is available in your area.

- Grow what you will eat—As "talk-about-able" as it might be to grow exotic veggies, if no one around your table will eat them (read: beets), it is little more than an exercise in ostentation. When choosing seeds or plants, check out those things that might be particularly expensive at your local market: blueberries, raspberries, fresh tomatoes, etc. You know you're hooked when you spend your winters pouring over local seed catalogs with friends.

- Go organic—As much as possible, avoid petroleum-based fertilizers and chemical pesticides. By composting, rotating crops, mulching, and using cover crops—remember, even the land was to be given a Sabbath rest every seventh year (Lev. 25:3–4)—you can keep your soil happily fruitful and able to provide the micronutrients so essential for a well-rounded diet.

- Save seeds—As plant biodiversity is rapidly declining, more gardeners are investing in seed banks and seed exchanges in order to help preserve heirloom varieties of very old vegetables, fruits, and grains.

- Share—By coordinating neighborhood gardens we can build community and ensure everyone has just enough zucchini. Also keep in mind that most food banks regularly face notorious shortages of fresh produce.

In this chapter we have considered ten tangible steps toward doing ecotheology: staying rooted, cultivating awareness, practicing centering prayer, keeping the Sabbath, living simply, resisting consumerism, eating justly, conserving water, reducing waste, and keeping a garden. We acknowledge the seeming inadequacy of these small changes in the face of the planet's ecocrisis. We also recognize their pressing necessity. German scientist Georg Christoph Lichtenberg (1742–1799) once said, "I cannot say whether things will get better if we change; what I can say is that they must change if they are to get better." Indeed it is only an accumulation of "seemingly" small changes that will heal the world. To overlook the importance of each action is indicative of human narcissism and of a lack of trust in God's mysterious economy and the power of resurrection. In 1961 Martin Luther King Jr. boldly declared, "Every step toward the goal of justice requires sacrifice, suffering, and struggle; the tireless exertions and passionate concern of dedicated individuals."[137] Every step by every individual toward justice, toward establishing the commonwealth of God, and toward the creation of a new heaven and a new Earth is valuable. As human creatures we have a unique capacity for—and as Christians we have been called to—both responsibility and hope. In our struggle together as co-creators of God's future shalom, what matters is that we act.

137. Martin Luther King Jr., "The Future of Integration," New York University, February 10, 1961, cited at "MLK Week," New York University (website), http://www.nyu.edu/life/events -traditions/mlk-week.html.

9

Earthen Vessels

Greening the Church

Dr. Seuss's classic *The Lorax*, beloved by many, is set among the green, lush, untouched world of the Truffula Trees, Brown Bar-ba-loots, and the Swomee-Swans. An entrepreneurial "Once-ler" discovers that the soft underbelly of the Truffula Trees can be exploited to make clothes known as "Thneeds," offering the potential of great wealth. Thus the Once-ler cuts down all the trees in the land in order to make as many Thneeds as possible. In so doing, a number of the Swomee-Swans, Brown Bar-ba-loots, and Humming-Fish lose their homes under the lush shade of the Truffala Trees. Enter the Lorax. Seeing what the Once-ler has done, the Lorax foretells that his exploitation can only lead to the destruction of their world. The prophecy becomes true: toxins accumulate on the land and in the air, the landscape becomes uninhabitable, and the integrity of the ecosystem is destroyed. The world of the Lorax is devastated. Years later, a small child encounters the sad, isolated Once-ler who lives in a boarded-up house overlooking a once beautiful world. The Once-ler speaks:

> "But *now*," says the Once-ler,
> "Now that *you're* here,
> the word of the Lorax seems perfectly clear.
> UNLESS someone like you
> cares a whole awful lot,
> nothing is going to get better.
> It's not."[1]

---

1. Dr. Seuss (Theodor Seuss Geisel), *The Lorax* (New York: Random House, 1971), 58.

As people who care "a whole awful lot," we continue in this chapter our investigation into "doing" ecotheology, moving from the personal ecopraxis of the last chapter to ways we might "green" our local churches and communities. *The Lorax* offers a profound lesson for this journey; its childlike simplicity can cut through our sophisticated denial. The ruin of one part of the web of life—humans, land, streams, ecosystems, Truffula Trees, Brown Bar-ba-loots, or the Swomee-Swans—can have far-ranging effects. Mark Wallace writes that "the gradual destruction of one life-form eventually results, in a ripple-like effect, in the degradation of the whole ecosystem that originally supported the lifeform now under siege."[2] If ecological *degradation* can ripple out into the whole created world, then so can ecological acts of *solidarity, stewardship,* and *discipleship.* And if personal actions can make a difference, how much more the good works of entire Christian communities.

Archbishop Desmond Tutu said, "The first law of our being is that we are set in a delicate network of interdependence with our fellow human beings and with the rest of God's creation."[3] We approach this chapter out of a conviction that most local churches need a deeper grasp of their own connection to God's Creation. As we grow in that awareness, we can more clearly see that Christ's church and God's world do not live in parallel universes: the church inhabits the Earth and the Earth inhabits the church. As the church begins to understand this mutuality, it just might find itself answering the call of the Once-ler.

Greening Leadership

God's Word is in all creation, visible and invisible. The Word is living, being, spirit, all verdant greening, all creativity. All creation is awakened, called, by the resounding melody, God's invocation of the Word. This Word manifests in every creature.

—Hildegard of Bingen[4]

"Green" is an almost universal symbol or metaphor for ecology and the Earth. It speaks to newness and nourishment, verdancy and vivacity, freshness and fecundity. In the twelfth century, Hildegard of Bingen coined the term *viriditas,* meaning "greenness." To "green" is both an intransitive and transitive

2. Mark I. Wallace, "The Green Face of God: Christianity in the Age of Ecocide," *CrossCurrents* 50, no. 3 (2000): 311.
3. Desmond Tutu, *The Essential Desmond Tutu,* ed. John Allen (Glosderry, South Africa: David Philip, 1997), 6.
4. *Meditations with Hildegard of Bingen,* ed. Gabriele Uhlein (Rochester, VT: Bear & Co., 1983), 49.

verb.[5] And green is a common theme in Scripture. At the end of Genesis 1, God provides "every green plant for food" (v. 30). Psalm 23 sings of "green pastures" (v. 2), and Proverbs declares that "the righteous will flourish like green leaves" (11:28). Joel casts a hopeful vision for animals: "Do not fear, you animals of the field, for the pastures of the wilderness are green" (Joel 2:22). Finally, in the Bible's last chapter we come across the image of a fruitful "tree of life," which has leaves "for the healing of the nations" (Rev. 22:2).

Green Pastors

Advocating for congregational "green leadership" is challenging for a number of reasons. First, we know we are addressing a burdened community of leaders and pastors, overextended by pastoral responsibilities and long lists of what they would do if they had more time. Is it really sustainable to worry about the spiritual health of our people *and* about recycling? Second, we know that each local church has any number of justice issues worthy of attention. Why should Creation care be prioritized on our mission, outreach, and compassion agendas instead of those issues focused on human well-being? We are certainly mindful that kindling interest toward Earthcare inevitably forges new complications for the local church and its leaders. Nevertheless to attend to ecopraxis in all its potential requires that we explore greening the church. The task before religious leaders is to create a sense of urgent hope and possibility within our congregations without resorting to guilt, cynicism, or hyperbole. All of us are in different places with this work—there is no right "next step" for everyone. What matters is that every leader—with boldness, faith, and vision—leads her or his community in taking the next step, whatever it may be.

Leadership begins with the practice of integrated living. Luke Gascho recalls growing up in a small country schoolhouse/church, with large windows on the east side through which the sun shone during Sunday morning worship. His father, a pastor and dairy farmer, would preach after a full week of caring for the small farm. Gascho comments: "I knew the man who stood behind the pulpit treated all the animals with gentleness and managed the land in ways that brought health to the soil. How wonderful to have harmony between the spoken and lived messages. . . . I heard two messages—one from the pulpit and one from the windows—and they were not in conflict with each other."[6] Because of the integrity of his father and the integrity of God's world, Christ's grace and the beauty of the Earth harmonized in a single

---

5. See *OED*, "green, v.1." For example, "French tarragon greens in the spring" (intransitive); "Sunlight and rain green the leaves on the plant" (transitive).

6. Luke Gascho, *Creation Care: Keepers of the Earth* (Harrisburg, VA: Herald, 2008), 143–44.

Tension Point: Politics

We've sought, as a writing team, to represent a generous Christianity that makes space for multitudinous shades of the political spectrum. But when it comes to actual, face-to-face, in-the-flesh living, especially for a congregation, replicating kind generosity toward the other is downright difficult, if not impossible.

Our team came toe-to-toe with this challenge on numerous occasions. At times, our ideological and political convictions about certain social and economic concerns made hospitable dialogue challenging, especially pertaining to the role of politics in contending with the ecocrisis. As a team, we rarely agreed politically.

As the church of Jesus, however, evangelicals with different political affiliations must learn how to love one another while disagreeing over politics—a task that does not get accomplished easily. We reject the notion that everyone must affiliate with *our* political party in order to care for the Earth. Our hope would be that anyone, from any political persuasion, would care deeply for God's Creation and make space for others.

- Some political and social commentators contend that among people of faith, both evangelical and mainline, their political perspectives inevitably "trump" their faith convictions. To that end, we wind up with "red" (Republican) churches and "blue" (Democrat) churches. Do you agree with that assessment? Why or why not?
- What are the implications of our political differences when it comes to the care of Creation?
- What would it mean if our churches became safe places for political differences to be engaged in hospitable, loving ways? How might it affect our ability to deal with the ecocrisis?

melody in that small, one-room schoolhouse/church. Greening a congregation or community is more effective when leadership is personally invested in its own ecopraxis.

One place to start is the weekly sermon. Within worship, the Word is proclaimed, a message holding the capacity to inspire gratitude and motivate action throughout the week. One practice the preacher or teacher can adopt is to weave ecological themes, anecdotes, or illustrations into sermons, planting the idea of Creation care in the hearts and minds of listeners. For a whole year, a pastor friend of ours experimented with making a connection between the Lectionary texts she preached from every week and some aspect of earthkeeping. Addressing Creation care in this way throughout the year roots it in our theology and encourages creative and wide-ranging application. A group of students from our seminary brought a whole month of summer sermons on earthkeeping to their Quaker congregation. On successive weeks they were able to address simplicity, consumption, and listening to the book of Creation.

Green Teams

Although the ongoing support of leadership (both publicly and personally) cannot be underestimated, another critical place to gather energy is at a grassroots level—form a "Green Team," "Creation Care Committee," or another name that resonates within your congregation. Much can happen from small beginnings. After interviewing a wide variety of denominational executives, lay leaders, and other professionals, one writer concluded that the most important need for a thriving earthkeeping ministry is "at least one individual who is totally passionate and who is willing to put in serious time . . . although ideally there would be a team of at least two or three individuals who could form a core group of support."[7] The process of identifying people who share a common passion revolves around spreading the word in the bulletin, newsletter, on a Facebook post; having informal conversations over a cup of coffee; and connecting people in small groups around their mutual interest. In other words, rather than focusing on tasks to be accomplished, invest ample time to build relationships. The Green Team need not be ecologists or master gardeners or ecotheologians; they can be farmers or amateur gardeners or kayakers. Often all that is needed is to provide an outlet for the energy that is already there. Many denominations have resources available for congregations, both to help organize a Creation care committee and to offer materials for children, youth, and adult education.[8] Whether a church is denominational or nondenominational, there is little need to reinvent the wheel since so much good work is currently being done.[9]

The surest way for a Green Team to experience burnout and disintegrate (along with any energy the broader congregation may have around Creation care) is to be overly focused on tasks and agenda items. Any resource or program is best used in service of the wider dream of helping people lead more integrated, faithful lives. While many items can fill the agenda for a Green Team, the most important is prioritizing relationships. An essential part of relationship building is communicating well. Green teams cannot afford to become isolated committees doing their work alone. In order to keep Creation

7. Karla Hignite, quoted in *Greening Congregations Handbook*, ed. Tanya Marcovna Barnett (Seattle: Earth Ministry, 2002), II.12.

8. See "Appendix D: Resources by Denomination," in *Greening Congregations Handbook*, appendices 17–41.

9. For a step-by-step pathway to greening your congregation, see "Strategy Pathway," in *Greening Congregations Handbook*, II.31–37.

care from becoming compartmentalized, seek an integrated vision for Creation care in every dimension of the church's life. Inviting the whole church into the work can be as simple as sharing a Creation care vision statement with the congregation, asking for their input, and keeping them informed of the team's activity. Team members can build intentional relationships with other groups in the church, listening carefully to discern how others might be supported in "greening" their areas of ministry. One member of the Green Team might be a liaison to the worship or education ministry teams, helping envision and plan preaching series or adult courses on topics related to care for Creation.[10] Another member might work in cooperation with the building committee, reminding folks to think ecologically when windows and toilets need to be replaced. Partnering with the grounds committee could raise questions about how weeds are handled or green space is managed.

Communicating well helps build unity and consensus on the team and within the congregation, forging a partnership rooted in relationship rather than a compartmentalized program.

Greening Land and Space

> The parish is the arena for the earthing of heaven locally. That is our local mission. World mission is the earthing of heaven globally.
>
> —Bishop James Jones[11]

The Green Team can influence how a congregation engages Creation as a community in concrete, practical ways. In my (Jen's) church, a representative from our Earthcare group (we call it Integrity of Creation) meets with the board of trustees to suggest eco-friendly practices like low-flow toilets and to protest spraying petroleum-based RoundUp™ on the dandelions in our front lawn. We have requested an energy audit of our building, proposed a space for a community garden, and entered a lottery for solar-panel installation. A committed group of individuals can function on a variety of levels and in multiple, creative ways to encourage an entire congregation to rethink their relationship to the Earth and the space their building occupies.

10. For an example of integrating creation themes in small groups, the Mennonite Central Committee has published *Simply in Season*, a cookbook with a free downloadable study guide. People start by eating together in small groups and enjoying food, faith, and fellowship. Along the journey they are exposed to justice for farmworkers and ways they can change their own buying, cooking, and advocacy practices. See Mary Beth Lind and Cathleen Hockman-Wert, *Simply in Season*, expanded ed. (Scottdale, PA: Herald, 2009).

11. James Jones, *Jesus and the Earth* (London: SPCK, 2003), 92.

Bioregional Discipleship

Recently Ched Myers has been advocating for a new form of discipleship within the church: *bioregional discipleship*. Myers believes that as Christ-followers, we are called toward solidarity with the poor and marginalized: "We live in an historical moment that demands serious, sustained engagement from Christians. Both our love for the Creator and the interlocking crises of global warming, peak oil and water, and widening ecological degradation should compel us to make environmental justice and sustainability integral to everything we do as disciples and citizens."[12] It is possible to make shifts in the paradigms and habits of our homes, local churches, and denominations. His language is sharp but compelling, calling children of God to "take a stand of passionate solidarity with a Creation that is enslaved to our dysfunctional and terminal civilizational lifeways."

Bioregional discipleship is praxis oriented and involves, among other disciplines, the *ecological reading of Scripture* and *watershed ecclesiology*. The ecological reading of Scripture involves re-reading texts from a new perspective, paying special attention to narratives that speak toward land and nature. Ellen Davis states that unless we can approach the text with a proper understanding of Earth as neighbor, our ability to understand Scripture will be compromised. Reading the text rooted in place would mean knowing the place we read from (both our bioregional and cultural/social location) and stretching our minds to reimagine the land as a home to be cherished rather than as a topic to be analyzed. This singular effort would make us better readers of Scripture.[13] Adopting an ecological hermeneutic, which might seem counterintuitive to our other learned hermeneutics, might be a helpful exploration for a small group, a Bible study, or simply as an exercise for preaching pastors.

Myers's vision of watershed ecclesiology is based on the concept that the spaces we occupy as church are well positioned to function as places to learn about our bioregional space as well as how to defend and restore those landscapes.[14] The proverbial maxim of bioregionalism comes from Gary Snyder: "The world is places." Places have unique habitats, economies, ecologies, and environmental factors. No two places are the same. This emerging sensitivity to local places brings a strong critique to the Western idea of "Nature" as a unifying, homogenous reality that permeates the created order; such an understanding of Nature, therefore, assumes that the conventions and realities that apply to

---

12. Ched Myers and Chris Grataski, "World Water Day 2013: A Call for 'Watershed Discipleship,'" *Ched's Blog*, March 22, 2013, http://www.chedmyers.org/blog/ched?page=1.

13. See Ellen F. Davis, *Scripture, Culture, and Agriculture* (Cambridge: Cambridge University Press, 2009), 22.

14. Since bioregions are organized by ecological rather than political boundaries, one common way to distinguish between them is by watersheds.

one place are always true of every other place. Nature here is like Nature there. Bioregionalism critiques that worldview by insisting that each region is unique and should be known on its own terms by those who make their home there.

There are many ways our churches might become places for knowing the bioregions in which we make our homes. One simple idea is to devote a bulletin board or a Facebook page as a place for resources, including links to websites and organizations, such as the local watershed council. Physical and virtual information centers are excellent places to highlight some of the practical objectives of bioregionalism: to ensure that political boundaries align with ecological boundaries, to highlight the unique ecology of a particular bioregion, to encourage consumption of local foods and the use of local materials, and to promote the cultivation of native plants in sustainable harmony with the bioregion. Perhaps one month the congregation could focus on the ecology unique to its bioregion. What are the native plants? Animals? Bodies of water? One Earthcare team provided flowers for Sunday worship from the wetland on their property. During the service they named the native plants in the "bouquet" beside the altar and invited members to gather immediately following the service to learn about the plants. A resource table set up after worship could also provide people with information. Maybe a nature hike could be offered or a Sunday school class that focuses on educating participants about local foods or native plants. Many communities have organizations that would be very willing to help educate the congregation. It is surprising how many "experts" and "practitioners" there are within our own congregations who would be willing to share their knowledge and resources.

The purpose of learning about our bioregions is to "re-inhabit" that space *as* church. Once a congregation has learned about their place, part of loving that place is engaging it on a spiritual level. One way to make that connection is to hold a worship service outdoors, among a grove of ash trees, on top of a hill, by a cascading river, or as the sun is rising on Easter morning.

Church Buildings

The Green Team might start the task of bringing a greater awareness of Earthcare to the congregation by exploring your church building's ecological footprint. The US Green Building Council, which promotes sustainable practices in buildings, offers the following list of impacts on the environment due to buildings. In the United States alone, buildings account for:

73 percent of electricity consumption,

39 percent of total energy use,

38 percent of CO_2 emissions,

40 percent of raw materials use (3 billion tons annually),
40 percent of waste output (170 million tons annually), and
14 percent of potable water consumption.[15]

What can congregations do to lessen their carbon footprints? How can the use of our buildings be maximized? For many church communities, a building is used on Sunday mornings but lays dormant and silent the rest of the week. What other organizations might be able to share the space? Perhaps the church can open the space to a local advocacy group, or allow the commercial kitchen to be used by groups learning to can from their gardens.

Certain members of a Green Team may be interested in evaluating the building from an economic perspective: what costs can be reduced by minor and often inexpensive updates? Can we weatherize windows, fix door seals, make windows as up to date as possible, keep the building cooler in the winter, and minimize use of air-conditioning in the summer? Can we save on water costs by minimizing lawn space?

Churches might consider consumption: how much paper do we use for bulletins every Sunday and where do the coffee beans for fellowship hour come from? Or waste: what do we do with food scraps after a potluck supper? How about lawn clippings?

One year, the Integrity of Creation committee from my (Jen's) church organized small groups during the Lenten season around the theme of living simply. Following that experience, the church voted to change its plan to pave the newly-purchased property to the west of the building as an overflow parking lot. Our collective Lenten experience had caused us to look at the land in a different way and to value the trees and topsoil rather than seeing the land for what it could yield—additional parking spots. The next year, the group worked in cooperation with the children's ministry team to facilitate a Creation-themed Vacation Bible School curriculum.

"Automobility" and Neighborhood

In gazing down the road to consider the future of the local church we are confronted with the dependence of churches on fossil fuel and the automobile. It is fascinating to reflect on the changes that oil and the automobile have brought to Christianity in the West. One author asserts: "Hydrocarbon energy changed the faith at least as much as Gutenberg's printing press."[16]

15. Ashley Katz, "Green Building Facts," US Green Building Council, July 1, 2012, http://www.usgbc.org/articles/green-building-facts.
16. Brandon D. Rhodes, "Re-Placing the Church: Missional Opportunities in the Emerging Energy Crisis" (DMin diss., George Fox Evangelical Seminary, 2013), 1. What follows is adapted from his work.

"Automobility," according to Sidonie Smith, is "the configuration of people, machines, landscape, urban geography, and culture that attends the increasing dependence upon the gas engine for transport in industrial and postindustrial societies."[17] Modern suburbia in America was created for and is dependent on the automobile; already by the 1920s the motorcar was becoming a necessity for the middle class and its flight to the suburbs.[18] Automobility, notes Brandon Rhodes, "created a geography, an architecture, an economy, and a culture around itself."[19] In spite of efforts by municipalities to increase the availability of public transportation, most suburban families cannot survive without a car, and usually own two or more cars. Cars continue to form the suburban culture of America, with its massive shopping malls and clover-leafed interchanges and single-family dwellings. And automobility and its suburban landscape have squeezed the suburban church into its mold. Few suburban churches can survive without sufficient spaces in their parking lots. Even more telling is how the automobile makes it possible for Christians to drive past the church in their neighborhood to attend one more to their taste. Automobility, therefore, reinforces the consumerism already so ingrained in our churches.

More and more people are beginning to ask what might happen if (when?) automobility is threatened or curbed. What transpires if the warnings about peak oil—that point in history when the global production of oil reaches its maximum rate—prove even partially true?[20] Although numbers are debated, it is estimated that the earth once contained 2 trillion barrels of oil; to date we have burned almost half of it and are currently consuming 87 million barrels a day.[21] Doomsday scenarios abound, as, on the other hand, does a (wishful) confidence in human ingenuity and technology to fix the problem. A more likely scenario—or at least one between diametrically opposite pessimistic and optimistic poles—is one of soft collapse or a long descent, dictated by a deteriorating energy return on investment (EROI). Instead of survivalism, a more healthy response is local preparedness for the decline in energy through a focus on transition and resilience.[22]

17. Sidonie Smith, *Moving Lives* (Minneapolis: University of Minnesota Press, 2001), 185.

18. Kenneth T. Jackson, *Crabgrass Frontier: The Suburbanization of the United States* (Oxford: Oxford University Press, 1985), 157–71. According to Purdue professor Jon C. Teaford, *The American Suburb* (New York: Routledge, 2008), 30–31, suburbia certainly existed before the rise of automobility, but it became a dominant feature of the American landscape after World War II.

19. Rhodes, "Re-Placing the Church," 5.

20. Richard Heinberg, *Peak Everything* (Forest Row, UK: Clairview, 2007), 1–22.

21. Sonia Shah, *Crude: The Story of Oil* (New York: Seven Stories, 2004), xvi, 177; US Central Intelligence Agency, "Country Comparison: Refined Petroleum Products—Consumption," World Fact Book, https://www.cia.gov/library/publications/the-world-factbook/rankorder/2246rank .html, accessed August 15, 2013. Even if "unconventional oils" like tar sands or oil shale are fully extracted, fossil fuels remain, ultimately, a limited resource.

22. Rhodes, "Re-Placing the Church," 110–15.

It seems to us that phrases like "local preparedness" and "transition and resilience" raise vital issues for the Christian church. Rasmussen states that we have two assignments: "We must meet certain 'adaptive challenges,' and we must create 'anticipatory communities' as part of the successful negotiation out of the fossil-fuel interlude."[23] The ecocrisis in general, and our dependence on fossil fuels in particular, are pressing congregations to consider ecclesiology and the nature of the church. To wit, how essential are locality and place to the practice and existence of Christian community? What steps might churches take to localize their ministry geographically, for example, in neighborhoods? What "spiritual" resources does Christianity bring to the table to support people and communities as they face the realities of these seemingly inevitable transitions and as they grapple with building resilience into their futures?

Greening Worship

A community of churches in Africa known as the Association of African Earthkeeping Churches (AAEC) has brought together worship, the sacraments, and earthkeeping in unique ways. At their baptism, novices confess their sins against the Creator *and* the Creation and commit themselves to a discipleship of earthkeeping.[24] Every year African earthkeepers turn out in the thousands to celebrate the *maporesanyika*—earth-healing—ceremony, in spite of whatever setbacks due to drought or frost they might have endured the previous year. During a tree-planting ceremony that includes the sacrament of Eucharist, one of the AAEC leaders proclaims: "Jesus said: 'I leave you my followers, to complete my work!' And that task is one of healing! We, the followers of Jesus, have to continue with his healing ministry. So, let us all fight, clothing and healing the earth with trees!"[25] Marthinus Daneel offers these excerpts from the liturgy of the tree-planting Eucharist:

> Look at the stagnant water
> where all the trees were felled
> Without trees the water-holes mourn
> without trees the gullies form
> For, the tree-roots to hold the soil—
> are gone!

23. Larry L. Rasmussen, *Earth-honoring Faith* (New York: Oxford University Press, 2012), 183.
24. Marthinus L. Daneel, "Earth-Keeping Churches at the African Grass Roots," in *Christianity and Ecology*, ed. Dieter Hessel and Rosemary Radford Ruether (Cambridge, MA: Harvard University Press, 2000), 540.
25. Ibid., 534.

There were forests
abundance of rain
But in our ignorance and greed
we left the land naked.
Like a person in shame
our country is shy
in its nakedness.

Our planting of trees today
is a sign of harmony
between us and creation
We are reconciled with the earth
through the body and blood of Jesus
which brings peace.
He who came to save
All creation.[26]

Worship is connected to confession of guilt and sin, an awareness of the broken Earth, a proclamation of hope in Christ's work on the cross, the celebration of the Eucharist, and the practical act of planting trees. Humanity is connected with God and the entire cosmos. Worship is indispensable for bringing a deeper awareness of Creation care to the people of God.

The "Work" of the Church

Writing in the middle of the second century, Justin Martyr outlines the basic elements of an early Christian liturgy.[27] Justin's model of worship revolved around three core acts of service that were to be presided over by the community's leader: proclaiming a message from Scripture or serving the Word of God (see Acts 6:4); serving the table of the bread and wine of the Eucharist; and serving "orphans and widows, and those who are . . . in want, and those who are in bonds, and the strangers," by making sure contributions collected during worship were distributed.[28] The word "liturgy" is derived from *leitourgia*, which is literally the "work of the people."[29] It is what the church does when it gathers. These liturgies are the communal scripts of a gathered people, a way of narrating their historical narrative. We all practice a liturgy of some

26. Ibid., 539.
27. *St. Justin Martyr: The First and Second Apologies*, trans. Leslie William Barnard (New York: Paulist Press, 1997), I.65–I.67, pp. 70–72.
28. Ibid., I.67, p. 71; see also Gordon W. Lathrop, *The Pastor* (Minneapolis: Fortress, 2006), 66.
29. *OED*, "liturgy, n.," says that *leitos* is apparently a derivative of *laos*, "people," plus *ergos*, "that works."

sort—some are loud, fast, and trend-driven; others follow a specific theological heritage; and still others allow space and silence for reflection—and our liturgy mediates a certain story of the world. Our theology of liturgy is a statement about what it means to be the church.

The essential power of worship is the act of remembering who we are. Stanley Hauerwas and Samuel Wells write that corporate worship "is the most regular way in which most Christians remind themselves and others that they are Christians. It is the most significant way in which Christianity takes flesh, evolving from a set of ideas and convictions to a set of practices and a way of life."[30] Liturgy is a preparation for life. That is, over time the church *becomes* its weekly practices, what it says to itself week in and week out. Paul Santmire reminds us that what the church *does* is inextricably connected to *who* the church believes it is. "The doing of the church flows from the being of the church. The works of the church flow from the grace given to the church. The life of faithful discipleship grows from the rich soil of faithful communal ritual. The church at work is totally dependent on the church at worship."[31] Because Christ's body of redeemed people is reminded of its identity in worship, it is able to live incarnate lives on the Earth, caring for, loving, and serving in the most tangible of ways. Work and worship go hand in hand. This is why examining the church's practices, liturgies, and rituals is a profoundly important assignment for leading our churches and communities into green living.

Liturgies, though historical, change with time. Our culture has forced new ways of "doing" the work of liturgy; for the first time in history, we can say, "Turn *on* your Bibles," or, we can offer gluten-free, egg-free, dairy-free Eucharistic elements. We can craft our prayers and liturgies in ways that help us question and deconstruct those actions and habits of daily life that objectify and exploit. If liturgy is truly preparation for life, then, as we raise our voices together, we long to become what we practice with words in worship. We can declare, for example:

> We confess our sin and the sin of this world,
> > clinging to the values of brokenness,
> > we lay waste to the land and pollute the seas.
> Have mercy on us, heal and forgive us,
> > setting us free as agents of your reconciling love in Jesus Christ.

30. Stanley Hauerwas and Samuel Wells, "Christian Ethics as Informed Prayer," in *The Blackwell Companion to Christian Ethics*, ed. Stanley Hauerwas and Samuel Wells, 2nd ed. (Oxford: Wiley-Blackwell, 2011), 7.

31. H. Paul Santmire, *Nature Reborn: The Ecological and Cosmic Promise of Christian Theology* (Minneapolis: Fortress, 2000), 76.

Some Green Team members may be interested in infusing worship with Creation themes. In the summer, my (Jen's) congregation holds an outdoor worship service that our Integrity of Creation committee is responsible for designing and organizing. The point of the service is to bring the congregation in contact with our own place. At other points during the year, we have focused on bringing the natural world into our worshiping space: boughs of pine on the communion table; we use our sanctuary walls as gallery space for an artist's paintings of flora and fauna; we have asked a talented poet in our congregation to write Creation-themed liturgy for a particular season.

Eucharist

In her autobiography Sara Miles chronicles her surprising journey from atheism to Christianity. Her conversion, she recounts, was realized at the Lord's Table: "One early, cloudy morning when I was forty-six, I walked into a church, ate a piece of bread, took a sip of wine. A routine Sunday activity for tens of millions of Americans—except that up until that moment I'd led a thoroughly secular life, at best indifferent to religion, more often appalled by its fundamentalist crusades. This was my first communion. It changed everything."[32] The Table does change everything. A little bread and a little wine may seem insignificant, but it epitomizes and re-creates God's gracious love in physical form. We become what we eat and drink.

In a letter to nuns grieving the loss of one of their sisters, Catherine of Siena (1347–1380) wrote about the presence of the Trinity in a uniquely Eucharistic way: "The Father is her table. The Son is her food. . . . The Holy Spirit waits on her."[33] These metaphors of table, food, and service illustrate well the wonder of Holy Communion. The table is the *Lord's* Table. In all the other tables of the world, our place is predicated upon class, gender, race, or our ability to *earn* a seat.[34] But this Table is different; it cannot be earned. It is the Lord's Table, not a denomination's table, not a church's table, not a pastor's table. Our hope stands upon the idea that this simple, weekly act—Table, Food, Service—has the power to re-create God's people for mission in a broken world.

To gather around the Table, to taste the abundant *food* of Jesus's body and blood, to be reminded of the Service we have received and of our calling to serve in return—the sacrament we call Holy Communion—is a profoundly "green"

32. Sara Miles, *Take This Bread* (New York: Ballantine, 2008), xi.
33. Catherine of Siena to the Nuns of San Gaggio near Florence and to the Nuns of Monte San Savino [March 1376], in *The Letters of St. Catherine of Siena*, trans. Suzanne Noffke, OP (Binghamton, NY: Medieval and Renaissance Texts and Studies, 1988), Letter 62, p. 199.
34. Marva J. Dawn, *Powers, Weakness, and the Tabernacling of God* (Grand Rapids: Eerdmans, 2001), 98–100.

gift of grace and responsibility. Churches can consider a number of creative ideas that can help stimulate renewed thoughtfulness toward God's Creation in the sacrament of the Lord's Table. When celebrating World Communion Sunday on the first Sunday in October, some churches utilize Communion elements that come from foreign lands by people who were paid equitably for their labor. This practice helps us reflect on the geographical, economic, and environmental implications of our food economy. Congregations might commission one person or family to be the "breadmaker" each week, giving them an opportunity for creativity and simplicity. If available, use wines or juices that are grown and made locally. Or, local communities might share an *agapē* feast. *Agapē* feasts in the early church were open-tabled meals that gave abundant opportunity for community building, feeding the poor and disenfranchised, and demonstrating the prospect of God's manna society, where there is "just enough" for everyone.

The Eucharist encompasses many of the themes we have addressed in this book. It is a celebration of the mystery of God's redemption for the whole Creation through the death and resurrection of Jesus Christ; it is a reminder of the Spirit's continued presence in our midst and in the whole created order; it is an eschato-logical confluence of what has brought us to this moment (past), of who we are and where we are located (present), and of a partnership with God in co-creating what can be (future); it is a space to repent, to receive God's forgiveness, and to be converted to a new way of living; it is brokenness—a broken body, a broken Body, a broken world—and healing; it is a moment of wide-eyed thanksgiving to God for the grandeur of Creation; it is a time to grieve the brokenness and groaning of the Earth and all its inhabitants; it is a model of table fellowship and hospitality, where all—children and adults, rich and poor, insiders and outsiders, Republicans and Democrats, libertarians and librarians, PhDs and GEDs—are invited; it is a commemoration of those not present at the Table—through illness, imprisonment, calling, death, or exclusion; it is, as Eastern Orthodoxy reminds us, the great convergence of Earth and heaven where the communion of saints, the *Sanctorum Communio*, unite in worship; it is a banquet of abundance, a joyous foretaste of the *agapē* feast to come; it is a call to serve, to feed the poor and the hungry, as Jesus fed the multitudes on the mountainside; it is bread for the journey—manna—a metaphor of sustainable consumption, of there being "just enough" for everyone; it is a physical reminder, in the wheat and grapes, of our connection to and dependence on the goodness of the land; it is an honoring, through the farmer and vinedresser, baker and winemaker, of vocation and the virtue of hard work; it is a representation to the world of unity and shalom; and it is a statement of discipleship, that we are what—and who—we eat.

By reimagining and greening worship, by reconnecting it to and embodying it in Creation, we are realigning ourselves with our heritage in the Bible
and Christian history. The Jewish celebrations in the Hebrew Scriptures and
the liturgical seasons of the church year were intimately associated with an
agrarian worldview. Today technology, gnosticizing, individualism, and consumerism have weakened that bond. To green worship is to return the church
to its roots and to reconstruct a countercultural community in mission.

Greening Mission

> The Church is the only society that exists for the benefit of those who are not
> its members.
>
> —William Temple[35]

When the children of Israel were languishing in exile in Babylon, longing
for their homeland, the prophet Jeremiah sent them these words of hope:
"Build houses and live in them; plant gardens and eat what they produce. . . .
But seek the welfare of the city where I have sent you into exile, and pray to
the LORD on its behalf, for in its welfare you will find your welfare" (Jer. 29:5,
7). Jeremiah urged the people to adapt to their unfamiliar surroundings, to
invest themselves in Babylon, since their well-being was wrapped up in its.
Dallas Willard once remarked, "Remember, in a pluralistic world, a religion is
valued based on the benefits it brings to its nonadherents."[36] A missional worldview involves striving for the common good—the commonwealth of God—of
an inclusive array of communities: families, neighborhoods, churches, cities
and towns, societies and cultures, *and* the whole community of life on Earth.

Mission and Earthkeeping

A momentous period in Protestantism began on July 9, 1706, when two
German Lutheran Pietists, Bartholomew Ziegenbalg and Heinrich Plütschau,
arrived as missionaries at Tranquebar on the southeastern coast of India. Their
undertaking deserves recognition as the first ongoing Protestant foreign mission work.[37] Why was the Tranquebar mission the first enduring Protestant
endeavor, coming as it did almost two centuries after the Reformation? Alister

---

35. Unknown source, though quoted frequently, e.g., Craig Brian Larson and Brian Lowery,
1001 Quotations that Connect (Grand Rapids: Zondervan, 2009), 304.
36. Quoted in Brian McLaren, *A Generous Orthodoxy* (Grand Rapids: Zondervan, 2004), 111.
37. Daniel L. Brunner, *Halle Pietists in England* (Göttingen: Vandenhoeck & Ruprecht,
1993), 102–3.

McGrath comments, "During its formative phase, Protestantism seems to have had little interest in the notions of 'mission' or 'evangelism.'"[38] One of the reasons Luther, Calvin, and later Protestants did not seek to reach out beyond the borders of Christendom was *theological*: We can trust God to convert the nations when (and if) God chooses to, they said. When William Carey suggested to local British Baptist ministers in 1792 that they spread the gospel to other nations, one older minister chastised him, "Young man, sit down. When God pleases to convert the heathen, He will do it without your aid or mine."[39]

It is remarkable how long it took Protestantism to grasp the human role and responsibility in evangelization and mission. Nor has Western Christianity been eager to recognize earthkeeping as one critical aspect of God's mission on Earth. However "mission is the result of God's initiative, rooted in God's purposes to restore and heal creation. 'Mission' means 'sending,' and it is the central biblical theme describing the purpose of God's action. . . . God's mission embraces all of creation."[40] A "sending" theology calls God's people to responsibility. Not infrequently one hears earnest Christians state, implicitly or explicitly, "Can't we trust God ultimately to save us from the ecological mess we're in?" To answer in the negative is perceived as a lack of faith. Admittedly the Bible gives numerous instances of God's gracious intervention in the affairs of the world; however, much more often—as with Jesus's call to discipleship—the Spirit beckons us to make God's mission here on Earth our mission. Our firm conviction is that God loves the whole Creation, that its salvation, healing, and shalom are all part of the mission of God, *and* that God summons us to responsible partnership in that enterprise.

To move in this direction, we must expand our concepts of mission and poverty. Many in the Christian community identify "mission" as something we (the privileged) do *for* the poor (the underprivileged). This widespread, often subtle perspective hinges on characterizing poverty solely in economic terms and has often resulted in well-meaning Christians doing more harm than good through their outreach efforts. Steve Corbett and Brian Fikkert state that Christians must embrace their "mutual brokenness" with those they seek to come alongside. Unless they come to such a realization, their "mission" might do little more than exacerbate their own "god-complexes" and enhance "the feelings of inferiority and shame" of the economically underprivileged.[41] John Perkins says, "We need the person of Jesus Christ to transform not just the poor but also ourselves."[42]

38. Alister E. McGrath, *Christianity's Dangerous Idea* (New York: HarperOne, 2007), 175.
39. Ibid., 176–77.
40. Darrell L. Guder et al., *Missional Church* (Grand Rapids: Eerdmans, 1998), 4–5.
41. Steve Corbett and Brian Fikkert, *When Helping Hurts* (Chicago: Moody, 2009), 64–68.
42. John Perkins, foreword to ibid., 12.

At the heart of missional earthkeeping is a spirit of humble mutuality that recognizes the interdependence of God's created order and resists a truncated understanding of poverty. Bryant Myers proposes a more encompassing theology of poverty: "Poverty is a result of relationships that do not work, that are not just, that are not for life, that are not harmonious or enjoyable."[43] This understanding of poverty means that our relationships with God, ourselves, others, society, and Creation are broken. It is God's mission, through the incarnation, death, and resurrection of Jesus Christ, to bring salvation and healing to *all* of these relationships. To be sure, evangelism is a part of God's mission and the gospel of Jesus but so are earthkeeping and the struggle for ecojustice. These enlarge our perspective and experience of poverty and shalom, brokenness and salvation, enabling us to participate in the whole mission of God on Earth.

Community Building

One Saturday morning I (Dan) ran into the owner of a local coffee shop, who had opened the shop to provide a welcoming gathering space for his neighborhood. With the coffee and conversation flowing fruitfully, he was now turning his entrepreneurial heart in another direction. He had just signed a lease on a large, vacant urban lot, about a mile from where I live, that he planned to turn into an expansive community garden. The lot is next door to a Head Start Daycare and across the street from low-income housing. I responded enthusiastically, "That's wonderful! I know that my intentional community and I would love to be involved from the ground floor. When's your next leadership meeting? May I come?" He replied forthrightly, "Actually, our goal is to help organize the neighbors closest to the garden. Our experience is that when we have too many educated white folk involved, the neighborhood is less likely to take ownership. Hopefully we can welcome you into partnership further down the road." Only slightly offended, I knew straightaway that his approach was the right one.

My entrepreneurial friend is prioritizing the value of community building over bringing a community garden to swift fruition; indeed he is acknowledging the long-term benefits of nurturing relationships in comparison to a short-term focus on concrete results at any cost. With the ecocrisis and other economic and social pressures staring us in the face, it is easy to feel compelled to take (any) action at the expense of building relationships. But it will take a community—in every meaning of the word—to engage these challenges; and, from most accounts, community in modern society is breaking down. Authors Robert Bellah, Robert Putnam, and many others have addressed the social disintegration in

---

43. Bryant L. Myers, *Walking with the Poor*, rev. and expanded ed. (Maryknoll, NY: Orbis, 2011), 143.

North America.[44] The collapse of connectedness has broad-ranging ramifications. Putnam testifies that the scarcity of social cohesion represents "one of the nation's most serious public health challenges."[45] Life is intended to be lived out in mutuality and relationship. When any part of the community of life is isolated or eradicated, the whole community of life suffers.

The importance of building community in the local church, whether through small groups or mission teams, is widely recognized. One way to think about small group opportunities in a way that builds relationship within and beyond the congregation is the community garden. All over North America churches and community groups are recovering their agrarian roots and getting their fingernails dirty . . . for the sake of others. In Ankeny, Iowa, a number of churches have united to create "Agape Garden," a 15,000-square-foot plot on which church volunteers in 2012 provided almost eight tons of vegetables for the local food bank, in spite of Iowa's widespread drought conditions that year.[46]

Others are using the garden to unite diverse constituencies around a common purpose to provide healthy food for families. One such outreach is Outgrowing Hunger.[47] Under the creative leadership of a local Christian college graduate, this newly formed group of volunteers scopes out unused parcels of land—private, public, or institutional—on which to plant gardens. Local community members and churches support these neighborhood gardens "where healthy food, resilient community, and economic opportunity spring up together." Their vision is grounded in a conviction that "a state of abundance exists in both the human spirit and the natural creation." A fundamental driving force is their desire to see "nutritional justice," especially for the economically challenged. In many marginalized communities, unhealthy food is cheaper and more easily obtained than healthy food, with far-ranging effects that include decreased productivity due to illness, behavioral and educational difficulties, and high rates of obesity and diabetes.

The wonder of a community garden is how it can bring all kinds of people together around a common dream of feeding each other and caring for Creation at the same time.[48]

44. Robert Bellah et al., *Habits of the Heart* (Berkeley: University of California Press, 1985); Robert Putnam, *Bowling Alone* (New York: Simon & Schuster, 2000); Peter Block, *Community: The Structure of Belonging* (San Francisco: Berrett-Koehler, 2008).

45. Putnam, *Bowling Alone*, 327.

46. Ben Lucas, "Food-pantry Gardens Wrap up Fall Harvest," *Des Moines Register*, October 4, 2012, http://www.desmoinesregister.com/article/20121005/NEWS/310050040/Food-pantry-gardens-wrap-up-fall-harvest.

47. Outgrowing Hunger, www.outgrowinghunger.org, accessed July 19, 2013.

48. For more on building connections between the local church and the land, see Fred Bahnson, *Soil and Sacrament* (New York: Simon & Schuster, 2013).

Community Organizing and Advocacy

Community organizing combines community building with effective action for the common good.[49] While community gardens can nurture relationships in the neighborhood and produce abundance for all to share, community organizing looks at the systems in place and their effects on people and neighborhoods. We are reminded of the oft-quoted words of Archbishop Dom Hélder Câmara: "When I give food to the poor, they call me a saint. When I ask why the poor have no food, they call me a communist."[50] Community organizing revolves around building power by organizing people around the common good and by helping them see their capacity to influence change, or their ability to act, even in the face of "oppressive" powers. In organizing, one sees the power of coming alongside in solidarity, of developing confident and articulate leaders, of bringing people together to act in the interest of their communities and the common good. John Perkins loves to quote this proverb: "But of the best leaders, when their task is accomplished, when their work is done, the people will remark: 'We have done it ourselves.'"

Community organizing sees the value in realistic, gradual change. It accepts the world as it is, filled with unjust power over, selfishness, and division; and it longs for the world as it should be—the commonwealth of God—a world of power alongside, of self-sacrifice, love, and equity. It recognizes that sometimes idealism can prevent us from pursuing or accepting "winnable" actions along the way. It prizes thoughtful strategy and knows that the more diverse the group that comes to the table, the greater the possibility of an effective and winnable outcome.

Like community building, relationship is at the heart of organizing. In one-to-one encounters we attend (with honest curiosity) to the other person's story and experience, body and heart, pain and joy, fears and dreams, and thereby exemplify the "good news" of her or his inherent worthiness and blessedness. The goal of listening intently and intentionally is to discover and act on a common, shared self-interest that moves us beyond any differences. By building relationships, people in the community are able to see past their isolation, to claim a sense of their own agency, and to step away from charity and on toward justice. In the last decades, many communities have suffered from the decline of "third spaces," places where people can build relationships other than at home or work. The church can play an important role in providing a

49. Thanks to Melissa Marley Bonnichsen, Terry Moe, and Melissa Reed for their help with this section. All of them are rooted in the day-to-day realities of community organizing.

50. *Dom Hélder Câmara: Essential Writings*, ed. Francis McDonagh (Maryknoll, NY: Orbis, 2009), 11.

safe third space. Larry Rasmussen writes, "In an important sense . . . an ethic of smaller-scale neighborly space matters *more* in a globalized world, not less."[51]

As our churches and Christian communities engage their environs, as they walk around and pray for their neighborhoods, as they learn the community's history and listen to the stories of its people, as they root themselves in the land, and as they come alongside the underprivileged, they will, by God's grace and the guidance of the Holy Spirit, discover ways to organize community for the common good of God's Creation.

Advocacy is another useful resource for the local Christian community interested in greening its mission. Advocacy involves speaking for or acting on behalf of those who are unable to speak or act—or prevented from speaking or acting for themselves—due to lack of privilege, the complexities of the system, or some other factor. Such work is fraught with uncertainty. It is difficult to know when it is appropriate to leverage one's privilege to advocate for others and when such an act removes their agency. Community organizing underlines the value of building power in people so that they speak and act for themselves. The Earth speaks a language few are able to hear or willing to learn. The psalmist writes of the voice of Creation: "The heavens are telling the glory of God; / and the firmament proclaims his handiwork. / Day to day pours forth speech, / and night to night declares knowledge. / There is no speech, nor are there words; / their voice is not heard; / yet their voice goes out through all the earth, / and their words to the end of the world" (Ps. 19:1–4). The Earth itself has few rights. Most ethical systems are oriented almost exclusively to the rights of humankind (although more people and organizations now are *advocating* for animal rights). When it comes to the well-being and health of ecosystems and rivers and forests, the whole of the other-than-human Creation, advocates are indispensable.

To advocate means providing a venue and organizing interested members of our churches and Christian communities to write letters or send emails or make phone calls to elected officials. It means attending open hearings and meetings to give voice to the voiceless. Brian Walsh and Sylvia Keesmaat write: "The one voice that is always drowned out in our cultural cacophony—until it screams at us through ecological disasters—is the voice of creation. It takes a certain meekness and receptivity to hear that voice."[52] To advocate for the Earth and for the underprivileged calls us as Christ-followers to listen . . . and to speak.

■ ■ ■

51. Larry L. Rasmussen, *Earth-honoring Faith* (Oxford: Oxford University Press, 2013), 181.
52. Brian Walsh and Sylvia Keesmaat, *Colossians Remixed* (Downers Grove, IL: InterVarsity, 2004), 194–95.

In this chapter we have addressed what it might look like to envision the ecocrisis as an "eco-opportunity" for originality and creativity in greening the local church. If care for Creation is going to percolate throughout our Christian communities, strong leadership is critical. As we have been emphasizing over the last chapters, "doing" ecotheology means we are as likely to act our way into a new way of believing as we are to ecotheologize our way into new patterns of discipleship. And what is true of individual Christ-followers is equally applicable to groups and churches. Through lessening a church building's ecological footprint and exercising bioregional discipleship, through corporate worship, preaching, liturgy, and Eucharist, through building community, advocacy, and being rooted in neighborhood, our local churches can create innovative "green" traditions that will change the nature of the church for a changing world. As we weave together theology and praxis, Dorothy Bass writes, "practices shape behavior while also fostering practice-specific knowledge, capacities, dispositions, and virtues. Those who participate in practices are formed in particular ways of thinking about and living in the world."[53] And just like the words of the Once-ler from *The Lorax*, unless our communities begin to care "a whole awful lot, nothing is going to get better. It's not."

---

53. Dorothy C. Bass, "Ways of Life Abundant," in *For Life Abundant*, ed. Dorothy C. Bass and Craig Dykstra (Grand Rapids: Eerdmans, 2008), 29.

Part IV

Last Things

10

Living As If

Resurrection Hope

The Jewish phrase, *tikkun olam*, is appearing often in ecotheological conversations. It was first used in the classic rabbinical teachings known as the Mishnah (c. 220 CE) to refer to legal protection for the disadvantaged, such as women involved in divorce proceedings or slaves seeking freedom. Later, medieval Jewish mysticism connected *tikkun olam* to a story about Earth's origins. In the beginning, there was only darkness. In order to create, God, out of love, had to give up space in order to make space, to "contract" (*tzimtzum*). Then the world emerged as an immense ray of light, which was gathered and held in great vessels created for that very purpose. But the light was so vast that the vessels broke into shards, and the wholeness of the world was scattered into a thousand fragments of light, lodged in people and events. According to the story, we are each born with the capacity to find the hidden light, to lift it up, and in doing so to restore wholeness to the world.

And so, *tikkun olam* has come to mean "repairing the world." But too often *tikkun olam* feels staggeringly unreachable. The facts we face regarding the crisis of the planet are so overwhelming that many of us opt into detachment, denial, or a paralyzing sense of helplessness. Where do we, individually and collectively, discover the hope to be healers of the world?

The Journey to Hope

> So this is where we begin—by acknowledging that our times confront us with
> realities that are painful to face, difficult to take in, and confusing to live with.
>
> —Joanna Macy and Chris Johnstone[1]

Even some of the most ecologically conscious folks I (Jen) know can be
debilitated by eco-numbness. Suzanne gardens, composts, uses her car infrequently, eats low on the food chain, recycles, upcycles,[2] collects and reuses gray
water (water from her sinks, shower, and washing machine), powers her home
with solar energy, and still—after participating in our church small group
focused on simplicity and Earthcare during Lent—felt an overwhelming sense
of hopelessness regarding the approaching crisis. "I feel so depressed," she
confessed, tears filling her eyes. "How could I ever do enough?" Our psyche
and emotional stability are susceptible to being overwhelmed by the problems
and crises in the world. "Compassion Fatigue" (or "Secondary Traumatic
Stress"), first discovered in the 1950s among emergency room nurses, is a clini-
cally diagnosed psychological hopelessness and depression that arises from
ongoing firsthand exposure to trauma, disease, famine, and even ecological
degradation.[3] Evidence suggests that the more a human encounters pain and
suffering the less they are capable of carrying the burdens of compassion for
that issue. Indeed when it comes to carrying the weight of the ecocrisis on
our individual and collective shoulders, we have found that Suzanne is not
alone in her lack of "hope."

What Hope Is Not

It is useful to establish what hope is not. Authentic hope is not the same
as optimism. The OED defines "optimism" as "hopefulness and confidence
about the future or success of something." This definition seems to imply
that our own agency or action is capable of bringing about the future we seek
(confidence), or that optimism rests on a kind of wishful thinking or hopefulness. Joanna Macy and Chris Johnstone write that hopefulness is when "our
preferred outcome seems reasonably likely to happen," which parallels the OED
definition of optimism.[4] The problem is that much of the ecological evidence
suggests that the preferred outcome or future success of life-as-we-know-it is

1. Joanna Macy and Chris Johnstone, *Active Hope* (Novato, CA: New World Library, 2012), 2.
2. "Upcycling" is turning useless stuff into new products that are useful and better for
the environment.
3. Susan D. Moeller, *Compassion Fatigue* (New York: Routledge, 1999).
4. Macy and Johnstone, *Active Hope*, 3.

very *uncertain*. We find it difficult to be confident about the future given the way humanity currently resides on the Earth. Something more than hopefulness, optimism, or wishful thinking must animate us.

Nor is true hope escapism, even when it is dressed up "spiritually." I (A. J.) vividly remember attending the funeral of a classmate when I was seventeen years old. James had died tragically at the hands of a deadly concoction of drugs and alcohol. At his service, he lay there all dressed up in coat and tie—clothes James rarely if ever wore. I sat by myself in the back, fearful, watching people slowly come to see him for the last time. Three hours passed. Once the room emptied, I went to my friend's casket, and touched his face and hands. He was so cold, and the moment felt so hopeless. Later, at his funeral, the priest had preached about hope and what we can expect in the afterlife. I came away with the impression that James was dressed up because he was being taken into the clouds to be in the presence of the One who made him. I have thought about that sermon, and how much I needed hope in that moment. I wanted reassurance that if James had jumped off the deck of the sinking Titanic (that is this world), he would land safely in a lifeboat that would bob him along to the shores of heaven.

At times of loss we need that kind of hope. But problems arise when escapist versions of hope are projected unwisely into our daily lives of responsible discipleship. There beliefs in a distant and disconnected heaven—"Heaven's morning breaks, and earth's vain shadows flee"[5]—can be truly detrimental. Often such a disembodied spirituality wrongly portrays resurrection hope as an *escape* from the material and the mundane. This is not real hope, even when it is dressed up. It is escapism . . . and denial.

If genuine, wide-eyed hope is not wishful thinking, hopefulness, or confidence; if it is not escapism or denial, then what is it? Paul's prayer for the Romans was that they "may abound in hope by the power of the Holy Spirit" (Rom. 15:13). Adapting a model by Macy and Johnstone, we will set forth a journey that, by the power of the Holy Spirit, just might enable us to abound in hope.

Hope Is Rooted in Gratitude

Our first step toward hope is to become rooted in gratitude. Gratitude is fundamental, first, because it recognizes the centrality of grace and of our dependence on God. In the New Testament grace (*charis*) unleashes thanksgiving (*eucharisteo*)—as seen in the beginning of many of Paul's Letters (e.g., Rom. 1:5–8; 1 Cor. 1:3–4; Phil. 1:2–3). Gratitude, then, is theocentric. Grounded in

---

5. Henry F. Lyte, "Abide with Me" (1847), http://library.timelesstruths.org/music/Abide _with_Me/, accessed July 24, 2013.

God's faithfulness, it is our humble response to God's creative and constant work in our lives. Instead of striving to become "more" than we are, gratitude provides a sense of fulfillment in who we already are. Beginning from a point of grace makes it less likely that we will respond to the ecocrisis out of guilt and shame. Because of gratitude we are more able to shift our mindfulness "from what's missing to what's there" as we "cultivate our ability to experience gratitude."[6]

To adopt a spirit of gratitude is, secondly, to become a learner: "No truth, no matter how profound, will find its way into a heart that is absent of gratitude," writes Erwin McManus.[7] Creation teaches us gratitude. We behold the natural world as a gift of grace. Gratitude fosters a wonder at little things, the apparently inconsequential details of our daily world. When we take time to slow down and notice God's everyday wonders in the world, we become aware of God's character and are compelled to gratitude. Joseph Sittler called these commonalities "grace notes."[8] To behold these indispensable notes of grace in Creation is an essential aspect of an ecological acumen, of seeing the way God sees. Grace and gratitude pull the rug out from under our anthropocentric grandiosity and illuminate how dependent our well-being is on the well-being of even the most seemingly insignificant elements of the created world.

Finally, gratitude has the ability to improve our resilience for facing the pain and reality of the ecocrisis.[9] By focusing on the gifts God has provided, we enhance our satisfaction with life as it is, and we then desire less. Gratitude imposes a valuable limit on "affluenza" and our thirst for more. To learn to be grateful enriches our sense of well-being and of being "graced." Every weeknight that I (Dan) am home I walk over at 9:30 p.m. to Don and Karen's house next door. We light a candle and practice "examin." Examin is a simple spiritual exercise in which each of us shares a "desolation" and a "consolation" from our day. It causes me to reflect on God's active presence in my life and in their lives, in both highs and lows. And in just ten to fifteen minutes I walk home more grateful than I came. Gratitude strengthens our resilience for the next steps of our journey to hope.

This call to gratitude is not a pious "tip of the hat" to God, nor a mere formality that a book that calls itself Christian *ought* to include, nor a perfunctory "opening act" to what really matters: ecopraxis. Without gratitude, without grace, without God, all of our ecopraxis will be without hope.

6. Macy and Johnstone, *Active Hope*, 48.
7. Erwin McManus, *Uprising* (Nashville: Thomas Nelson, 2003), 114.
8. Peter W. Bakken, "Nature as a Theater of Grace: The Ecological Theology of Joseph Sittler," in *Evocations of Grace*, ed. Steven Bouma-Prediger and Peter Bakken (Grand Rapids: Eerdmans, 2000), 16–17.
9. Macy and Johnstone, *Active Hope*, 43–44.

Hope Is Honoring Pain

After gratitude, the next step on the journey to hope is honoring pain. Macy and Johnstone underscore that "*pain for the world*, a phrase that covers a range of feelings, including outrage, alarm, grief, guilt, dread, and despair, is a normal, healthy response to a world in trauma."[10] It may be healthy, but acknowledging pain and despair is profoundly countercultural in suffering-denying and death-denying North America. To despair is literally the negation (*de*) of hope (*spērare*). Facing into the despair of the ecocrisis, as difficult as it is, honors those who suffer and the Creation that groans. Rather than denying the existence of suffering, we see it, and in seeing it we honor it. To honor pain is deeply "spiritual." One example is the mother of Jesus. Richard Rohr writes that Mary "teaches us by the way she stands at the foot of the cross. Not a word is spoken; she simply trusts and gives space and silence. She is present. . . . Faith is not for overcoming obstacles; it is for *experiencing* them."[11] Compassion, the act of being present to and embracing the suffering of another, is "an essential and noble capacity" in the work of ecological healing.[12]

A vital resource for honoring pain is grief and lament. Walter Brueggemann, describing Hebrew prophets, declares: "I believe that the proper idiom for the prophet in cutting through the royal numbness and denial is *the language of grief*, the rhetoric that engages the community in mourning for a funeral they do not want to admit. It is indeed their own funeral."[13] The first (minority) world today is afflicted with royal denial as we ignore the groaning of Creation. Steven Chase writes, "It *is* sad: the true pain of the earth today is our denial of her pain."[14] And yet it is indeed our own funeral.

Jeremiah, the weeping prophet, modeled a "ministry of grief" on many levels.[15] He publicly wept for those leaders who hid insolently behind "these deceptive words": "This is the temple of the LORD, the temple of the LORD, the temple of the LORD" (Jer. 7:4). Jeremiah grieved for himself—"My joy is gone, grief is upon me, / my heart is sick" (8:18)—and for Creation:

> I looked on the earth, and lo, it was waste and void;
> and to the heavens, and they had no light.
> I looked on the mountains, and lo, they were quaking,
> and all the hills moved to and fro.

10. Ibid., 67.

11. Richard Rohr, *Radical Grace: Daily Meditations*, ed. John Bookser Feister (Cincinnati: St. Anthony Messenger, 1995), 154.

12. Macy and Johnstone, *Active Hope*, 67.

13. Walter Brueggemann, *The Prophetic Imagination*, 2nd ed. (Minneapolis: Fortress, 2001), 46.

14. Steven Chase, *Nature as Spiritual Practice* (Grand Rapids: Eerdmans, 2011), 133.

15. See Brueggemann, *Prophetic Imagination*, 46–57.

> I looked, and lo, there was no one at all,
>   and all the birds of the air had fled.
> I looked, and lo, the fruitful land was a desert,
>   and all its cities were laid in ruins
>   before the LORD, before his fierce anger. (4:23–26)

Prophets (ancient and modern) are often known for their unrelenting critique and unequivocal tongue. Too often we forget their grief, even as we neglect to grieve.

Lament is how we raise our voice in sorrow or even protest when our hearts have been broken. It is prevalent in the Old Testament as both an individual and communal act of grief. In his reflections on Lamentations, Ron Ruthruff, who has worked for decades with house-less and street-involved youth and families, writes that lament is "the ancient poetry of truth-telling, an act of survival that testifies to the human requirement to speak the unspeakable, to find speech in traumatic numbness, and . . . to assert boldly the sheer act of pain."[16] The pain in Lamentations at the destruction of Jerusalem is palpable:

> Pour out your heart like water
>   before the presence of the Lord!
> Lift your hands to him
>   for the lives of your children,
> who faint for hunger
>   at the head of every street.
> Look, O LORD, and consider!
>   To whom have you done this?
> Should women eat their offspring,
>   the children they have borne? (Lam. 2:19–20)

The language of lament is audacious. We squirm at its rude rawness, its uncensored brazenness before God. Yet Ruthruff tellingly observes, God is strikingly silent in the book of Lamentations. Far too often, the voice of God, enfolded in the praises of the powerful, suppresses the cries of the invisible and disregarded. Lament sees, bears witness to, and intones the silent tears of the overlooked.

Who will honor the pain of the Creation and all those suffering from its degradation? Who will grieve for them and give voice to their lament?

---

16. Ron Ruthruff, "Theology of Suffering: Exploring the Importance of Lament," presentation notes, Soul Formation Academy, Mt. Angel, Oregon, March 13, 2013.

Hope Is Seeing Reality

The third step, seeing reality, is about learning to "see" in two ways: what is and what could be. To see "what is" is integral to honoring pain. It involves facing the reality of what is really there, both the beauty of life—which we often miss because of the hectic pace of our lives—and the distressing effects of the ecocrisis—which we deny because of the pain it elicits. Human greed, addiction, "affluenza," attachment, consumption, classism, sexism, racism, and ecological degradation are frightening realities to embrace. The "reality of reality" causes us to drift emotionally toward eco-numbness, and we come face-to-face not only with the ecocrisis itself but also with our own plunge into indifference.

To see the reality of what is, both in the world and in our hearts, we must turn toward it with what Catherine Keller calls "'metanoic' consciousness."[17] Then with the psalmist, the prophets, and Jesus (Luke 19:41–44), we grieve and lament, trusting in the conviction that reality is where we encounter God, that in the act of seeing what *is*, we meet Jesus Christ. In his *Ethics*, Dietrich Bonhoeffer writes:

> In Christ we are invited to participate in the reality of God and the reality of the world at the same time, the one not without the other. The reality of God is disclosed only as it places me completely into the reality of the world. But I find the reality of the world always already borne, accepted, and reconciled in the reality of God. That is the mystery of the revelation of God in the human being Jesus Christ. What matters is participating in the reality of God and the world in Jesus Christ today, and in doing so in such a way that I never experience the reality of God without the reality of the world, nor the reality of the world without the reality of God.[18]

Only having seen and faced the reality of "what is" will we be able to engage our hearts and minds to imagine a new reality, "what could be." To begin to see the reality of what could be necessitates becoming aware of our community, or communities.[19] Starting with the smallest communities we

---

17. Catherine Keller, "Eschatology, Ecology, and a Green Ecumenacy," *Ecotheology: Journal of Religion, Nature, & the Environment* 5, no. 2 (Jan. 1997): 98. In "Talk about the Weather: the Greening of Eschatology," in *Ecofeminism and the Sacred*, ed. Carol J. Adams (New York: Continuum, 1993), 47, Keller defines metanoic consciousness as "facing up to the *man*-made apocalypse, resisting the North American array of post-utopian cynicisms, pessimistic determinisms, reactionary Christian messianisms, and business-as-usual realisms."

18. Dietrich Bonhoeffer, *Ethics*, trans. Reinhard Kraus, Douglas W. Stott, and Charles C. West, ed. Clifford Green (Minneapolis: Fortress, 2005), 55.

19. Macy and Johnstone, *Active Hope*, 89–91.

belong to and expanding outward, we belong to families, Christian communities, neighborhoods, bioregions, the human society, and, ultimately, the whole web of life. As we become increasingly aware of our membership in these expanding communities, we see both the resources they have to offer and our responsibility to each. We are not alone on this journey toward hope, and seeing reality as it could be means seeing our rootedness in these communities.

"What could be" also encompasses visualizing a new reality, what Jesus called the kingdom or commonwealth of God. As we will see, it means "living as if" this reality *is* reality. It means trusting the abiding, co-creative power of the Holy Spirit, participating selflessly in all of the communities to which we have been called, and preparing for the welfare and well-being of the seventh generation to come.

Anthropologist Gregory Bateson used to tell this now widely circulated story: The dining hall at New College (a misnomer if there ever was one; New College is one of Oxford's oldest colleges) was constructed in the fourteenth century with enormous oak beams supporting its roof. About five hundred years later, the college learned that those beams were filled with beetles and that beams of that size were almost impossible to obtain. Unbeknownst to most of the college fellows, the college was endowed with other properties across the country. So they called in the college forester and asked if he had any oaks on those lands. He replied, "Well sirs, we was wonderin' when you'd be askin'." He informed them that when the dining hall was built, a grove of oak trees had been planted to replace the beams when it became necessary. Forester after forester had handed on this plan for nigh on five hundred years, saying, "You don't cut them oaks. Them's for the College Hall."

And Bateson would conclude his story by asking, "What about the next time? Has a new grove of oaks been planted and protected?" Though the story is (somewhat) apocryphal,[20] it reinforces the importance of seeing "what could be"—and preparing for it—for our own sakes, for the sake of generations to come, and for the sake of every community to which we belong.

Hope Is Living "As If"

The last step on this journey is to live "as if" the future we envision, which is nothing less than the commonwealth of God that Jesus proclaimed and gave his life to bring to fruition, is a "reality" that we can partner with God

---

20. Dylan Thuras, "Oak Beams, New College Oxford," original text by Stewart Brand, Atlas Obscura (website), http://www.atlasobscura.com/places/oak-beams-new-college-oxford, accessed July 25, 2013.

in bringing about. Macy and Johnstone refer to living "as if" as "active hope." Passive hope "is about waiting for external agencies to bring about what we desire." Active hope, on the other hand, "is about becoming active participants in bringing about what we hope for." Active hope is oriented toward practice and does not require optimism to move forward: "The guiding impetus is intention; we *choose* what we aim to bring about, act for, or express. Rather than weighing our chances and proceeding only when we feel hopeful, we focus on our intention and let it be our guide."[21] Active hope—living in dependence on the Holy Spirit *as if* God's kingdom is indeed among us (Luke 17:21)—empowers us to live through paralyzing feelings of denial and indifference. When those emotions come, as they inevitably will, we return to an active hope set in intentionality and in God's grace.

Living "as if" draws us into engaging our imaginations and participating in creating a future that is different from our present. Such a hope is available to people in both the first (minority) world and the majority world. Leonardo Boff writes of the power of active hope for the marginalized: "Through imagination, society and the oppressed dare to transcend their prison and envision a world different from this perverse one that denies them participation and life."[22] Authentic hope is not about guarantees or certainties. It is about intentionality and agency, about living as if we can help animate the commonwealth of God, as if we can help bring heaven to Earth. Quaker futurist Elise Boulding writes, "We are in no way prophesying or predicting or compelling the future by this kind of imaging, any more than we are compelling the future when we pray. The enactment of the future depends on what we do, how we individually and collectively respond to what we envision."[23]

The great prophets of the Hebrew tradition refused to run away from predictions of desolation and despair—Jeremiah narrates the undoing of the world (Jer. 4); Isaiah describes ecological devastation (Isa. 24); Hosea tells the story of economic corruption in a world of greed; Joel and Amos record environmental catastrophe. Yet none of the prophets left their people—or leave us as readers—without an image of the people of God being restored to relationship, characterized by the health and fruitfulness of the land. The biblical text consistently nourishes hope without circumventing despair. If hope is not about escapist optimism, then only after we have seen the depths and dimensions of the problem can we see the depths and dimensions of a

21. Macy and Johnstone, *Active Hope*, 3.
22. Leonardo Boff, *Ecology and Liberation*, trans. John Cumming (Maryknoll, NY: Orbis, 1995), 104.
23. Elise Boulding, "Turning Walls into Doorways," *Inward Light* 47, no. 101 (Spring 1986), cited in Macy and Johnstone, *Active Hope*, 171.

hope-filled future. Rabbi Tarfon wrote, "It is not upon you to finish the work. Neither are you free to desist from it."[24]

Living in Hope

When asked if I am pessimistic or optimistic about the future, my answer is always the same: if you look at the science about what is happening on earth and aren't pessimistic, you don't understand data. But if you meet the people who are working to restore this earth and the lives of the poor, and you aren't optimistic, you haven't got a pulse. What I see everywhere in the world are brilliant, caring people willing to confront despair, power, and incalculable odds in order to restore some semblance of grace, justice, and beauty to this world.

—Paul Hawken[25]

Florinda is nursing her babies, twins about six months old. Her other four children are scampering about under the watchful eye of her extended family. Their rural Mozambican home has a few scattered thatched-roof huts, some chickens, and a simple plot of land for growing maize. Florinda is a single mother; her husband died of an unknown illness (probably AIDS) while working the mines in South Africa. A few years ago she learned that she is HIV positive. On this day a team from the Sustainable Home-Based Care (SHBC) program is visiting her. Tomás and Carolina, who live in the neighborhood, have been trained to offer compassionate care and hope to women like Florinda. They bring salves for the sores on her chest, make sure she is taking her antiretroviral drugs to arrest the effects of HIV in her body, and walk through a series of questions to help keep her on the journey to wellness. The caregivers begin and end their time with Florinda in prayer, seeking God's blessing and healing.

Carolina and Tomás are two of over seventy trained volunteers who provide care for 756 beneficiaries. The volunteers and other associates form the Kuhanha Association in Iahambane Province. Kuhanha means "to live," "to have life." The program of home-based care is "sustainable" because the volunteers, in addition to being caregivers, also work together in specific income-generating activities that support their work: raising chickens, pigs, or goats; growing sweet potatoes, cassava, black beans, maize, or peanuts; or keeping bees for honey. Over the last year, the Kuhanha Association has earned over

24. Cited in Paul Kivel, *Uprooting Racism*, 3rd ed. (Gabriola Island, BC: New Society, 2011), xvi.
25. Paul Hawken, *The Ecology of Commerce*, rev. ed. (New York: Harper Business, 2010), xxi–xxii.

five hundred dollars—a significant amount in Mozambique—which they use to provide transportation to the hospital and food for the beneficiaries. Tomás, Carolina, and almost every one of the volunteers *are themselves HIV-positive.*

While Nathan, the director of a Christian relief and development organization in Mozambique, and I (Dan) were driving to observe different Christ-centered ministries like SHBC, I was overwhelmed by a profound sense of hopelessness and helplessness. As we passed tens of thousands of disadvantaged Mozambicans on the road, I grieved over how limited their prospects were for thriving. In an existential moment of paradox I felt both shame over my privilege and thankfulness for being privileged. But Nathan challenged me to see otherwise. He pointed out that most of the Mozambicans and other Africans he works alongside are authentically joyful and grateful. He spoke of how author Andrew Zolli described "hardy" and "resilient" people as those who (1) believe that the world is a meaningful place, and (2) have a keen sense of their own agency in that world, even in the face of failure.[26] After a lengthy theological debate over the first point—I was still struggling with whether or not the world is a meaningful place—I had no choice but to grant him the second, that to be resilient requires a sense of agency. My encounter with Tomás, Carolina, and the scores of volunteers who are serving the suffering out of their own suffering was indisputable confirmation of the power of agency. In spite of what I might consider insurmountable hardship, they *lived as if* they could influence their world in the name of Jesus Christ for the common good. And in their small community of Iahambane Province, they are . . . and the world is different because of it.

■ ■ ■

It seems apropos to conclude this chapter and the book with this story of agency and hope from Mozambique. The ecocrisis is too daunting to face on our own; we can no more do this work in isolation than we can be optimistic about our future. The story of *tikkun olam* reminds us that, even if we feel incapable of making a significant difference, we are nevertheless exactly what is needed to heal a fragmented world. Our task is not to take on every shard but to bring healing to that particular place in which we are located at this particular moment in history.

In another moment in history, an unpretentious carpenter chiseled and fashioned Galilee's native wood, went to and fro with his disciples in ordinary

26. "A Shift to Humility: Andrew Zolli on Resilience and Expanding the Edge of Change," *On Being with Krista Tippett*, May 16, 2013, http://www.onbeing.org/program/a-shift-to-humility-andrew-zolli-on-resilience-and-expanding-the-edge-of-change/5501, accessed July 7, 2013.

wooden boats, cried tears in an olive grove, and endured an ominous piece of Roman wood. Brokenness and sin entered Creation through an act of disobedience under a tree in Eden, just as wholeness and restoration came through an act of obedience on another tree just outside Jerusalem. Jesus Christ is our *tikkun olam*—repairer, healer, renewer—the One who emerged from the tomb making possible the renewal of all things. Christians throughout time and space have *leaned* and *relied* on that resurrection, but now we must *practice* it, by living "as if" with resurrection hope.

Acknowledgments

By its very nature this project has been a collaborative effort. Besides the obvious writing collaboration between the three of us, we have many others we want to acknowledge and to whom we are profoundly grateful. We owe a great debt to The Association of Theological Schools, which gave us a Lilly Theological Research Grant for collaborative research; the Association's confidence in our proposal shocked us into reality and propelled us toward action. Along the way, various friends and associates have read a chapter or two and given us concrete feedback. Our work is better and more nuanced because of their input (although their feedback in no way implies approbation). In no particular order, we heartily thank Nathan and Deanna Glancy, Laura Simmons, Steve Delamarter, Kent Yinger, Loren Kerns, Cherice Bock, Jill Firmin, Jim Martin-Schramm, Don Ottenhoff, Janel Kragt Bakker, Steven Chase, Tom Johnson, William P. Brown, Eric Lopez, Scott Ables, Fletcher Harper, Steve Bouma-Prediger, Melissa Reed, Melissa Marley-Bonnichsen, Terry Moe, Dick Harmon, Robyn Hartwig, Russell Joyce, Mark Cartledge, Jeffrey Lamp, Brandon Hubbard-Heitz, Michael Chan, Aaron Friesen, Steve Overman, Rick Lindroth, Paul Ede, and Genny Rowley. We are indebted to Bob Hosack, Lisa Ann Cockrel, and the rest of the Baker Academic team, including Susan Matheson. We are grateful to the staffs of the George Fox University library, the Alcuin Library at St. John's University, the Clemens Library at the College of St. Benedict, and the Bodleian Library at the University of Oxford. Finally, we express our deep appreciation to the students, past and present, who helped create and continue to participate in the Christian Earthkeeping concentration at George Fox Evangelical Seminary. They, and learners everywhere, are the raison d'être of this work.

I (Dan) extend thanks to George Fox University for granting me a sabbatical during the 2012–13 school year and to the faculty and staff at my seminary for their grace and support. During the winter semester of 2013 I had the privilege of being a research scholar at the Collegeville Institute for Ecumenical and Cultural Research in Collegeville, Minnesota; thanks to the staff, Don Ottenhoff, Janel Kragt Bakker, and Carla Durand, and to my fellow scholars for their support and timely counsel. The Seminary Stewardship Alliance of Blessed Earth provided an opportune seed grant to support my research. I am grateful to my intentional community, Urban Abbey, for their love and prayers and for taking care of the garden and our chickens while I was off gallivanting. My involvement as a GreenFaith fellow helped inspire this work. My friends at EcoFaith Recovery and Salt and Light Lutheran Church have been encouraging green companions. My family—Philip, Amber, and Rachel—have loved and carried me. I dedicate this book to my granddaughters, Kenley and Dylan; my fierce love for them compels my passion for the world they will inherit. And lastly, to Jen and A.J.: it has been a remarkable journey, one that has changed me. My delight in you as gifted students has morphed into unreserved gratitude for your collegiality and friendship.

I (Jen) am grateful for the exercise in catharsis this writing project brought with it. I spent countless hours in coffee houses, my office, and the back porch reflecting on my own experience of place, rootedness, and connection to creation. I am a more integrated individual because of the opportunity I had to do my own work while contributing to this text. There is no one in my life who deserves more thanks than my husband, Peter. He has supported me unconditionally during the past two years as this work has been culminating. Without his encouragement, feedback, and partnership, my contribution to this project would have been sorely lacking. I am grateful as well to my congregation, First Congregational United Church of Christ in Corvallis, and my colleague Elizabeth Oettinger, who have allowed me the space to write and teach while I have the privilege of ministering to them. My parents, Bob and Karen Butler, are the folks who made me who I am. As young people are prone to do, I have underappreciated them most of my life. But as I get older, I am profoundly grateful to be their daughter. My Moses Fury was born just as we embarked on the final stages of editing this text. Already he has become my greatest teacher. For him I am determined to journey toward hope, to live "as if," and to participate in the healing of the world. Finally, to Dan and A.J., with whom I have spent the better part of two years drinking coffee, arguing, crying, and laughing, I am proud of what we created together and honored to have been on this journey with you.

I (A.J.), wholeheartedly want to thank my incredible wife, Quinn, and son, Elliot, for the fervent grace they've extended, allowing me the space to pour my heart, soul, and countless hours away from the dinner table into this very important writing project. There's nowhere I'd rather be than in the garden out back with those two. Without their loving support, this book would have been an impossible task. Friends have been key dialogue partners in my ecological mindset: Matthew and Nancy Sleeth, Amos Yong, Laura Leavell, Keith Jagger, Jeffrey Lamp, Cheryl Bridges-Johns, and Mark Cartledge have been particularly helpful and gracious to engage my work. Furthermore, I will forever be in debt to the theological, moral, and spiritual formation afforded me at each of the institutions I've had the privilege to attend: New Hope Christian College (Eugene, Oregon), George Fox Evangelical Seminary (Portland, Oregon), and the University of Birmingham (UK). Each of these outstanding institutions not only formed my mind and heart but also challenged and affirmed me and all of my academic and pastoral passions. Of course without the loving support of my church, Theophilus, this project would not have happened. Finally, and not least importantly, I wish to acknowledge my coauthors, Jen and Dan, who have both helped me see God's world afresh. It goes without saying that their influence in my life has been immeasurable, and I am thankful to God for both of them.

All three of us pray, ultimately, that this work brings glory to God, inspires diverse Christ followers to thoughtful action, and plays a small part in the restoring and stewardship of God's creation.

Select Bibliography

This represents a *very* select bibliography. We did not want the list to be overwhelming, so we focused predominately on texts we have used or referenced appreciably in our seminary courses. Also, we have only listed books, and have, for the sake of brevity, omitted many worthwhile journal articles, documentaries, podcasts, and other resources.

Bauckham, Richard. *The Bible and Ecology: Rediscovering the Community of Creation*. Waco, TX: Baylor University Press, 2010.

Berry, R. J., ed. Environmental Stewardship. London: Bloomsbury, 2006.

Berry, Wendell. *The Art of the Commonplace: The Agrarian Essays of Wendell Berry*. Edited by Norman Wirzba. Berkeley, CA: Counterpoint, 2001.

Boff, Leonardo. *Cry of the Earth, Cry of the Poor*. Translated by Phillip Berryman. Maryknoll, NY: Orbis, 1997.

Bouma-Prediger, Steven. *For the Beauty of the Earth: A Christian Vision for Creation Care*. 2nd ed. Grand Rapids: Baker Academic, 2010.

Brown, Lester R. *Plan B 4.0: Mobilizing to Save Civilization*. Rev. ed. New York: W.W. Norton, 2009.

Brown, William P. *The Seven Pillars of Creation: The Bible, Science, and the Ecology of Wonder*. New York: Oxford University Press, 2010.

Chase, Steven. *Nature as Spiritual Practice*. Grand Rapids: Eerdmans, 2011.

Davis, Ellen F. *Scripture, Culture, and Agriculture: An Agrarian Reading of the Bible*. Cambridge: Cambridge University Press, 2008.

Deane-Drummond, Celia. *Eco-Theology*. Winona, MN: Anselm Academic, 2008.

DeWitt, Calvin B. *Earthwise: A Guide to Hopeful Creation Care.* 3rd ed. Grand Rapids: Faith Alive Christian Resources, 2011.

Dillard, Annie. *Pilgrim at Tinker Creek.* New York: HarperCollins, 2007 [1974].

Edwards, Denis. *Breath of Life: A Theology of the Creator Spirit.* Maryknoll, NY: Orbis, 2004.

Erlander, Daniel. *Manna and Mercy: A Brief History of God's Unfolding Promise to Mend the Entire Universe.* Mercer Island, WA: The Order of Saints Martin and Teresa, 1992.

Gauscho, Luke. *Creation Care: Keepers of the Earth.* Harrisonburg, VA: Herald, 2008.

The Green Bible. San Francisco: HarperOne, 2010.

Guroian, Vigen. *Inheriting Paradise: Meditations on Gardening.* Grand Rapids: Eerdmans, 1999.

Hall, Douglas John. *Imaging God: Dominion as Stewardship.* Grand Rapids: Eerdmans, 1986.

Hessel, Dieter T., and Rosemary Radford Ruether, eds. *Christianity and Ecology: Seeking the Well-Being of Earth and Humans.* Cambridge, MA: Harvard University Press, 2000.

Horrell, David G. *The Bible and the Environment.* Sheffield: Equinox, 2010.

Horrell, David G., Cherryl Hunt, and Christopher Southgate. *Greening Paul: Rereading the Apostle in a Time of Ecological Crisis.* Waco, TX: Baylor University Press, 2010.

Kingsolver, Barbara. *Flight Behavior: A Novel.* New York: HarperCollins, 2012.

Leopold, Aldo. *The Sand County Almanac.* New York: Oxford University Press, 1949.

Longacre, Doris Janzen. *Living More with Less.* 30th anniv. ed. Edited by Valerie Weaver-Zercher. Scottdale, PA: Herald, 2010.

Maathai, Wangari. *Unbowed.* London: Arrow, 2008.

Macy, Joanna, and Chris Johnstone. *Active Hope: How to Face the Mess We're in without Going Crazy.* Novato, CA: New World Library, 2012.

Martin-Schramm, James B., and Robert L. Stivers. *Christian Environmental Ethics: A Case Method Approach.* Maryknoll, NY: Orbis, 2003.

McFague, Sallie. *Super, Natural Christians: How We Should Love Nature.* Minneapolis: Fortress, 2000.

McLaren, Brian D. *Everything Must Change: When the World's Biggest Problems and Jesus' Good News Collide.* Nashville: Thomas Nelson, 2009.

Merchant, Carolyn. *The Death of Nature.* New York: Harper & Row, 1989 [1980].

Moe-Lobeda, Cynthia D. *Resisting Structural Evil: Love as Ecological-Economic Vocation*. Minneapolis: Fortress, 2013.

Moore, Kathleen Dean, and Michael P. Nelson. *Moral Ground*. San Antonio: Trinity University Press, 2010.

Myers, Bryant L. *Walking with the Poor*. Rev. and exp. ed. Maryknoll, NY: Orbis, 2011.

Northwest Earth Institute. *Seeing Systems: Peace, Justice and Sustainability*. Portland, OR: NWEI, 2014. (The Northwest Earth Institute, www.nwei. org, has produced a number of excellent discussion courses. We have also used *Hungry for Change: Food, Ethics, and Sustainability; A World of Health: Connecting People, Place and Planet;* and *Voluntary Simplicity*.)

Rasmussen, Larry L. *Earth Community, Earth Ethics*. Maryknoll, NY: Orbis, 1997.

———. *Earth-honoring Faith*. New York: Oxford University Press, 2012.

Sabin, Scott C. *Tending to Eden: Environmental Stewardship for God's People*. Edited by Kathy Ide. Valley Forge, PA: Judson, 2010.

Santmire, H. Paul. *The Travail of Nature: The Ambiguous Ecological Promise of Christian Theology*. Philadelphia: Fortress, 1985.

Schut, Michael, ed. *Simpler Living, Compassionate Life: A Christian Perspective*. Harrisburg, PA: Morehouse, 2009.

Sittler, Joseph. *Evocations of Grace: The Writings of Joseph Sittler on Ecology, Theology, and Ethics*. Edited by Steven Bouma-Prediger and Peter Bakken. Grand Rapids: Eerdmans, 2000.

Sleeth, J. Matthew. *Serve God, Save the Planet: A Christian Call to Action*. White River Junction, VT: Chelsea Green, 2006.

Snyder, Howard A., and Joel Scandrett. *Salvation Means Creation Healed: The Ecology of Sin and Grace*. Eugene, OR: Cascade, 2011.

Van Dyke, Fred H., et al. *Redeeming Creation: The Biblical Basis for Environmental Stewardship*. Downers Grove, IL: InterVarsity, 1996.

Wirzba, Norman, ed. *The Essential Agrarian Reader: The Future of Culture, Community, and the Land*. Lexington: University Press of Kentucky, 2003.

Woodley, Randy. *Shalom and the Community of Creation: An Indigenous Vision*. Grand Rapids: Eerdmans, 2012.

Wright, N. T. *Surprised by Hope: Rethinking Heaven, the Resurrection, and the Mission of the Church*. London: SPCK, 2007.

Wright, Richard T., and Dorothy Boorse. *Environmental Science: Toward a Sustainable Future*. 12th ed. San Francisco: Benjamin Cummings, 2012.

Index